Capitalist China
Strategies for a
Revolutionized Economy

Capitalist China
Strategies for a
Revolutionized Economy

Jonathan R. Woetzel

John Wiley & Sons (Asia) Pte Ltd

This publication is designed to provide accurate and authoritative information in regard to the subject
matter covered. It is sold with the understanding that the publisher is not engaged in rendering
professional services. If professional advice or other expert assistance is required, the services of a
competent professional person should be sought.

Other Wiley Editorial Offices

John Wiley & Sons, Inc., 111 River Street, Hoboken, NJ 07030, USA
John Wiley & Sons Ltd, The Atrium, Southern Gate, Chichester PO19 8SQ, England
John Wiley & Sons (Canada) Ltd, 22 Worcester Road, Rexdale, Ontario M9W 1L1, Canada
John Wiley & Sons Australia Ltd, 33 Park Road (PO Box 1226), Milton, Queensland 4064, Australia
Wiley-VCH, Pappelallee 3, 69469 Weinheim, Germany

Library of Congress Cataloging-in Publication Data:
ISBN: 0-470-82108-6

Typeset in 10.5/13 points, Times by Linographic Services Pte Ltd
Printed in Singapore by Saik Wah Press Pte Ltd
10 9 8 7 6 5 4 3 2 1

To Aeri and Dominic

Contents

ACKNOWLEDGMENTS

I gratefully acknowledge the support of McKinsey colleagues in Greater China and throughout the world who worked with me to develop many of the insights that follow. To them go my thanks and best wishes. I would particularly like to thank Steve Shaw, Tony Perkins, Paul Gao and Perchow Joseph Chang for their thoughtful contributions. Gordon Orr, Jacques Penhirin, Greg Gibb, David von Emloh, Chris Gradel and Emmanuel Pitsilis also provided insightful comments. Josh Dowse and Jeanne Subramaniam helped to focus my prose with their excellent editing. Carlo Yu and Benedikt Zeumer provided accurate and timely research.

I would further like to thank my interview partners, who provided terrific insights based on their rich experience and noteworthy accomplishments in the challenging China market.

Finally, I owe the most to my wife for her loving support, without which this work would not have started, let alone reached completion.

Jonathan Woetzel
January 16, 2003

FOREWORD

China has in the last decade become a true center of global economic growth. Always seen as a market with potential, China's rising consumer incomes now make it a must-win opportunity for global companies. China's low-cost manufacturing capability and vast human resources are increasingly shaping industries worldwide through exports, as it supplies developed markets and competes with emerging economies. China has already surpassed the United States as the world's leading destination for foreign direct investment. China's growth increasingly plays a role in shaping regional Asian economics and politics. Chinese companies already participate in the Fortune Global 500 and almost every major global corporation has representation in the country. And looking forward, growth in services, labor productivity and infrastructure development promise yet more changes ahead.

However, winning in China has never been easy. The list of prominent failures is long and received wisdom is that profits are elusive in what must be a long-term play for any investor, domestic or multinational. Competition is fierce in sectors where global players have entered – for example, the cheapest consumer electronics in the world are available in China. Chinese exports are in turn rapidly driving down prices globally. In less open sectors, China's regulatory and legal framework is often sketchy, reflecting the lack of a commercial history. The financial sector, in particular, is still driven by government imperatives, skewing the playing field towards local favorites. And few if any companies have all the people and resources needed to win on the ground.

McKinsey has been actively serving both local and multinational companies in China since 1985 to meet and overcome these challenges. Our initial offices were opened in Hong Kong in 1985, followed by Taipei in 1991, Shanghai in 1993, and Beijing in 1995. Today we have over 150 consultants and 20 partners in the four locations, which combined make up our Greater China Office.

I have personally supported our China initiative for many years as a Board member of the Qinghua University Business School in Beijing and more recently as a member of the Shanghai Mayor's International Business Leader Advisory Council. These positions have offered me an opportunity to see first hand the dramatic and impressive changes that China has made in less than a decade. On many of my trips to Asia, I have combined visits to China with visits to India. The relative acceleration of China in the last decade has been truly astounding and has fundamentally reshaped the way Indian businessmen view opportunities in the international and domestic economy.

In this book, Jonathan Woetzel, a Shanghai-based director with over 15 years of experience in our Greater China Office, draws on our collective knowledge to present insights into what has been driving the Chinese economic phenomenon and what it takes to win in this environment. His and his colleagues' perspective is broad-based, covering China's rapidly evolving high-tech revolution, the restructuring of traditional industries like autos, energy and steel, and the emergence of the service economy as sectors including retail, financial services and media gradually open up to competition. The book seeks to provide an understanding of both what is driving change in these sectors and where future sources of competitive advantage may lie. Several of our clients and notable businessmen also provide, through in-depth interviews, their own personal perspectives on key success factors in China.

On behalf of McKinsey & Co., I hope the book provides helpful support to your thinking about China and its opportunities and challenges. We believe that winning in China is possible and that careful attention to the country's uniquely competitive market environment can lead to success. In fact, we might even suggest that winning in China will be *the* mark of a truly global company in the 21st century.

Rajat Gupta
Managing Director,
McKinsey & Co.

1

Why China is Changing

C hina evokes contradictory images. To some it means a market of a
billion consumers and an emerging grassroots democracy whose
leaders survive only as long as they deliver the goods. To others it
is a black hole for investment, a Communist dictatorship ready to explode
and precipitate another Asian financial crisis. In fact China is all of these
things. Its dynamic economy exists superimposed on a legacy of 40 years of
bureaucracy, not to mention 4,000 years of imperial rule. Private
entrepreneurs coexist with Communist party mandarins. And while profits
go to the winners in the competitive sectors of the Chinese market, state
enterprises continue to benefit from official and unofficial subsidies.

Yet reform has now moved to the point where it is unstoppable. Central
planning created the state enterprise system, a cradle-to-grave scheme of
entitlement, marked, not surprisingly, by extreme inefficiency. But with the
launch of reform in the late 1970s, planning has been rolled back. Private
and semi-private players now control the bulk of the economy. As a result,
productivity has risen dramatically, and China has become one of the
greatest economic success stories of the 20th century. Looking forward,
there are even greater challenges. Investments required to grow the economy
are enormous. The government expects over US$300 billion will be needed
every year. And the social costs of growth are increasing as well. Stopping
reform now would place an unbearable burden on the government to sustain
investment and manage social pressures on its own.

Thus China's government is continuing to move quickly towards a
market economy. The banking sector is being reorganized along commercial
lines. State enterprises are lining up to launch public stock offerings and
their managers to receive stock options. The government is putting in place
national health, pension, housing and educational schemes to free enterprises

from the burden of funding employee welfare. While foreign investment continues to grow, Chinese companies are starting to diversify abroad as well. Moreover, with China's accession to the World Trade Organization (WTO), the playing field will change. Multinational corporations will have unprecedented freedoms to establish their own operations, acquire Chinese companies and even tap the Chinese capital markets.

Could anything go wrong? Banking and capital markets reform are major risks. The amount of money required to stablize the Chinese banking system is estimated to range anywhere from 20 to 40% of GDP. The stock market, while developing quickly, is clearly inflated and sell-offs could quickly depress the economy. WTO membership will not affect all sectors of the economy uniformly. Some sectors such as consumer electronics are already highly competitive. Others like telecom services are not directly included in WTO provisions.

But these risks affect only the pace, not the direction, of reform. Simply put, there is no credible alternative to pursuing the market-based model of economic development. Companies and investors should recognize the uncertainties inherent in any rapid transition of this magnitude. But the real challenge will be to profitably participate in what promises to be the most dynamic market in the world.

1.1 MOVING TO A MARKET ECONOMY

The central driver of China's economic progress over the last two decades has been government's progressive withdrawal from direct management of the economy while introducing competition. The state sector has shrunk dramatically as whole sectors of the economy have transitioned to private control through privatization and individual business start-ups. Meanwhile, China's productivity has improved measurably and China's GDP per capita has more than doubled over the past decade. Chinese companies compete internationally and China has become the most favored destination for direct investment in emerging markets. However, maintaining growth will require even more investments while managing a tricky social transition. Government has realized that pushing reform to include market-based funding mechanisms offers the best and, in fact, only chance to continue this rate of economic progress. This in turn will challenge China's corporate sector, both foreign and domestic, to increase its efficiency and productivity to keep China's economy on track.

CHINA'S INVESTMENT-HUNGRY ECONOMY

With 1949 and the Communist liberation, China began a unique experiment in economic development. Neither fully embracing Soviet-style central planning, particularly following the Sino-Soviet split in 1958, nor adopting capitalist market thinking, Chinese economic policy made national self-sufficiency its primary goal.[1] By 1976, trade had shrunk to an all-time low and foreign investment was almost nonexistent. Even within China, trade and internal mobility were highly restricted. The economy was designed to be highly cellular, with thousands of independent local economic entities that could survive on their own in the event of war or invasion. Mao's Third Line of investment buried steel mills in remote backwaters and placed refineries operating on marginal assets in the remote northwest. The political and military infrastructure was in fact the only national network that existed until the beginning of reform. The Party held a monopoly on power and, with no established code of law, its decisions were final.

Yet after the chaos of the Great Proletarian Cultural Revolution (1966–1976), China's political unity found itself at risk. After 30 years of, at various times, autarchy, central planning and anarchy, the Chinese people were not receiving the benefits they had been promised by their political leaders for more than a generation. The devastating Tangshan earthquake in 1976 brought home just how badly China's leaders had let its people down as rescue efforts took months to unearth the dead and tens of thousands died in the aftermath. Mao's death in 1976 presented a unique opportunity to make a decisive change in political direction.

Deng Xiaoping's return from the political wilderness delivered this change and then some. Shortly after taking power in 1978, he and Zhao Ziyang announced the Four Modernizations. These represented a fundamental change in economic policy, stating that the army, agriculture, industry and foreign trade all needed to be fundamentally rethought. Efficiency was essential if growth was to be achieved – a thought encapsulated in Deng's most famous line, it "doesn't matter if the cat is black or white as long as it catches mice". Beijing also realized that change could not be micromanaged, given the central government's low funding ability and the long tradition of decentralized economic management. Leading economists saw the central government not as an administrator of the economy but as a policy-guidance arm, approving major projects, consolidating fragmented industries, and encouraging new technologies, much as Japan's Ministry of International Trade and Industry formerly did. By using the stick of real bankruptcy or forced merger along with the carrot of access to public capital markets, the government sought to get large state companies off its books. And by setting the boundaries in which competition could occur (for instance, import tariffs) and by picking up the pieces after the battle was over (managing layoffs and retraining workers), Beijing could foster a more productive and competitive environment.

Reform in the countryside was the starting point. The collective farms were abandoned in favor of so-called sideline farming. Agricultural productivity boomed and rural incomes rose dramatically in the early 1980s. The cities came next, as state-owned enterprises (SOEs) were told they must stand on their own as the traditional supply and distribution functions of the state withered away. Where the government used to set supply contracts and prices, appoint managers and control investments, with the publication of the 14 Enterprise Freedoms in the early 1990s, enterprises were formally given the rights to decide their own purchases, production plans, personnel arrangements and finances. Entrepreneurs meanwhile were allowed to set up businesses on their own or in the form of a collective. The typical collective started as a shareholding enterprise divided among three or four families from a local village and operating under the auspices of the village or county government.

Foreign investment was seen to be another important tool to introduce competition into the economy. Foreign investment was expected to bring not only capital but also intangible assets such as advanced technologies, management know-how and trained employees that would help China develop a more advanced economy and increase its competitiveness in the global economy, primarily by pushing local companies into performing better.

Now, 20 years later, the results of this transformation are increasingly evident. Through investments in human capital, infrastructure and technology, China's economy has in fact become increasingly productive.[2] Productivity in the industrial sector grew at over 10% annually throughout the 1990s, over three times the rate in the developed world (Exhibit 1.1). This was in large part due to the leapfrog effect of adopting new technology. China did not have to repeat decades of incremental improvement that the West went through. For example, improvements in infrastructure allowed manufacturers to relocate production further into the countryside and employ rural workers where they lived. The same approach is also emerging in services where the application of modern formats may in future lead to a leap in productivity.

Human capital is also significantly better developed than in the 1980s. At the top of the pyramid, China's leading universities produce talent to match that in other parts of the world (at an employed cost of $5,000–$10,000 per annum). Close to half a million scientists and engineers graduate from Chinese universities each year, providing an enormous talent

Exhibit 1.1   The transition of China's economy is fueling huge productivity improvements

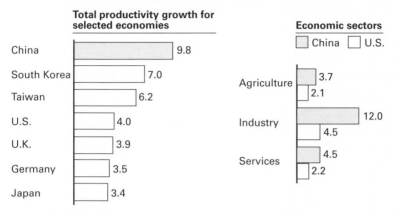

Labor productivity growth (CAGR in percent, 1990–2001)

Total productivity growth for selected economies

China	9.8
South Korea	7.0
Taiwan	6.2
U.S.	4.0
U.K.	3.9
Germany	3.5
Japan	3.4

Economic sectors

☐ China   ☐ U.S.

	China	U.S.
Agriculture	3.7	2.1
Industry	12.0	4.5
Services	4.5	2.2

Source: China Statistical Yearbook; Bureau of Labor Statistics

pool for R&D and manufacturing operations. Students returning from abroad supplement this talent pool. Over the decades, hundreds of thousands of Chinese graduates have studied overseas. The global recession, combined with China's continued stability, has encouraged many of them to return to China. They bring not just skills, but also capital. And at the primary education level, China, as measured by the United Nations, has literacy rates of 90%, around 30% higher than in India. While the majority of the mass labor force remains rural, both urban and rural residents have the basic (or greater) skills to be employable.

And most importantly, China's economy is fundamentally more competitive. Collective, private and foreign enterprises accounted for over 50% of industrial output in 2001, reflecting how far reform has moved. Among the so-called collectives are multi-billion-dollar groups with global operations. Greater freedom has proved more of a challenge to the state sector as many enterprises failed to seize the opportunities presented them. Their role in the economy has shrunk accordingly – the SOEs' share of China's GDP has decreased from 80% in 1978 to less than 30% in 2000. This is in line with government expectations if not policy. An official of the Development Research Council, the think-tank of the State Council, recently asserted that China did not want to shrink the share of government spending in the economy. On the contrary, what it sought was to move the government to a more stable funding base than the revenues of state enterprises – that is, taxation of commercial enterprises.

This initial success has created a demand for even greater levels of investments. China is today a medium-sized economy with a Gross Domestic Product (GDP) equivalent to that of Italy. What makes it distinctive is its growth. By 2010, it is expected to almost double in size to rival Germany. With continued growth it will surpass Japan by 2020. This level of growth is both a political and an economic necessity. An entire generation has been raised to expect increases in their standard of living and a better life for their children. And without growth, commitments government has made to social, environmental and educational programs will go unmet.

Massive investments will be needed to generate this level of growth. Relying on current assets is simply not practical as, in many cases, existing stock is sub-scale and inadequate to meet rising demand. As a result, government has made investment a high domestic priority whose importance is expected to further increase over the next few years. As a percentage of GDP, investment has grown from 40% to 45% in China over the last five years. The Economist Intelligence Unit believes this ratio will increase to 50% over the next five years as China continues to modernize. In contrast, this ratio averages about 20% for industrialized countries such as the U.S., and about 25% to 30% in newly industrialized countries in East Asia, such as South Korea. Given that China's GDP could grow by 7% to 8% annually over the next five years, over this timeframe, an estimated US$1.6 trillion needs to be invested.

NO TURNING BACK FROM REFORM

Government is responding to this challenge by moving decisively to adopt market-based mechanisms to raise and channel investments. China's growth is largely domestically funded. Foreign investment forms no more than 10% of total investment requirements today and is expected to remain around this level in the future. China's thrifty consumers have long boasted one of the world's highest savings rates at over 40%. The challenge is to deploy it productively. Only by rigorously applying market-based return criteria can government be assured that the forecast huge investments are properly deployed. And only by productively deploying them will government be able to manage its social challenges. This in turn implies massive changes to China's banking and financial systems.

The process of transforming China's banks from instruments of policy to commercial enterprises has been long and slow. In 1949, the People's Bank of China (PBOC) assumed the functions of all existing Chinese and foreign banks. Three specialized banks were formed under the PBOC – the

Agricultural Bank, the People's Construction Bank and the Bank of China. This system lasted for 30 years until, in 1979, the three specialized banks were spun off from PBOC. But they remained government controlled and subject to directed lending. Foreign banks only began to be allowed in China in the early 1980s – Nanyang Commercial Bank, a Bank of China Hong Kong affiliate, was the first "foreign" bank to offer banking services in Shenzhen. In 1984, PBOC became China's official central bank, its remaining commercial lending operations being put into a new bank – the Industrial and Commercial Bank of China (ICBC), now the largest bank in China. In 1985, many smaller Chinese banks were created. By the 1990s these smaller banks had begun to grow and accounted for over 10% of deposits. This gave them a substantial presence but they were still not a threat to the PBOC-derived incumbents. In 1994, Beijing passed the Commercial Banking Law, which made it a crime for local officials to pressure banks to make policy loans. The government created three policy banks to assume responsibility for directed lending and policy loans (China Export-Import Bank, State Development Bank, and China Agricultural Development Bank). In 1995, the big-four ex-PBOC banks were told they were now expected to operate as proper commercial banks responsible for their own profit-and-loss accounts.

However, commercial practices were slow to take hold. The state banks have, since the founding of the central planning system, been immune from market pressures. With periodic government bailouts, the banks have had no accountability for bad lending decisions. And with no individual managerial incentives or pressures to improve the quality of decision-making, bank executives respond primarily to political pressures and personal greed. As a result China's state banks are weighed down by non-performing loans (NPLs). Independent analysts say NPLs remain as high as 40% to 50% of the portfolio. The implication is that a one-third writeoff and recapitalization of the banks would amount to anywhere between 20% and 40% of China's GDP.

Realizing the importance of a sound financial system for the country's economic future, the government has in the past few years tried to restructure the banking sector more aggressively. Recent announcements have declared that the banks would be privatized through stock market listings. At the same time, in 2001 the government issued Renminbi (RMB) 270 billion ($32.6 billion) in special bonds to partially recapitalize the big-four state banks to deal with NPLs. A portion of these NPLs was split off into Asset Management Companies, to be restructured and sold off. In tandem, the carefully designed opening of the banking sector to private and foreign participation is intended to stimulate this transformation by allowing internationally experienced human capital and best practices to flow unimpeded into the sector. Private investors are now being allowed to set up banks in cities where there are no local banks and to buy, at least partially, into some banks.

With these clear signals, the leadership of the big-four banks appears to have recognized the need for change. On a province-by-province basis, the banks are putting in place more commercially oriented practices (for example, credit and collection policies), aided by almost unlimited consulting support from international banks. (Citibank, for instance, has all but transferred its core business process design to Bank of China.) The growth of the new generation of banks in China (examples include China Merchants and CITIC) who lack the burdensome legacy of the big four provides an additional stimulus for change. Progress may be slow, but reform has started.

The painful process of bank reform has led China's government to recognize that capital markets may be more efficient mechanisms for intermediating capital between supply and demand – particularly in terms of addressing investors' insistence on returns. Accordingly, the government is instituting policies to support the development of a robust and liquid capital market. Chinese companies are increasingly turning away from traditional banking credit to equity and bond financing, and Chinese individuals are putting a growing share of their money into stocks and fixed-income instruments rather than deposits. China's capital markets will have significant opportunities to expand, and become an increasingly important source of funding for Chinese companies (Exhibit 1.2).

China's equity markets have developed in three phases that highlight the tradeoff between control and growth that is the regulator's dilemma. The early 1990s featured an emphasis on control, including elimination of the T-bill futures market in 1995 and the rectification of financial institutions in early 1994. This followed the abolition of market price controls in May 1993 and the entry of institutions into the market in 1993. However, after a brief period of freedom, controls were reintroduced in 1999 following the introduction of the Securities Law, and a planned sale of state shares was suspended in 2001.

In 1990, the Shanghai and Shenzhen stock exchanges were opened with great fanfare. In December 1991 came the first Initial Public Offering (IPO) – Shanghai Electronic Vacuum. In 1992, the first closed-end fund was set up and the B-Share market was launched for international investors to participate. A formal regulatory body – the China Securities Regulatory Commission (CSRC) — was founded in 1992. In 1993, Tsingtao Brewery became the first Chinese company to be traded on the Hong Kong Stock Exchange. Trading was restricted – in 1993 domestic retail and institutional investors were allowed to invest only in A-shares, domestic SOEs and listed

Exhibit 1.2 Sources of Funding in China (US$ billions)

							Forecast			
100% =	189	231	259	251	292	295	324	348	374	402
Bank loans*	60%	57%	59%	55%	49%	55%	49%	42%	36%	30%
Capital markets { Bonds*	16%	14%	19%	21%	18%	23%	24%	25%	27%	28%
Capital markets { Stocks*	4%	11%	5%	7%	20%	7%	12%	18%	23%	28%
FDI	21%	18%	17%	16%	13%	15%	15%	15%	14%	14%
	1996	97	98	99	00	01	02	03	04	2005

* Includes funding from both domestic and overseas sources

Source: China Statistical Yearbooks; EIU; McKinsey analysis

companies were prohibited from trading stocks, and commercial banks were barred from operating trust investment and securities businesses.

This experimental phase came to a close in July 1994 when equity issuance was abruptly suspended for seven months. A moratorium was imposed on new IPOs and strict controls were placed on the number and size of rights issuances. But by 1996 the regulator had allowed domestic equity issuance to go back to pre-1994 levels, in part to cool down the secondary market. The CSRC assigned a quota to the planning commissions of the various provincial governments. These in turn allocated the quota to IPO candidates in their own provinces, mostly to state-owned enterprises, and further selected the lead underwriters.

The third and current phase of standardization can be said to have started with the key reform initiatives in July 1999, intended to move China's bourses towards international standards. These included the replacement of the quota system for IPOs with an expert-review panel, the introduction of new investors, and more aggressive regulatory action. In early 2000, the listing quota was abolished in favor of an expert-review system. All IPO candidates now have to go through a one-year preparatory phase before an application can be submitted. Investment banks must submit these applications on behalf of the candidates and selected members from an 80-member expert committee review the qualifications of the candidates. The CSRC also controls the number of IPO applications that an investment bank can submit, based largely on the total number of deals that the bank accomplished in the previous year. This transformation has opened up the IPO approval system to a wider range of companies while retaining the CSRC's control on the process through the preparation period, the allocation of application slots to underwriters, and control over the quality of final approvals.

The CSRC has also introduced new investor classes. Since 1999, the ban on state enterprises buying equities from the primary markets has been lifted, insurance companies have been allowed to invest up to 15% of funds in equity markets, and up to 50% of new listings can be placed with institutional investors. The A- and B-share markets have been effectively merged since 2001 and, in future, domestic institutional investors will likely be able to participate in international markets. At the same time, foreigners will gain controlled access to the A-share market through Qualified Financial Institutional Investors. Finally, the delisting of Shanghai Narcissus and Yuejinman in mid-2001 showed fresh resolve on the part of the regulator to improve the quality of China's listed vehicles, as did the regulations on decreasing state-owned shares in the stock market, which came into effect in June 2001.

Looking back after a decade of development, the capital markets experiment appears to have been a qualified success. Within a decade of coming into existence, China's capital markets have grown to be Asia Pacific's second-largest after Japan and the largest among emerging markets. According to Goldman Sachs, China's domestic stock market will reach approximately $2 trillion (65% of GDP) by 2010. Domestic market capitalization has grown at over 40% from $43 billion in 1993 to $580 billion in 2000, a third of which is tradable (the balance is held by the state or individuals not registered for active trading). As a percentage of GDP, market capitalization has soared from 10% in the early 1990s to over 50% in 2000. For a relatively nascent market, this compares well with Taiwan (70%), Malaysia (120%) and Singapore (160%).

China is, in fact, emerging as a leader in state-industry privatization globally as it tries to establish a modern corporate system based on shareholding and other forms of private ownership. Reflecting the early stage of the market, 55% of equity issued annually in China is in the form of IPOs. In contrast, IPOs amounted to less than 30% of stock issued on the New York Stock Exchange (NYSE) in 2000. Average annual equity issuance has grown from $5.4 billion in 1993 to over $17 billion in 2001, amounting to an average growth rate of 16%. The number of listed companies has also grown dramatically at over 20% per annum, from 223 in 1993 to over 1,200 by the end of 2000.

This is not to say that there are no challenges – on the contrary, China's stock markets have a long way to go to achieve world-class standards of liquidity and regulation. By 2002 a bubble had clearly formed, with price-earnings ratios of over 40 the norm. Private companies still face barriers to accessing the stock markets. Of the 1,200 listed companies, fewer than 200 have collective or private ownership. And by global standards most of China's listed companies are relatively small, with a market capitalization of $500 million and average issuance of $100 million in 2000. Large Chinese companies such as China Mobile, China Unicom and China National Offshore Oil Company still turn to overseas capital markets to raise funds. Chinese companies tapping overseas markets in Hong Kong have been much bigger than the typical domestic listing, with average market capitalization of $12 billion and $1.7 billion in issuance volume in 2000 reflecting these companies' issuance. Of the top seven listings of Chinese companies between 1997 and 2001, five were international, reflecting the inability of China's domestic markets to channel large IPOs (for instance, around $3 billion). But they also reflect the intangible benefits associated with an international listing, such as prestige, the impact of good corporate governance and the receipt of foreign currency.[3]

RAISING THE CORPORATE GAME

With the capital markets and more commercially oriented banks taking over the traditional government role of funding, China's government expects that China's corporate sector will raise its game to raise productivity and sustain China's economic growth. China needs strong companies to deploy the savings of its consumers effectively. If low profits and corruption are allowed to fritter away these resources, a historic opportunity will be missed. Improved performance will in turn provide the revenues government needs to meet its urgent social priorities.

Government is moving to unleash the productivity potential inherent in Chinese enterprises by fundamentally changing the conditions under which business operates in China. Transparency and accounting regularity are high priorities – the CSRC has mandated regular reviews of accounting for listed companies and the rotation of auditors. Government shares of listed enterprises are being sold down, both to pay for social programs and to remove the pernicious influence of majority state control. And China's political structure itself is evolving to manage these risks as the economy moves forward. Without stable, transparent and accountable government, business will pay a high price in frictional costs. Thus entrepreneurs are now being invited to join the Communist Party, in part to build confidence that their wealth will not be turned against them in a political change of winds.

With these changes, Chinese state enterprises will be less able to rely on the not-so-hidden-hand of the government to sustain them in good times and bad. As state banks are required to make better lending decisions and stock markets become more choosy about who they let onto the exchange, SOEs must shape up or ship out. And even the most famous companies can fall by the wayside. China's department stores have been among the first bankruptcies even though they are still highly visible pillars of the society. In early 2002, Haier, one of China's most respected state companies, came under attack for its expensive expansion in the U.S. at a time when its market share at home was declining.

Foreign investors for their part will also face new opportunities and challenges. Most will benefit from ever-expanding opportunities in China, notably through its entry into the World Trade Organization (WTO) as China will continue to seek Foreign Direct Investment (FDI) after its WTO accession. According to official publications by the State Council, going by the average contribution of FDI to GDP growth, China will need $250 billion in foreign investment, if it wants to achieve 7% to 8% annual GDP growth during the Tenth Five-Year Plan period (2001-2005). Regulatory change following WTO accession will open up investment opportunities previously not available (for example, in financial services).

In the age of globalization, China's WTO accession will also give multinational corporations (MNCs) greater scope and flexibility in capitalizing on competitive advantages China offers across industries. This is already manifested in the shifting nature of FDI to China, from labor-intensive to capital-intensive and then technology-intensive businesses. As an example, in 2000, 90% of Whirlpool's production in China was for export. For Motorola it was 45%, for Hewlett-Packard 42% and for Hitachi 39%. Foreign Invested Enterprises' (FIEs') share of export of high-technology products from China increased from 61% in 1996 to 82% in 2000. Global companies are also building global R&D and service centers in China. Motorola has R&D investments of more than US$200 million and employs over 1,300 researchers in China. GE Capital has its North Asia Back Office Center in Dalian which serves Japan, Korea, Taiwan and Hong Kong.

But WTO accession also means equal footing for all market players. So foreign-invested companies will no longer benefit from favorable treatment. Foreign investors who were the first to enter China have benefited from government-arranged deals. In Shanghai, Volkswagen was guaranteed sales to taxi companies by the Shanghai city government in the early years of its joint venture. Kodak secured a virtual ban on imports by its competitor Fuji for a three-year period as a condition of its investment in domestic film processing. These deals are no longer allowed under WTO rules. Neither will be preferential tax, land and other economic incentives.

The development of China's capital markets as a major source of domestic funding may also diminish the relative importance of FDI in satisfying China's need for capital over time. As Chinese companies grow larger and improve their performance, more of them will be able to get funding from international capital markets. The opening-up and improvement of China's capital markets will also induce more foreign investors to participate in China's growth through them. On the other hand, the development of a well-functioning, open capital market will also be positive for FDI in China as it means more exit options for foreign investors, especially venture capitalists, through IPOs, for example.

A simple calculation may reveal the limits of FDI (MNC) expansion. Foreign companies currently control about 10% of China's economy. According to estimates by Morgan Stanley, this figure could reach 20% in five years if we simply extrapolate the historical trend. This makes the share of economic growth captured by foreign investors as a group disproportionately high. It will be even more so for previously restricted industries, such as financial services. The opportunity to capture a disproportionate share of growth will likely diminish once the foreign participation rate in the economy reaches a "steady" state. Logically, this will also reflect increased participation by local companies. In fact, China may increasingly begin to resemble the United States in the relative openness and competitiveness of most sectors of its economy. Understanding where and how this transition is happening is key to any company's success in China, whether foreign or domestic.

✳   ✳   ✳

China's development over the last 20 years has brought much economic benefit and created interests with a major stake in the continued successful development of the economy. Government leaders recognize that their continued leadership requires further economic success. After 20 years of this pace of change it is not surprising that there are stresses in the system. China's continued success will depend not only on how the government demonstrates its awareness of these stresses and its ability to handle them, but also on whether the emergent corporate sector proves able to compete on a world stage.

1.2 CHINA IN THE WTO: WHAT WILL REALLY CHANGE?

by Stephen M. Shaw and Tony Perkins

China's accession to the WTO was greeted with both excitement and skepticism. WTO entry will usher in dramatic change in some areas such as distribution and financial services. In other areas, however, change will be modest at best. In some it might even be negligible. To understand why, it is important to look not only at what the agreement says but also at what it doesn't say. For example, the licensing of new telecom service entrants, Renminbi (RMB) convertibility, the freeing up of interest rates, the viability of China's banking system – these are all major issues not talked about in the WTO deal but which will fundamentally affect the rate and nature of real change.

WTO-induced change in China will be an additional force applied to an already dynamic business terrain. In some industries, rapid or fundamental change is already under way; in others, it is not. Thus, any early and sweeping conclusion that WTO accession will allow foreign corporations to overtake Chinese companies is generally misplaced: the situation is much more complex. Some sectors of China's economy already have formidable Chinese enterprises (for instance, oil, telecom services, rail, transport). They may be inefficient by world standards, but they have strong legacy positions, high aspirations, and — in the WTO sunset period agreed to for most sectors — a big head start. Other sectors have fast-growing, aggressive, medium-sized Chinese companies – some private, some almost private – that have shed or segregated their SOE obligations (some examples are TCL and Konka). They have very low-cost structures, are well managed and are not afraid to go global.

In fact, of the players in this market, one could argue that today's mid-sized Chinese companies already competing in sectors less controlled by the government could be the big winners in the post-WTO economy. Most terms of the U.S.-China agreement ensure that reduced barriers to competition and investment will be phased in over two to five years, giving Chinese companies a significant lead in strengthening entrenched market positions and capturing many newly available opportunities.

In such a scenario, three significant outcomes of the negotiations surrounding China's entry into WTO are possible. The largest single fundamental change is the opening of distribution. This clearly creates new possibilities in the sector and paves the way for investment and modernization. But, perhaps more importantly, it affects how every business that is make-sell by nature goes to market. Further areas of "explosive" industry growth and hence great opportunity are the Internet, banking, insurance and securities.

In a number of industries, major change is apparent only on the surface (Exhibit 1.3). A closer look reveals that only moderate or relatively small degrees of fundamental change are likely in the near term because in some areas of the economy, markets are currently pretty open or fairly competitive, either due to lack of government control from the outset (for example, consumer packaged goods) or because existing deregulation has led to an already competitive marketplace (for instance, consumer electronics). In still other areas, the government has already taken a tough restructuring stance to create corporatized competitors (for example, telecom services and oil) and thus is already driving rapid change. WTO entry will only accelerate this change incrementally.

THE TRANSFORMATION IN DISTRIBUTION AND RETAIL

WTO accession will perhaps have the largest impact on this broadly defined commercial arena. The phasing out of restrictions on distribution and distribution services for most products will have a two-fold impact. First, it

Exhibit 1.3 China's WTO accession impact varies by sector

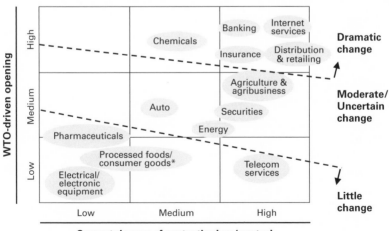

* Excluding liquor and tobacco; these industries have been highly controlled
  and will likely continue to be

Source: United States–China Business Council; McKinsey analysis

will provide opportunities to pursue distribution and/or retailing as a business in itself. Second, and perhaps more importantly, it will provide companies with the classic degrees of freedom to compete in crucial areas such as after-sales support and channel management that can become major sources of competitive advantage. Given the antiquated nature of distribution in China, the opportunities for innovation are huge – both in distribution services themselves, and, more importantly, in how companies in a variety of industries compete with each other.

In retail, the opening up of distribution might well facilitate the growth of nationwide retail networks by allowing economies of scale. The only way a chain retailer can compete with non-chain retailers in China is to achieve economies of scale in buying and distribution; for instance, by buying nationally from one company. WTO accession could provide a more level playing field for entrants against incumbents. The decline in tariffs will discourage smuggling, thus choking an important source of supply for local "mom & pop" stores. Professional retailers will benefit not only from this diminished "cost advantage" but also from the opportunities for competitive pricing as the large costs incurred in third-party distribution disappear.

In terms of creating distribution/retail businesses, it is unclear who will be the natural owners or the winners. To consider an example: Will the current infrastructure owners, given their control of assets and ties with the government, be in an advantaged position in terms of modernizing their services and integrating transportation? Or could another type of player snatch victory from their hands? Quite possibly, very effective logistics businesses with national scale could develop, leveraging network scope and scale economies. A proliferation of players with such aspirations may bring about consolidation over time. For example, a number of manufacturers of specialized products, such as Procter & Gamble, have built enough scale to set up proprietary distribution channels within their sectors and could choose to develop a class-leading offering.

Regardless of how the end-game plays out, the sector is set for tremendous turmoil and innovation as, over time, manufacturers, distributors and retailers strive to achieve the supply-chain efficiency and effectiveness of developed markets.

EXPLOSIVE GROWTH IN THE INTERNET

The Internet and e-commerce: Post-accession, this will clearly become an open field for both domestic and foreign players. Internet-based activities are fundamentally hard to control and e-commerce is a fast-moving market. Attempts to control Web-based content and e-commerce will only drive the market to other shores. Generally, PC-Internet penetration drives the growth of e-commerce. In China, however, PC penetration is very low — about 2.3% in 2002. The penetration of mobile phones, on the other hand, is much higher; close to 7% in 2002. With the advent of technologies such as Wireless Application Protocol (WAP) and 3G, mobile phones (and perhaps other devices such as Personal Digital Assistants and television) are likely to drive Internet penetration in China.

It is not clear whether local or foreign companies will be the winners in the e-commerce market, but we venture to say that partnerships between the two might prove a winning combination. Foreign companies have the technology, brands and skills; Chinese companies have the local content, language capabilities and local connections. An Amazon.com can't win in China because it has few foreign-language capabilities. But an Amazon.com in partnership with a Chinese company would be a hard combination to beat. For example, in 2001, eBay purchased Eachnet, a Chinese auctions provider based in Shanghai, providing a handsome return to its initial venture capital backers.

The barriers to growth will be fulfillment and payment. No one yet has the distribution capability to deliver products reliably across China and the penetration of credit cards is low. Japan overcame the distribution barrier by using convenience stores: wholesalers deliver goods to convenience stores where they are picked up and paid for by customers. But, again, China has no national network of chain stores. E-commerce players will thus have to find multiple partners to build physical and financial distribution networks.

Another barrier could be that China (and Asia in general) has still to sort out e-commerce transaction-based protocols and regulation for security of consumer information, encryption, and recognition of digitized signatures, for example. But once this happens, and once non-proprietary distribution/ delivery services become more modernized, the opportunities for e-commerce are almost boundless.

BREAKING THROUGH IN FINANCIAL SERVICES

International banks, financial services firms and insurance companies have a lot to gain from WTO-induced changes in banking, securities and insurance.

In **banking**, accession to the WTO will sweep away the severe restrictions on foreign banks, leaving Chinese banks open to strong competition in the areas of financial talent, quality clients, new business and technology. For foreign banks, this adds up to major growth opportunities in both consumer and corporate banking. In corporate banking, foreign banks will have the leading edge in transaction-based businesses and cash management services.

Foreign banks will also have the advantage in consumer banking; that is, personal services such as investment products, credit cards, and auto financing. In fact, in retail banking, we could envision a decided shift in favor of foreign banks, with affluent customers moving their business to them in search of better service and security. In the five years till full market opening, the local banks have a lot of ground to cover to become world-class players – they now have more incentive than ever to embrace aggressive improvement programs.

Securities, previously closed to foreign investment and foreign banks, will be opened up considerably, creating unprecedented access to China's escalating securities market. But the degree and rate of change will be decided by three factors. First, the degree to which the Renminbi becomes convertible. This pivotal issue has not been clarified, despite all the buzz about WTO terms, but convertibility is bound to happen before long. The second pivotal factor is how China's securities market evolves and matures. Though growing rapidly, this market is still embryonic. Finally, the degree to which the banking sector can be reformed and non-performing debt can be converted to equity will have a crucial impact on the development of the securities market after accession. All three factors are highly related and it is hard to predict whether the required conditions for success will develop quickly or slowly. What is clear, though, is that, post-accession, the playing field will be more open than ever and many new players will emerge.

Insurance will also open up a great deal. Currently, the sector is dominated by local companies due to the geographic restrictions on foreign companies (they are allowed to operate only in Guangzhou and Shanghai), and to other restrictions such as the need to operate through joint ventures with government-approved Chinese partners.

The lifting of these and other restraints will surely lead to the entry of a large number of life insurance players. These players are more likely to invest in existing Chinese insurance firms (currently starved for capital), rather than build a business from scratch. Since product offerings will still be restricted by regulation and investment vehicles will be rather limited, they will have to gain competitive advantage primarily by building professional sales and marketing capabilities to win new and retain existing customers. The international life insurers are likely to be much more aggressive in China than their property and casualty counterparts, given the relatively low penetration in China of lucrative "life" products.

WHERE CHANGE IS LESS THAN MEETS THE EYE

In many sectors, reading between the lines shows that what may be required is less excitement and a little caution.

Take **automotives** and **auto components**. On the face of it, this sector seems set for massive change given the dramatic reduction in tariffs. Reduced tariffs will considerably lower car prices. In fact, this is already happening, based on the expectations of manufacturers. The biggest real change, however, will likely be the opening up of distribution. With the rights to distribute and sell goods themselves, local manufacturers will have greatly improved market access and a chance to better manage the customer experience. Changes in distribution will also have a significant impact on parts management and business system design for automobile makers and maintenance centers.

Actual change in competitive positioning, however, is likely to be less than dramatic. True, many of the small, loss-making car producers will lose ground as imports flood in. In fact, imported products over time will "set the bar", and form the basis for competition for local assemblers. But many new manufacturing entrants are unlikely since it will be hard to dislodge the rather efficient, large-scale joint-venture manufacturers such as SAIC-Volkswagen. Certainly, in the sunset period to 2006, local players will work harder than ever to gain further scale and productivity, and reach world-class product, manufacturing and service standards.

In **energy**, it's instructive to look closely at the **oil industry**. Like autos, this sector has remained heavily controlled, both upstream and downstream, given its long-recognized status as a strategic industry. In the last few years, in an effort to dramatically improve the efficiency of its large integrated incumbents, the Chinese government has begun to corporatize them through asset restructuring and public listings; for instance, of China National Offshore Oil Corporation, Sinopec and China National Petroleum Corporation (See box '**Creating Global Oil Majors**'). This reflects the government's view that incumbents need to significantly modernize and greatly improve their productivity.

The WTO agreement will build on this major initiative, most prominently in the area of retail and distribution. However, when these areas are eventually opened to foreign players (some years after accession, and conditionally even then), they may find that the opportunities are limited since Chinese incumbents will have built on their already strong positions. Chinese incumbents will retain control of attractive retail and wholesale assets and will aggressively try to consolidate their strengths in those parts of the value chain which foreigners, by and large, have not been able to enter, such as exploration, production and refining. The government's hope is clearly that

Chinese players will have consolidated their market presence in the sunset period before foreign companies can build an advantage in distribution.

Unlike in most other sectors, large-scale opportunities for international oil companies in wholesale and retail will thus be scant. Possible joint-venture partners will grow from just one source – the Chinese government. The pressure on currently inflated downstream margins that WTO accession will create may encourage local players to make significant deals with multinationals. That said, there might be larger opportunities in natural gas than oil. Natural gas is highly attractive as a source of clean energy and Chinese players do not have the well-developed infrastructure that would prompt protectionist sentiments on the part of the government.

How WTO accession will play out in **chemicals** is highly uncertain. It is hard to sensibly predict a clear development path for this sector, given its current status and the publicized changes from WTO accession. While the government has encouraged local participation through tariff barriers, Chinese players today still lack economies of scale. If the government lowers and finally eliminates tariff barriers as promised, China will be inundated with chemical imports at world prices, due to global overcapacity in a number of major chemicals. It is difficult to see how sub-scale Chinese players could compete viably in such a scenario.

Ultimately, the timing of competitive changes will likely depend more on the pace of product-specific market development than on regulatory sanctions, though certainly the market can be accelerated through access to cheap imports. For instance, commodity manufacturers that must incur significant transportation costs to get their products to market will have large opportunities in a market relatively safe from low-cost import competition. However, mega-dollar investments in local production will be required to truly tap the local market potential. Such investments are predicated on a Chinese market that is truly world-scale and reasonably accessible by transport.

For most chemicals, such markets are at least five years away from China's current stage of development. In fact, this appears to have been taken into consideration in the strategy of the global majors, who have staked their claims to key petrochemicals hubs across the country but have notably refrained from aggressive investments, particularly given the recent history of intense competition and poor returns in chemicals globally and in Asia-Pacific.

Ultimately, then, in a post-WTO world, little may change in five years but it seems safe to say that, in 20 years, the competitive landscape will be concentrated around a handful of world-scale hubs with world-class facilities. Who will be investing and operating those hubs is a completely different (and, at the moment, unknowable) matter.

Creating Global Oil Majors

In the 1990s, the Chinese government decided to initiate an aggressive program of industry restructuring, management change, and an introduction of international and private-sector capital in the oil and gas sector.[4] In some ways the sector was an ideal candidate for reform – it boasted attractive world-class assets, large domestic companies and a promising market situation. Conservative estimates put China's oil and gas investment requirements for 2000 to 2010 at over $50 billion. Much of this was because China's infrastructure had not kept pace with demand. Domestic energy marketing and transport infrastructure were woefully inadequate, with largely sub-scale terminals and depots, no long-distance pipelines and poor road and barge transportation. Manufacturing was likewise far from adequate to meet China's energy needs. China imported over 600,000 barrels per day (bpd) of refined petroleum products, primarily diesel and fuel oil in 2001, making it the largest importer in Asia.

The first major step was to corporatize the state refining and upstream bureaucracy, in the process establishing Sinopec, CNPC and China National Offshore Oil Corporation (CNOOC) as independent commercial entities in the early 1990s. Sinopec was formed by grouping together the existing refining assets of the various provinces. At the time it was seen as a holding company formed primarily to facilitate negotiations with foreigners on new refining investments. Several years later, the marketing assets of the provinces were integrated into Sinopec as well. CNPC represented the onshore upstream assets of the country while CNOOC controlled offshore.

Market pricing for crude oil and refined products was the next step and was introduced gradually. At first entirely controlled by the state, in the mid-1990s oil prices began to be linked to international levels. Crude prices were the first to be reformed, through a series of adjustments to bring them in line with traded Singapore prices. Refined products followed as an adjustment process gradually brought Chinese prices in line with international levels, although monthly adjustments were still made by hand by the State Economic Commission. This began to reveal the economic inefficiencies of refineries, situated far from markets, on top of declining reserves.

Then, in 1997, the State Council decided to reform Sinopec and CNPC, hitherto upstream and downstream monopolies, into vertically integrated oil companies. The express objective of the reform was to form internationally competitive entities that would be able to generate profits and support Beijing's broader economic reform program. Sinopec was to own both upstream and downstream assets in southern and coastal areas while CNPC would control the north. CNOOC would retain its offshore oil exploration monopoly but still consider downstream investments.

Despite the reform, each company still retained a distinctive profile. CNPC clearly remained the dominant upstream player in China, with the lion's share of attractive assets and current production. In particular, Daqing, the historic heart of China's upstream industry, continued to supply over 30% of total Chinese upstream production and 50% of CNPC's own supply. The Tarim Basin also provided CNPC with the greatest prospective reserves in China, amounting to over 10 billion tons. CNOOC, the offshore oil company, was the only challenger to CNPC but its volume was dwarfed in total reserves, annual production and new finds. Sinopec for its part controlled only the rapidly declining Shengli fields and a collection of played-out basins in the interior of the country. In its favor though was its effective control of the majority of the refining and marketing assets in the major markets of the south and east. CNPC meanwhile was left with only the slow-growth north and interior markets for its upstream supplies.

The three major oil companies – CNPC, Sinopec and CNOOC — then all announced plans to list internationally in 1998. CNOOC was expected to list first given its smaller size yet still attractive assets, experienced management and profitable track record. However, poor preparation, an unrealistic offer price and weak investor relations forced it to reschedule at the last minute, leading to the replacement of the lead underwriter and embarrassment all round. As it turned out, PetroChina, CNPC's listed company, would be the first to list on the New York Stock Exchange in the spring of 2000 following an intensive period of preparation and restructuring. The IPO was a success and six months later Sinopec would follow.

By the end of 2000, all three companies were listed and the government moved on to the next stage of its reform plan – opening up the markets to competition, both domestic and international. This marked a reversal in the government's attitude to foreign investment in the sector. Regulators had historically prevented foreign companies from entering the Chinese market. Beginning in the early 1980s, MNCs have sought access to upstream and downstream opportunities with limited success. The early bid rounds in upstream oil failed to yield any successes and resulted in more than a few spectacular failures. Much of the time the offered acreage had already been extensively worked over by Chinese drilling crews. Only offshore, where China lacked technology, were foreigners given the opportunity to explore in relatively prospective areas, and several finds were made.

Downstream, foreigners were blocked from most of the attractive marketing opportunities, in particular through the establishment of Article 18, which explicitly prohibited investment in retail stations. As for refining, foreign interest was limited given the poor worldwide refining environment, and a prohibition on owning over 50% of these assets or on getting access to the most attractive ones.

But once China entered the World Trade Organization (WTO) in 2001, it committed to a new series of market-opening moves in downstream areas. Tariffs on refined and petrochemical products were to be slashed. Retail would be opened up in three years and wholesale in five to both international and domestic players. The opening of wholesale was a particularly tough move as the historic oligopoly exercised by Sinopec and CNPC produced fat profits for both.

Cumulatively, these moves have basically opened the Chinese energy sector to competition. Whether and how the incumbents respond will have a huge impact not only on their survival, but also on the success of the entire state-enterprise reform program. All the large Chinese companies are still at a significant competitive disadvantage in what is a fast-consolidating global industry. Market analysts note that their public stocks trade at significant discounts to Western counterparts. While large in China, their revenues are less than 10% of a giant such as ExxonMobil. Only by continuing to take unpopular but necessary restructuring moves while aggressively investing in new growth opportunities created by the booming domestic market can they survive.

Agriculture and agribusiness: This is another area in which WTO accession seems to promise dramatic change. Tariffs will decline and export subsidies will be eliminated. Private trade will be allowed, as will be the import and distribution of products, without the necessary involvement of a state trading enterprise or middleman. Quotas will be relaxed, pricing will be decontrolled and foreign companies will be allowed to enter. However, there will be no opening of floodgates, since quotas, while increasing in volume, will still exist. In fact, it is hard to see how the Chinese government can live up to the terms of the current agreement.

From a narrow U.S. perspective, American stakeholders have sought targeted concessions so that their farmers will have a new (and very large) market for their goods. However, it will be very difficult indeed for the Chinese government to throw open agricultural commodities markets en masse. This would cause an even more severe dislocation of China's population from rural to urban areas than that already under way, despite widespread current government intervention and protection. Clearly, the government will have to walk a tightrope between early and fast liberalization versus a gradual opening up that would help mitigate even more dramatic and politically dangerous dislocation of the rural population. In fact, while quota increases are dramatic in percentage terms, in many cases absolute amounts of allowed imports often comprise only a small fraction of total consumption. For example, though the quota for corn imports will rise from 250,000 metric tons to a total of 7.2 million metric tons, consumption of imported corn in China amounts to only 0.2% of total corn consumption today.

EVOLUTION, NOT REVOLUTION

Sectors in which evolutionary rather than revolutionary change is likely are telecommunication (telecom) and telecom equipment, consumer goods and pharmaceuticals.

In **telecom and telecom equipment**, notwithstanding the publicity given to the opening of service businesses, very little will change. This sector has been restructuring for some time and WTO accession will only accelerate the already fast pace of change.

In telecom and other communications services, China Telecom has already been carved into vertical slices and the new entities intend to compete with each other. The richer PTAs[5] are becoming fairly independent in their operations and new entrants are building presence. China Netcom and other Internet players are building capability and other ministries, such as Radio, Film and Television, and Railways, have concrete plans to use their networks commercially. WTO accession will open telecom services to partial foreign ownership of existing players. However, there is no assurance that local companies will sell stakes, nor is there any indication of how new licenses will be granted.

The opening up of the telecom equipment sector will intensify competition. But there will be no significant upheaval since major international players have already staked out their positions reasonably well. Here, it is important to note China's unspoken policy to support domestic players through non-tariff barriers (for example, local-preferred buying practices) and the "standards" issue (that is, the hard-to-resolve question of what are the right equipment standards for China). WTO rules will make it harder for local players to perpetuate the standards issue, but the "buy local" behavior on the part of local service providers is likely to remain strong.

While a major industry shake-up is unlikely, this is not to say that WTO implementation won't prove quite beneficial to all players. Telecom equipment makers will be able to integrate sales of imported and locally made products via a single salesforce. Managers will no longer have to deal with explicit quotas and tough export requirements and will thus be free to focus on the fast-growing China market. Finally, tariff reductions will allow the integration of Chinese plants into a global manufacturing strategy – decisions on where to manufacture can be based more purely on business economics.

Reduced tariffs may also benefit late entrants, such as Japanese and Korean handset makers. Instead of further investments in plants in China to gain market access, they will be able to ship products from their existing world-scale facilities, and focus instead on building Chinese sales and marketing infrastructure. Similarly, data equipment vendors will have an attractive choice in how to invest-they can build plants, or they can invest in local sales capability. Original Equipment Manufacturers (OEMs) will continue to find China an attractive manufacturing base.

In **consumer electronics and personal computers** too, WTO-induced change will be relatively minor, as these markets have been opening to competition over time, and are already quite competitive in an absolute sense. For example, a number of local television makers (for example Haier, TCL, and Konka) are already competing intensively, and prices for color televisions in China are lower than those in the U.S. or Western Europe. In fact, it could even be said that local manufacturers, who import many components, are becoming tough exporters as falling tariffs further reduce their cost of goods.

In personal computers, the landscape is similar. Local players such as Legend are overtaking foreign competitors, who, till now, have been playing largely in the gray market (landing imported PCs into China, despite regulatory proscriptions). As the PC market in China continues to grow quickly, foreign players such as Dell and HP are setting up shop to manufacture in China. And like many other sectors, the liberalization of PC sales and distribution will allow producers to compete on more dimensions, further intensifying competition in an already competitive sector.

The picture is not very different in **consumer non-durables/packaged goods**. Processed goods and other consumer goods manufacture has not been considered a strategic area by China, and thus has never been a target for much government control or intervention. Consequently, a large number of foreign and local players are vying for share in this market. Most major players, from Nestlé to Unilever to Procter & Gamble, already have a considerable presence in the Chinese consumer goods market. This market tends to be inherently local (especially for processed food products) and the behavior of MNCs tends to be consistent with their behavior in the rest of the world: trying to build brands and distribution presence in urban centers while tailoring products to local tastes.

With the exception of liberalized distribution, we do not think that much will change for existing players after China's accession to the WTO. However, new entrants or small current players in the market may gain some advantage. Currently, their lack of scale prevents them from setting up proprietary distribution capabilities – which the major players have done. The entry of new distribution players may allow minor marketers to get to market almost as efficiently as major competitors.

Pharmaceuticals is another sector that has been open for some time. At least 25 global pharmaceuticals firms are operating in China through joint ventures or wholly foreign-owned enterprises (WFOEs) today. The sector has already been evolving in line with changes in the Chinese medical insurance system. The main area of interest post-WTO is likely to be over-the-counter products for three reasons: the opening up of distribution; an expected improvement in the enforcement of intellectual property laws; and an expected increase in private spending on healthcare. Also, WTO accession may create better opportunities for locals and multinationals alike to brand and export traditional Chinese medicines, including acquiring and licensing internationally famous Chinese products. Yet again, WTO accession will only increase competition in an already competitive Chinese market.

✳   ✳   ✳

What does all this add up to for CEOs pondering the implications for their companies of China's accession to the WTO? The short answer is that anyone playing a China card based on the WTO accession will have to be very vigilant. Accession is often seen solely as an economic event. In fact, it is a socio-political one. Some forces in the Chinese government want to drive change and modernization – for them, WTO accession will force change rapidly enough to let the economy prosper. As long as these forces are in power, the government will live up to the deal. But if the social impact of accession is very adverse, it could give a currently silent minority the ammunition for slowing economic reform. Clearly, calculated risks have been taken, with clear downsides. Any company planning major moves in China based on assumptions about the WTO agreement must be clear-headed about these risks and downsides.

REFERENCES

1. Chinese central planning was always a relatively loosely run affair. A Soviet planning official noted in the 1970s that the Chinese plan for chemicals included only 30 basic chemicals while Gosplan's equivalent tracked hundreds.

2. *Sources of China's Economic Growth, 1952–99*, World Bank Policy Research Working Paper 2650.

3. Nonetheless, these benefits could often be outweighed in the eyes of Chinese issuers by the much higher price-earnings ratios available in the domestic market. In early 2001, the A-share market traded at a PE of 54 compared to18 for Hong Kong-listed Chinese companies–so-called H-shares.

4. The power sector has also been mooted as a promising sector for reform since it also has profitable large companies with major investment needs. In April 2002, the State Council issued a framework under which reform is to proceed. This included the separation of the State Power national holding company into separate generation and transmission groups, the introduction of competitive power pricing to the grid and the tightening of emission standards. The restructuring of companies is not expected to be completed before the end of 2003 and competitive power pricing is not expected to be introduced until 2005, but it is a sign that this other major sector of the energy economy will begin to enhance its competitiveness.

5. PTA: Posts and Telecommunications Administration, the administrative branch of China Telecom in each of its provinces.

2

The High-Tech Revolution

High technology is the newest sector of China's economy. With a strong push from foreign investment and supported by China's abundant engineering talent and fiercely competitive domestic market, Chinese companies are leapfrogging to become global leaders.

China's consumer-electronics industry was one of the first to go global. Building on the core advantages of low-cost assembly and the world's fastest-growing market, China's consumer-electronics players are not only becoming manufacturers of choice for Western brands, but also rapidly building world-scale export businesses and buying up their falling Western rivals. Their leapfrog approach promises to do in 10 years what Japanese and Korean brands did in 40.

Likewise, China's semiconductor industry will grow to global significance, driven by similar factors that propelled Taiwan's rapid rise. However, China's unique characteristics, in particular its robust domestic demand and plentiful design talent, will lead to a more design-focused industry, and potentially a complementary relationship with Taiwan.

The challenge for all of these aspiring global leaders is as much organizational as it is strategic. As Liu Chuanzhi of Legend says, making the transition from entrepreneurial founder to global institution is the biggest challenge for Chinese high-tech companies. The winners will be differentiated by their single-minded focus on performance and their ability to manage through the inevitable ups and downs of China's high-growth economy.

2.1 TAKING CHINA'S CONSUMER ELECTRONICS COMPANIES GLOBAL

Fresh from the consolidation of the domestic industry, Chinese consumer electronics manufacturers are set on pursuing growth in developed markets. The large profit pools of these markets are attractive in their own right. Without access to them, Chinese companies will face increasing pressure from multinationals, which have finally learned how to compete in China. But globalization will be quite a challenge for Chinese companies. These companies lack the international brands and world-class operational skills of the successful global players. Leading global companies have taken decades to develop brands and skills of this order and it would require huge investments for Chinese companies to replicate their strategies. Instead, Chinese companies must try to accelerate the globalization process to take on the global majors on their own turf. Doing so will require innovative strategies that alternatively leverage technology shifts, mergers and acquisitions (M&A), and original equipment manufacturing capability, all while building on the inherent advantages of China as a home base.

THE GLOBALIZATION IMPERATIVE

China's consumer electronics companies are well aware of the need to go global and several are already doing so. One of the most famous, Haier, a white-goods producer, has already invested over $30 million in U.S. factories and expansion plans, and aims to earn one-third of its revenues from overseas production and another third from exports of the international Haier brand. Another white-goods company, Kelon, is building an OEM business in the U.S. and Europe while pushing its own brand in Asian markets. Still others are establishing manufacturing in the emerging markets of Brazil, Russia and Vietnam (Gree) or actively manufacturing for global brands and retailers such as Home Depot (TCL, Midea).

Why? First of all, things are tough at home. Huge domestic capacity investments pose the threat of overcapacity in China. While domestic market growth is still relatively high by global standards, annual increases in demand have fallen from double to single digits. Overcapacity is now over 30% in washing machines, 40% in refrigerators, 45% in microwave ovens and 87% in televisions.

Further, MNCs are posing a greater threat than ever to Chinese players. Some MNCs have built local presence and now have local manufacturing, solid knowledge of the market, local distribution networks and local management. Deregulation is also benefiting MNCs as government support is diminishing, import tariffs are being reduced, and the removal of marketing and distribution restrictions post-WTO provides greater access to the market.

MNCs now have the skills to outdo Chinese companies along the value chain. They now match local companies in low-cost manufacturing and have also localized their product development and service networks. Their advantages in product quality, latest technologies and key account management capability are starting to reverse the early dominance that locals achieved in the market. For example, Siemens, Electrolux and Samsung increased their collective share of the white-goods market from 6% to 22% between 1998 and 2000, largely at the expense of domestic leaders Haier, Kelon and Meiling.

To defend this home base, and create a viable platform for global competition, Chinese players will need strong global growth to achieve a size necessary to compete in this tough global industry. Companies like Haier, TCL and Konka are only 5% to 10% the size of a truly global player like Sony or Philips. International sales typically contribute no more than 10% of revenues compared to over 60% for a global player (Exhibit 2.1).

Expansion into developed markets offers the most leeway for Chinese players to reverse their fortunes. This might seem counterintuitive since the conventional wisdom is that developing markets are easier to penetrate

Exhibit 2.1 Chinese companies have ample room to grow through international sales

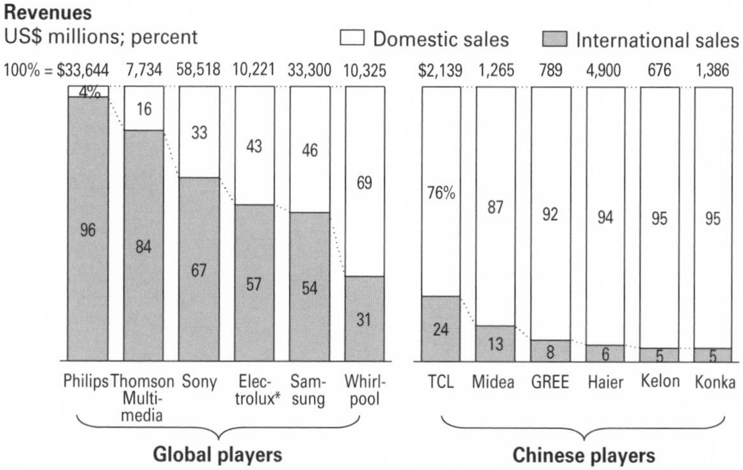

* All European sales considered domestic sales – consumer goods only

Source: Annual reports; Hoovers

because they are less competitive. The truth is that developing markets are as challenging to enter as developed ones: in many, multinational players are offering their latest products at very competitive prices. And while developed markets have their own challenges, they also have a lot to offer Chinese players. For one, there are the larger markets and profit pools. In white goods alone, the U.S. boasts a profit pool of over $2 billion, nine times that of China and 100 times that of Brazil. In brown goods, the U.S. profit pool is over $1 billion, 10 times the profit available in China and 20 times that available in Brazil. Developed markets also offer a wider range of sizable segments to target. In the U.S. the projection television market alone is larger than all the video products sold in India. The $400 million-worth of compact refrigerators sold in the U.S. in 2000 was twice the total value of all refrigerators sold in South Africa or Poland.

For another, strengths can be built from competing in these markets. Developed markets have more-demanding consumers who are early adopters of technology: Ericsson and Nokia took the lead in mobile phones thanks to European early adopters. Then, competing in these markets forces companies to innovate and improve. Developed markets are also often the source of new technology, talent and partnerships. Samsung, for example, partnered with Qualcomm in the U.S. to develop CDMA technology in its mobile phones.

Developed markets also pose difficulties that Chinese players will have to get past, including margin pressure and brand competition. A major difficulty is channel consolidation in advanced markets. In the U.S., for example, mass-market retailers control over 50% of the consumer-electronics market and the trend is accelerating, cutting the margins of new entrants. Some leading channels also have strategic partnerships, which creates entry barriers. U.K. retailer Dixons, for instance, maintains 10 global partnerships with companies such as JVC. Shelf space and product delivery are committed with long lead times (for example, 10 to 15 months in brown goods). Furthermore, new products may be co-developed with shared customer research and product engineering.

Consumer brand expectations are another major challenge for new entrants. Brand is an important purchase criterion in almost all consumer-electronics markets in developed economies: the majority of consumers find it risky to buy a brand they are unfamiliar with. Most would say the brand name is somewhat to extremely important in the purchase decision. Brand has the potential to drive replacement of products, and demanding consumers identify brands with features and value. In the U.S. home-refrigeration and laundry markets, the top five brands hold over 80% of the market. In Europe, in refrigeration products, over 80% of sales are from replacement purchases and consumers tend to replace old products with new ones of the same brand. Strong brands can also command price premiums, particularly in brown goods such as televisions, as Sony and others have demonstrated.

INSUFFICIENT EXISTING ADVANTAGES

However, to win in the developed markets, a new approach is needed. Low-cost labor will not be a sustainable advantage. Investing in the fully integrated approach that Chinese manufacturers have employed in the domestic market is likely to be prohibitively expensive and risky.

China has some existing advantages that will suffice for entry into global markets, primarily an inherent labor-cost advantage. This will certainly aid initial penetration. Wages in China are far below those of other exporting countries such as Korea and, while productivity-adjusted labor costs are on a par with Eastern Europe, increasing productivity will strengthen the labor-cost advantage given the low wages.

Lower break-even points can also provide a significant competitive advantage in overseas expansion. Traditional capital-intensive approaches often prevent new entrants from gaining enough volume to threaten entrenched market leaders. But Chinese entrants who use labor-intensive approaches have a sustainable cost advantage since, free from capital constraints, they can undercut market leaders who have little ability to retaliate given their costs of plant and equipment. This cost advantage has already helped Chinese consumer-electronics firms enter the low end of many U.S. markets.

However, while a low-cost advantage is sufficient for entry, Chinese companies will have to do more to gain global leadership. For one thing, they do not have a monopoly on China's low-cost labor. Multinationals are relocating their manufacturing to China: Sony, Philips and Panasonic are all manufacturing over 80% of production outside their home countries and China is a key manufacturing site for all. For another, low-cost manufacturing has always shifted over time from Europe to the U.S., to Japan, to Korea and Taiwan, and then to China. In the future, the Indian subcontinent and Africa could become low-cost manufacturing centers given their large, untapped markets and low labor costs (Exhibit 2.2).

In the long term, there are few examples of winning based purely on low costs. Japanese players enjoyed a low-cost position from the 1950s to the 1970s. But during this time they developed leading-edge technology, led lean manufacturing and quality movements, and invested in global branding. This gave them global leadership in automotives and consumer-electronics.

Exhibit 2.2   Global low-cost centers have periodically shifted and will do so again

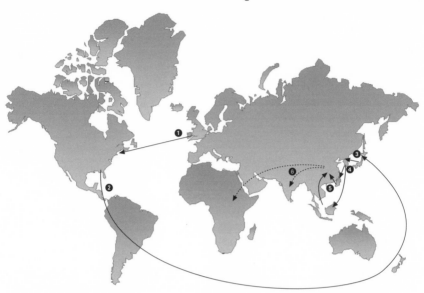

- **①** **Late 1800s** – American industrial revolution facilitates migration of global low-cost manufacturing center from Europe to U.S.

- **②** **1950s and 1960s** – Post-war Japan reconstructs itself as low-cost manufacturing base

- **③** **Late 1970s and 1980s** – As Japan emerges as a global heavyweight, neighboring Korea takes on mantle of low-cost manufacturing center

- **④** **Late 1980s** – Low-cost manufacturing moves to fast-growing SE Asian countries and Taiwan

- **⑤** **1990s** – Economic reform in China and huge consumer market transforms China into strong manufacturing base

- **⑥** **Future?** – India and Africa loom as potential low-cost manufacturing bases given large untapped markets and low-cost labor

Source: McKinsey analysis

Korean players did the same, building off their labor-cost advantages in the late 1970s and early 1990s. Taiwanese companies, in contrast, mostly failed to develop global brands and are now losing cost leadership to Chinese companies.

On the other hand, replicating the traditionally integrated Chinese business model in developed markets with traditional products also appears prohibitively expensive and risky. Chinese manufacturers have traditionally relied on a fully integrated business model in the domestic market. While initially using foreign technology, they have attempted to develop their own technology and products. Companies are generally heavily asset-based, with large manufacturing organizations. Almost all have their own distribution networks with large and cheap salesforces. In going overseas, only a few Chinese companies such as Haier have chosen to build factories in the U.S. Haier demonstrated the costs of this approach as its stock price has plunged in 2002 on speculation that its domestic cashflow, under threat from multinationals, would not be enough to sustain its losses from U.S. factories and brand-building investments.

LEVERAGING GLOBALIZATION TO WIN

Chinese companies must take advantage of the very forces of globalization which put them at risk in their home market to capture market share abroad. Changes in technology, regulation and corporate conduct all create unprecedented opportunities for Chinese companies to accelerate the multi-decade globalization process.

Leapfrogging Technology Shifts

Chinese companies have a unique opportunity to penetrate global markets by leapfrogging technology shifts. Consumer-electronics companies have traditionally followed a staircase approach to globalization (see box **'Samsung's Globalization Story'**). In the beginning, a national company meets the needs of global customers (for example, private-label retailers) through domestic operations. An office may be established to build market presence overseas but most revenues and investment are domestic.

The next step is that of "market learner": developing market understanding and determining which customer segments are attractive and servable. Consumer marketing capability is needed at this stage. Successful globalizers then move on to product development. Product selection, manufacturing technology and marketing are all tailored to meet the needs of specific segments. Finally, having achieved a dominant position in one segment, global leaders extend their brand globally and seek to develop innovative products to drive the industry.

Chinese companies can shorten this process by leveraging the unique opportunity that technology shifts in consumer-electronics provide. By focusing on new products that have not yet been identified with global leaders, Chinese companies can gain share and build brand recognition at an affordable price. In the same way that Sony broke through with the Walkman, Chinese companies can take advantage of recent rapid technological advances. In display technology, for example, one leading Chinese electronics group has prepared a well-thought-out plan to export

Samsung's Globalization Story

South Korea's Samsung is a global leader in consumer-electronics, with over $33 billion in sales; 50% of which is exported primarily to Europe and North America. Samsung is the leading global brand in CDMA mobile phones, microwave ovens, color monitors and components such as TFT-LCD screens. Samsung used the staircase approach to globalization and spent considerable time and money in doing so.

Starting with domestic operations, it acquired basic product-development skills through joint ventures (for example, with Sanyo) and over 50 technology licensing agreements. In the 1970s, it had joint ventures in consumer-electronics with Sanyo, NEC and Corning and licensing agreements with RCA, JVC, Kelvinator, Matsushita, Toshiba, Philips and Casio.[1] Branded exports began in the early 1980s and its overseas beachheads targeted price-sensitive customers and formed private-label relationships with companies like Sears and GE. In the U.S. it set prices at a significant discount to Japanese and U.S. competitors and acted as a private-label supplier to retailers and brands. Samsung used these early years to build its understanding of customer wants and perceptions of Samsung. How it learned from product display is illustrated in this quote from the Samsung Chairman's U.S. market research trip: "Prominently displayed were Sony, Bang & Olufsen... behind them were Philips, Panasonic ... in the back with "bargain sale" stickers were Samsung televisions and VCRs, often with a layer of dust dulling the high-quality finish."[2]

Through extensive consumer research and by building up its overseas sales and manufacturing organizations in the U.S., Germany, U.K. and Australia, Samsung slowly learned market needs. In the late 1980s it began targeted product development in high-profile, high-technology areas such as flat-screen monitors. It also significantly increased its overseas manpower. Its U.S. branch opened in 1977 and by the late 1990s Samsung was employing over 500 people at its New Jersey headquarters. R&D budgets also increased and, by the early 1990s, Samsung's aspirations led it to invest in products and technologies that would raise its brand profile (for example, digital high-definition televisions, and digital mobile phones.).

Finally in the late 1990s it launched global branding with aggressive advertising campaigns (for example, Olympics sponsorship), forming alliances with high-tech partners like Sprint, and launching a wave of cutting-edge products. Over $1 billion was invested in advertising in the late 1990s. In 2001 alone, its brand advertising budget rose to over $400 million. Channel focus shifted to category killers and mass-merchants were de-emphasized. Technology development allowed it to claim the world's first full line of digital televisions and the lightest mobile. Total R&D spend amounted to over 5% of sales and $7 billion from 1996-2000. Its brand was valued at $5.2 billion in 2000 by Interbrand.

plasma and projection televisions with liquid crystal display (LCD) screens to the U.S. The products are already being produced and sold in China, reflecting the surprising fact that China is now the new leading-edge market for many new consumer-electronics items from DVDs to mobile handsets.

Doing so, however, requires — in addition to leading-edge products — an established order-fulfillment capability, a solid understanding of the needs of the international consumer, and multiple international marketing and distribution partners. If any of these skills are missing, Chinese companies will exit the market as fast as they entered. Konka, for example, had an initially successful entry in the U.S., persuading mass-merchant retailers to give it major orders. However, it proved unable to deliver as promised and, with the loss of accounts and the concomitant publicity, beat a hasty retreat from the market. Other more successful companies are taking it step-by-step, penetrating the market through independent distributors serving discounter channels while investing in educational and training materials for the salesman. There is plenty of experienced salesforce management available – with no historical baggage – and Chinese companies can offer equity to the best talent to create a motivated team.

Pursuing M&A

A second globalization strategy is for Chinese companies to aggressively pursue M&A in developed markets. Buying up distressed and other low-cost assets provides a cost-effective way to access the channel and in some cases to gain valuable technologies. Attractive targets are companies that are relatively cheap but with usable assets or capabilities, especially brand, technology, and channel access. They must be able to move manufacturing to China and industry structure in the target market should be relatively concentrated to avoid destabilizing price wars at the time of the acquisition.

Globalization puts this strategy in reach of Chinese players who only a few years ago might not have had a chance to execute it due to the lack of opportunities or capital. Targets are increasingly plentiful as the same lower tariffs and elimination of subsidies that put Chinese companies at risk in

China also put additional pressure on independent mid-sized companies in Europe and North America. Financing is no longer the critical stumbling block – private equity firms globally are more than willing to provide risk capital if there is a compelling business case and capable management. However, the real barrier for Chinese companies is skilled global managers. As targets are typically in distress, this strategy often requires turnaround managers that only the most capable companies are able to muster.

For example, one Chinese company identified an attractive acquisition candidate in the U.S. in the late 1990s. The company had a relatively high value/price position and its brand was well known for quality and value. Financing was obtained from U.S. mezzanine sources and other private equity investors. A timetable was defined to move all manufacturing to China within two years and to accelerate component sourcing to almost completely replace U.S.-made components within three years.

However, after two years, localization had barely proceeded and profits were significantly below expectations. The key shortfall came in the lack of aggressive hands-on management. The Chinese owners had deferred to the original management team who, in turn, failed to take the difficult decisions to shut down U.S. manufacturing capacity and transfer critical design knowledge to China.

Realizing this, a board of combined Chinese and U.S. management was formed, substantial long-term incentives were established to retain key management in line with performance, and a tough set of performance evaluation metrics was put in place – some of which resulted in the U.S. CEO departing after six months. The Chinese company went on to set up a purchasing system in China to reduce material costs and establish a China organization to become a center for manufacturing, purchasing, quality, and logistics expertise in order to improve the performance of Chinese suppliers by, for example, cutting order lead times from two months to five weeks. These more radical moves turned the company around and put the business back on track.

OEM Partnering

Finally, Chinese companies can also pursue an OEM strategy to quickly build scale without corresponding investments in marketing. With the development of information technology, it is feasible to construct a global network that seamlessly links production in China to marketing and design in developed markets. Traditional players in developed markets find this model attractive as it allows them to outsource high-cost production, in turn creating greater price flexibility. For the Chinese company, they achieve scale without committing to the massive investments required in building their own international brand.

Cost and quality leadership, the ability to support multiple global customers and the ability to acquire the needed technology and capabilities are key success factors in this model. Low cost is required to secure initial contracts – usually requiring excellent supply-chain management and sourcing skills. Multiple customers are typically required to minimize dependence on any one company and gain scale over time. This strategy requires the least in additional skills from Chinese players. However, by the same token, it offers the least upside from the market. Returns can only come through expanding scale to achieve a position of global dominance around components and assembly.

The Galanz Story

Galanz, the largest global microwave producer with a global share of nearly 30%, is an example of globalization with an OEM strategy. Founded in 1978 as a textile company with 200 employees, in 1992 Galanz entered the microwave market. It recruited five microwave specialists from Shanghai, purchased an automated production line from Toshiba and produced 10,000 units in its first year.

Galanz then began manufacturing for OEM customers. It targeted customers seeking to lower their manufacturing costs but who were not yet ready to set up in China and wanted to focus on other parts of the value chain such as R&D and sales and marketing. Galanz maintained cost leadership while integrating into its customers' networks and lowered prices to gain market share and scale – the industry average pricing dropped by 18% annually in the late 1990s. Meanwhile Galanz's share climbed from 48% to 76% and volume more than tripled. As a result, Galanz's cost position improved to give it a 10% advantage over its nearest competitors. Standardized quality processes enabled Galanz to obtain industry certificates and thus OEM contracts.

Galanz also obtained critical manufacturing capabilities at low cost. It originally offered to manufacture microwave compressors for foreign companies at less than half their original cost. In return, it required those companies to move their production equipment to its production center in Shunde and to allow it to utilize extra capacity for its own production. By gaining technology and know-how for producing critical microwave components, Galanz was able to manufacture most components instead of importing them, thus further lowering its cost in its own production.

By 1995 Galanz had a 25% share of the domestic market and total sales of 250,000 units. Since then it has maintained this position while signing over 80 contracts with multiple OEMs. OEM sales represented over 60% of sales in 2000, and annual production capacity reached over 12 million units while domestic market share climbed to 70%. Sales climbed to over RMB 5 billion (over $600 million) and net profits to over RMB 450 million (close to $55 million). Galanz is now starting to launch branded products for markets such as South America, but still sticks to its OEM approach and is also rolling it out to other home appliances beyond microwaves.

✳   ✳   ✳

China's consumer-electronics manufacturers have little choice but to go global. Born into an industry that is essentially open to global competition, they must quickly gain scale in the only markets that will allow them to do so – the home turf of the world's multinationals. Winning here, however, will require developing fundamentally new approaches that go beyond competing on cost to capture the benefits of new technologies, acquisitions and OEM partnerships.

2.2 LEGEND: BUILDING A COMPUTER GIANT*

An interview with Liu Chuanzhi, Chairman, Legend Holdings

When people in most parts of the world want to buy a personal computer, they usually think first of the well-known brands: Compaq, Dell Computer and IBM, for example. Not so in China. There the branded PC of choice is called Legend. Never heard of it? Perhaps not for long, if Liu Chuanzhi has his way. Since 1984, Liu, the chairman of Legend Holdings, has built his company into China's (and Asia's) number-one manufacturer of PCs, with more than $3 billion in revenue. Legend expects to double that figure in three years.

Although still controlled by the state, Legend is a public company, and its shares trade on the Stock Exchange of Hong Kong. Liu is a

---

* Originally published in *The McKinsey Quarterly*, 2001 Number 3, and at www.mckinseyquarterly.com. Copyright (c) 2001 McKinsey & Company. All rights reserved. Reprinted by permission.

forceful advocate for going public and a pioneer in China in the use of stock options. In the following interview, conducted in Hong Kong by Allan Gold, Glenn Leibowitz and Tony Perkins, Liu discussed the challenge of shaping a successful market-based company in China and the prospects for Legend in the hypercompetitive technology sector.

Q **Please tell us about the origins of Legend and how you went about building the company.**

A I came out of the Chinese Academy of Sciences, where I was doing work on magnetic storage. But I had to put my designs to the side because there was no way to turn them into products. In 1984, when the market reforms in China were starting to take effect, the country's leaders called for the conversion of research and development results into products that could be marketed. I was excited about doing this type of work, but most people didn't understand it. Chinese people put scientific work on a pedestal, while commercial activities were looked down upon.

More important, although our company was a state-owned enterprise, we structured it as a private company from the beginning. I had to raise capital from banks and outsiders. The initial investment of 200,000 Renminbi[3] was so small that it was barely enough to get started.

The government did give me a very good opportunity. When I discussed terms and conditions, I requested the authority to make decisions myself. I didn't want the government to decide who would work for me. In addition, I had financial decision-making power. I could determine the wages and bonuses of our employees, and I didn't have to do so according to what the government told me.

As time went by, I wanted Legend to make its own PCs because we were technology experts. But, at the time, China was entirely a planned economy. The government wouldn't permit us to produce computers, because in China you had to have a license. The government felt that China had many factories, so why should it give a PC license to a company such as ours? I therefore crafted a strategy to go to Hong Kong, which didn't require a license. We set up a company in Hong Kong, at first to do trading, and we later set up a factory. When China's Central Planning Department saw that we had the capability, it gave us a license. So we went back to China.

Q **How much did you rely on Western technology? Are there Western companies you try to emulate or Western chief executive officers from whom you would like to learn?**

A   When we started to work as a distributor for foreign companies, we discovered that management was something we had to learn. So we learned from foreign companies while gaining an understanding of China's computer market. Our earliest and best teacher was Hewlett-Packard. It was as HP's distributor that we learned, rather thoroughly, how to organize sales channels and how to market. Later we did a lot of business for HP and helped it reach its leading position in China's computer market. We also studied the strategies of Intel and Microsoft. We constantly read foreign management journals.

Particularly good were the books by Andy Grove, Bill Gates and, especially, some Taiwanese businessmen, like Stan Shih.[4] But one key point is that I wanted to do things according to China's actual situation, not just blindly follow theory without considering reality.

As for the CEO I admire most; that would be Jack Welch. I studied at Crotonville – GE's management-training center – for two weeks. I hope to meet him the next time I take a trip to the United States.

Q   **Which brands do you distribute in China today?**

A   Our biggest business is HP laser printers and ink-jet printers. The second is Toshiba notebook computers. The third is Cisco networking products. We also distribute IBM minicomputers and Microsoft applications software.

Q   **Do Legend-branded products compete with these?**

A   While we distribute Toshiba notebooks, we also have our own branded notebook that has now become number one in the Chinese market. Several years ago, the market for Toshiba notebooks was very small in China – only a few thousand units a year. Later, after we became the exclusive distributor for Toshiba, we developed it into the number-one brand in China. But in the past two years, after we came out with our own branded product, our brand has surpassed theirs.

In addition, for laser printers HP is number one, while we're number two. This has created competition. Plus, in networking products, we compete with similar products we represent from Taiwan. Cisco's products are higher-end, so we don't compete with them. To compete more effectively as a manufacturer and a distributor, we decided to separate the branded-products business from the third-party distribution business. Legend Computer will retain its current listing in Hong Kong and focus on branded products. Digital China will be spun off as a new listed company to focus on the distribution of third-party products.

Q **What is the basis for Legend's success in China?**

A From a longer-term perspective, we focused on two areas, and in both cases we looked to U.S. companies as a model. One was to restructure as a publicly held company and sell shares. We believed that after we restructured, we could get onto the same track as publicly held foreign companies. This also enabled us to offer stock options to our employees, and I believe that it has had a very positive impact on their performance.

The second idea was to build a solid management foundation. We look at management on two levels. On one level, there are the nuts and bolts – marketing and promotions, channel management, product marketing, ordering, and logistics management – and we built these into the company. Then there is a deeper level that deals with what we call culture but might also be described as motivation and ethics, and this is more problematic than developing the nuts-and-bolts areas of management.

Q **Can you elaborate on the challenge associated with this aspect of management in China?**

A Americans already have a strong sense of the market, a strong sense of business ethics and a strong spirit of loyalty. In China, it hasn't been long since the market-opening reforms, so people don't have a strong sense of the market, and business ethics are underdeveloped.

How do you motivate a leadership team in China? State-owned enterprises have problems in this area because of compensation limits. When a key manager gets paid a low salary, he doesn't feel the need to bear responsibility, nor does he have the ability to take responsibility, because a lot of things are simply out of his control.

We have tried to instill a different culture at Legend. We hope that the highest managers at Legend will come to work with a desire to serve the company. What I mean by "a desire to serve the company" is something more than a desire for advancement – more than economic compensation and a better position. This is normal, but for Legend it's not enough. A Legend manager must first think of Legend as a career. If Legend does well, he'll do well. In China, there are two days a week of rest. But at Legend, most employees take only one day off, so that they can study. This is of their own free will.

Q And one important way you have addressed the motivation issue is the use of stock options?

A We started the options program in 1994. Actual distribution began around 1998, and we think it has had a huge effect. One of our company's missions is to integrate the needs of our employees with those of the company. To make them true masters, from a materialistic standpoint, options play an important role.

Ten percent of the employees in our listed companies have stock options. Our entire company has about 7.4 billion shares, and 740 million shares are set aside for employee stock options. All white-collar employees who have been in our company for more than two years get stock options. But when they reach upper management, they get a lot more.

Q Legend was one of China's first companies to be listed abroad. How would you assess its experience as a publicly held company?

A I think going public has had two major effects on Legend. The first is the ability to obtain capital; the other is dealing with shareholder pressure. The purpose of going public is not entirely to get the money. Dealing with shareholder pressure is a way to improve because shareholders demand transparency and systematic management.

So from one perspective, I regard this pressure as a type of motivation. Our company demands a special degree of transparency – the good, the bad; the shareholders must know everything. Legend's most fundamental objective is to serve the long-term interests of the shareholders.

Q Do you have any concrete examples of how Legend has become more transparent?

A The first example is the Hong Kong Stock Exchange, which requires semiannual performance reporting. But we report our performance every quarter, as is the practice in the United States. There are few companies in Hong Kong that do this.

The second example refers to an event that occurred in 1998, when some Chinese companies experienced internal problems. They took the money they had borrowed from the bank and lent it out at high interest rates to other people to earn profits. Later, when they were unable to collect on their loans, this created a problem. To let shareholders understand the details of our situation, in the evening of the day this incident occurred we held a conference call with our global shareholders to describe the financial situation. We explained that we had never borrowed money for the purpose of re-lending it and reassured everyone that if this were to happen we would tell them immediately. This may sound normal in the West, but it's not the case in China.

Q **Many publicly held companies are forced to lay off employees when times get tough, and the technology sector has been particularly hard hit recently. What do you think about using layoffs?**

A In principle, layoffs can be used at Legend, but I would be very cautious in using this approach, because culturally we're different from the United States. We could do this, but we wouldn't do it casually, because of the long-term impact it might have on the company.

If someone's performance at Legend is not up to standard, his superior will send him to the Human Resources Department to help him find a new job. If he can't find a new job within three months, we'll let him go. However, when undertaking major layoffs if sales drop, we will give those being laid off three months' pay. We won't send them from one department to another, because the company as a whole wouldn't need that many people.

Q **In contrast to the slowdown in the global PC market, the PC market in China continues to grow at a rapid pace. What are the biggest opportunities you have identified?**

A On the macro level, the Chinese market is starting from a low base. For example, only 4% of households in midsize cities currently have PCs. In large cities, this number is between 10% and 20%. In comparison with the United States, there is a huge gap, so the market potential is very big.

Another big opportunity comes from the fact that we understand the Chinese consumer better than foreign companies do and are better able to segment the market. Although American companies are strong in technology, they do R&D with a view to global markets – they haven't spent as much time conducting R&D for the Chinese market.

Just think about different product applications. The nature of written Chinese creates differences in the way IT products are used. For example, Americans are accustomed to using keyboards for input. Keyboards are suited just for alphanumeric input, not for ideographs. So computers in China must develop either voice input or a better way to input by hand. In addition, there is the way companies use computers. Financial statements in China are different from those in the United States, so software has to be developed differently. You need to have a deep understanding of how this type of product would be used by a Chinese company. This could be considered a weakness of American companies relative to Chinese companies.

We also view services as an important strategic area. For example, there are 10 million small companies in China that buy computers primarily for accounting, inventory, purchasing and payroll. Just buying a computer is not enough. A company of, say, 200 people needs to be networked. Plus, you need to make modifications to the software. We expect that this will be a profitable sector for us.

Q **What challenges does Legend face in its effort to expand market share and profitability?**

A The biggest challenge is that this industry changes so much. We can't be like U.S. companies that are in a position of leading the trends; the main thing for us is to keep up with the trends. Many American companies have taken different directions, so how do we assess which of them will become mainstream?

The second challenge concerns our business in China. Our market share is getting bigger and bigger. We have over 30% of the PC market in China. As we move forward, we'll reach our limit, so someday – probably after 2005 – we'll have to go overseas. The question is how we will do this: whether we will try to sell branded goods or take the OEM[5] approach.

When we analyzed the drivers of our past performance, we discovered that it was due to our having leveraged local competitive advantages, such as knowing how to make products that fit the needs of Chinese consumers. However, once we go overseas, these will no longer be advantages, so I will be very cautious.

Just look at the experience of the Taiwanese technology companies, almost none of which have built brands overseas. They haven't figured out how to compete with foreign brands overseas. I think we could take the path of Taiwanese companies that are original-design manufacturers,[6] or we could cooperate with Taiwanese companies.

Q **How is Legend using the Internet to expand its business or reduce costs?**

A   Up to now, we've used the Internet to reduce inventories, and by lowering inventories we lower costs. I don't have concrete figures, but it's very clear that in the computer industry the accumulation of inventory is the most important cost issue, because prices change so quickly.

Legend can also manufacture PCs according to customer needs and orders. This helps us tremendously because in the future our biggest challenger in China might be Dell. This year Dell is ranked sixth or seventh and, of course, one of its special features is its build-to-order system. So we're putting in a great deal of effort to prepare for this.

In our Beijing factory, we have six production lines, three of which are specially designated for build-to-order production. In China, we have several thousand distribution points, including 200 home-PC specialty shops and more than 3,000 dealers. Nearly all place their orders through the Internet. These orders are produced entirely to specification – for example, someone wants a 20-gigabyte hard drive, while someone else wants 10 gigabytes. We'll specially configure the computer. The costs of doing this are higher, but so are the profits.

Currently, our orders are only from businesses. We don't take orders directly from end users. China's underdeveloped bank-payments system and transportation infrastructure make business-to-consumer e-commerce almost impossible today.

Q   **What next for the Internet in China?**

A   The Internet definitely has a bright future in China. It is entirely possible that the Internet can change the way people live, as it has done in the United States. Chinese people are envious now of how Americans can go on-line to obtain the information they need, then go on-line for shopping. This is difficult in China right now. If we can improve the payments and transportation infrastructure, that would be a big boost for the development of the Internet. Right now, we're held back by these two problems, which I estimate will take about two to three years to solve.

Q   **What is your philosophy about grooming talent?**

A   It is important to Legend's long-term development to make the older generation of entrepreneurs, including myself, gradually pass the mantle to younger, more capable people who are open to new things. There are about a dozen of the older entrepreneurs who started out with me. They have a big gap in energy.

When I choose someone, I apply two criteria. The initial criterion is whether he could put the interests of the company first. The second criterion is talent, or ability. What I emphasize in talent is the ability to learn, to do well at different tasks. Can he learn from foreign companies? Can he learn from practical experience? I don't care whether he succeeds or fails at a particular task; what I care about is whether he is able to learn from his failure and what he does after.

Q **Have you adopted a particular management style?**

A When I first founded the company, I used the top-down approach within my leadership group. It was an authoritarian approach: what I said, those reporting to me had to do. This was because, at the time, I had a better understanding than those under me. Plus they had more of a planned-economy mentality and were thus quite rigid.

In the early 1990s, after a number of high-quality younger people joined the company, I changed my top-down approach to one I would call instructive or guiding, where everyone would discuss things. They would still act according to my wishes, but I provided guidance. Later, in 1994 and 1995, I gradually changed my approach to a participatory style, whereby my employees would present a plan and I would provide my input.

This gave the people around me a strong platform for making their own decisions. Our younger employees make many of the company's key strategic decisions. I gradually changed my role from that of director to that of movie producer. I put up the money; I say whether we should make a martial-arts film or a romance; but younger people are in the director's seat.

When the day comes for me to retire, I believe our investors will not be taken by surprise, because over the years, while I've been playing the leading role in name, it has been the younger people who have been doing the job. It will be a stable succession.

2.3 DESIGNING SUCCESS IN SEMICONDUCTORS

Overcoming a past marked by sluggish growth and dated manufacturing technology, China's semiconductor industry is now set for rapid development on the back of surging OEM demand. However, regional foundry overcapacity, technology acquisition constraints and the lack of local process technology render the prospects for large manufacturing investments highly uncertain. China's design sector offers much brighter prospects and, if linked with Taiwan, the world leader in manufacturing, could form a partnership that would profit both parties and create a new global industry standard.

SIGNIFICANT INVESTMENTS PLANNED

Foreign semiconductor companies have begun to invest significantly in China. Always an attractive market, China is now attracting global interest as a semiconductor manufacturing center.

By 2005 China will be the third-largest semiconductor market in the world next to the U.S. and Japan (Exhibit 2.3). In 2001 China was already a significant producer of global electronics, making 7% of electronic equipment produced globally and consuming 6% of global semiconductor production. Over the next five years domestically-made electronics goods will continue to fuel demand for semiconductors. China's production of electronic equipment is expected to grow at 11% a year in contrast to the global rate of 8%. Semiconductor consumption will correspondingly expand at the rate of 16% a year compared to the global rate of 10%. Both export and domestic markets will fuel the growth in demand. Expected GDP growth

Exhibit 2.3 China's projected semiconductor consumption (US$ billions)

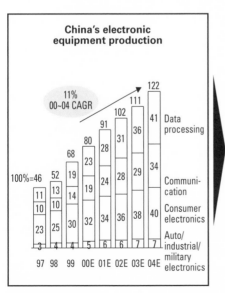

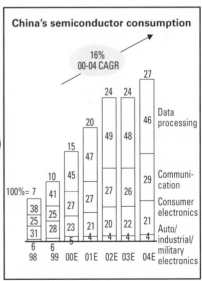

Source: Dataquest

of 8% a year will increase domestic purchasing power, which will drive up consumption of electronic equipment. Exports of cordless phones, DVD players, motherboards and hard disk drives – all of which need semiconductors – are driven by the development of Chinese export powerhouses, both under their own brands and as OEMs for multinationals.

However, today's Chinese semiconductor industry is woefully undeveloped. Domestic semiconductor companies and local joint ventures manufacture only 4% of China's own demand. China has five fabricating plants (fabs), most of them government-sponsored joint ventures. Production technologies are several generations behind the latest technology: no Chinese-owned fab in China has less than 0.35 micron technology when the leading-edge technology is 0.15 microns. The vast majority of China's semiconductor requirements are imported. In 2001, Intel was the biggest importer, accounting for 11% of imports or almost $1 billion in sales to China. Other large importers were Toshiba, Hyundai, Philips, Sanyo and ST.

International investors and OEMs are responding to this opportunity as they see establishing manufacturing plants in China as a new option to reduce dependence on Taiwanese plants. Taiwan appeals to OEMs because its plants have scale in operations and assets, access to strong end-equipment markets, and because the country has rich capital markets. However, Taiwanese talent is increasingly expensive, natural resources are almost gone and there are risks of natural disasters from earthquakes and typhoons.

Entrepreneurs have announced plans to invest in digital logic foundries providing CMOS or BiCMOS logic to fabless design houses or to selected Integrated Device Manufacturers (IDMs).[7] Multinationals have played it more cautiously, preferring to invest in distribution and assembly and test facilities as precursors to significant on-the-ground presence. IDMs such as IBM, Intel and AMD are localizing their A&T operations in order to save on shipping costs by being close to the end-customer and to enable better customer service.[8] By investing in China they can also capture a low-cost advantage in labor. Also, this step could eventually lead to fabrication investments. Only Motorola has taken a more aggressive approach and has invested in its own manufacturing capacity as part of an overall strategy to dominate the telecom market in China.[9]

These investments in China have been encouraged by a moderate easing of technology restrictions. The transfer to China from the U.S. and other countries of all but the most leading-edge processes is now allowed. Motorola was able to set up a 0.25 micron plant to produce digital DNA for wireless communications, automotive electronics and consumer products. Grace, a U.S.-registered semiconductor start-up, has 0.25 micron technology and can upgrade it to 0.18 micron. Similarly, SMIC, a Bermuda-registered start-up, broke ground in 2001 with 0.25 micron technology.[10]

China's government is also doing its part to attract investors. Government has removed import taxes on semiconductor equipment and technology imports, reduced the 17% value-added tax to 6%, and given new companies a tax holiday: no taxes are payable in the first two years of profitability and only 15% tax is payable in the subsequent three years. Three-year depreciation is allowed. The government has declared Shanghai the capital of China's semiconductor industry and fast-tracked approval of the SMIC and Grace fabs. Raising capital is also becoming easier. Technology companies such as Shanghai Belling are among the most highly valued on domestic bourses.

HOWEVER, PROFITS MAY BE ELUSIVE

However, the economics of China's new manufacturing facilities appears uncertain. Historically, Chinese manufacturing capacity has not earned its cost of capital and global conditions look increasingly difficult.

The first wave of manufacturing investments in China were in DRAM-only fabs, set up to provide OEMs such as PC manufacturers with commodity products. These DRAM fabs made products for large-volume commodity markets that were relatively easy to enter and where operational skills could be transferred at fairly low risk. However, the upside for these fabs has been constrained by high exposure to the semiconductor cycle. DRAM prices have proved far more volatile than foundry wafer prices, with most if not all of the value being captured in the early years of the DRAM technology's introduction. Chinese fabs typically had only a year or two of profits before the price wars hit. They then found it difficult to leverage DRAM skills into high-value segments due to the lack of process design capability. As a result, the big Chinese DRAM fabs in 2001 incurred huge losses, reflecting the global downturn in commodity prices and their inability to switch to higher-value product lines.

The economics of new fabs will largely depend on market conditions when they come on line. Global utilization of capacity and price levels are largely external factors that can swing value from negative to positive quickly. Foundry supply is already increasing faster than demand globally, particularly with new fabs in Korea, Taiwan and Malaysia. While growing foundry demand in China may be large enough to accommodate new fab investments, those already made, including Shougang, Grace, SMIC, and Huahong, could bring foundry supply and demand in China into balance by

2004.[11] Additional foundry investments will then need to find new customers or offer distinctive value propositions to win market share.

Longer term, China-based DRAM and foundry manufacturing strategies appear to be fundamentally limited by weak process design capability. Successful DRAM strategies require leading-edge process technologies. Players must strive to stay ahead of the curve in development, which means continually investing in leading-edge process technology and switching early into new products (for example, from 16 MB to 64 MB). Pushing out the new generation of DRAMs ahead of competitors is key to capturing price advantages. Even those players who attempt to be a cost leader by sticking with the old generation of products (for instance, 16 MB) seek to shrink their process technology as far as possible to reduce cost (for example from 0.35 micron to 0.25 micron). Winning in this strategy in China appears difficult given the early stage of China's process technology.

Likewise, the lack of a strong domestic process design industry severely constrains China's foundry opportunity. Without domestic process design expertise it is difficult to improve foundry productivity once the line has been installed. And with continued, albeit slightly lower, barriers to technology transfer, China remains limited in its ability to understand and develop cutting-edge semiconductor manufacturing equipment. Taiwan on the other hand has enjoyed much more freedom to transfer technology from the U.S. than China has today. As a result, it has developed a depth of experience that should allow it to maintain a clear lead in manufacturing technology.

DESIGN IS CHINA'S STRENGTH

Those looking to invest in semiconductors in China would perhaps do better by considering design. While China may be short of skilled process engineers, it has no shortage of low-cost designers. About 400,000 science and engineering students graduate each year in China (not counting the 50,000 current and former graduates who move overseas), and more than 5,000 overseas students and professionals return, bringing up-to-date Western knowledge and skills. This yearly addition of new engineering graduates is at least 15 times that of Taiwan's. And labor costs in China remain low: on average, high-tech workers are paid around $3,000 a year, with companies in the coastal areas paying more than those inland. Workers in China's semiconductor design houses receive an annual wage of around $10,000.

The challenge for design firms is to invest significantly in building their IP, market and manufacturing networks. First and foremost, design expertise needs to be built. While low-cost engineers are plentiful, cell libraries and IP still need to be acquired. Further, going to market in China requires an on-

Two Other Investment Options

Assembly and test is also a core China strength, reflecting its relatively labor-intensive character. By 2010, assembly and test companies will generate revenues of over $7 billion, packaging 80% of all chips consumed in China. Both international IDMs and contract A&T companies will localize most of the A&T manufacturing needs for semiconductor components consumed in China. Assembly and test services could also be exported. Today foreign companies also dominate assembly and testing; China has over 10 major foreign-owned A&T establishments.

And while China's distribution market is also potentially a source of value as it is expected to grow at over 35% per annum, it is also likely to be dominated by foreign players who bring experience in building and managing modern distribution centers and services as well as a global network of customers and suppliers. Foreign companies operate from foreign trade zones such as Shanghai's Waigaoqiao, or have formed local partnerships such as that between Tomen and Huahong. Avnet, for example, has been actively acquiring companies around China, beginning in 1995 with the acquisition of WKK Semiconductor in Hong Kong. Since then it has bought operations in Taiwan, Singapore, Korea and, most recently, in Shenzhen. It is hard to see how a new entrant could match these global leaders in what is a very scale-driven business.

the-ground capability. Sales representatives should be able not only to market the company's designs but also act as qualified technical reps to understand customer requirements and translate them into specific process design requirements. Supporting applications materials and technical personnel are needed to educate customers. Markets also tend to be highly concentrated, making the sale process time-consuming. Typically, qualification can take up to two years from initial chip design to customization, prototyping, performance testing and trial production. Payback on these investments depends on the ability of the design firm to penetrate a few highly attractive markets, in particular that for mobile communications. Profit is expected to be concentrated in a handful of largely globally driven segments: PCs, digital cellular phones, monitors, DVD players and optical disk devices. These are expected to account for over $300 million in industry profits by 2004. Mobile communications chips in particular are expected to grow at over 25% a year, accounting for roughly two-thirds of the $8 billion communications market by 2004.[12]

Fortunately, China's domestic OEM market creates precisely the demanding customers that are essential for the rapid growth of the design industry and that can support these kinds of investments. Semiconductor consumption is already close to Taiwan's current consumption and will soon surpass it. Domestic OEMs account for a growing share of total demand in China. As a share of purchasing by the top 10 users, their purchases grew from 36% in 1997 to 52% in 2000, led by local players such as Legend Computers, Changhong Television, and Konka. These players also are rapidly consolidating, thus achieving the scale necessary to support development of new semiconductor designs. In data processing, five players alone account for 60% of the market. In consumer-electronics and communications, the top five players account for 50% of the market. As these players seek to improve profit margins by sourcing low-cost components and to differentiate themselves through better products and customized solutions, they will need designers who can provide new solutions that meet their particular needs.

In fact, Chinese design companies are already beginning to supply Chinese OEMs with customized or standard components, thereby capturing a high share of end-use value and leveraging their direct access to customers. For example, Silicon Valley entrepreneurs and Chinese designers in Shanghai and Beijing founded Newave Technologies to provide low-cost components to Chinese OEMs. With a design center located in Shanghai, Newave has focused on relatively mature markets such as fixed line-switching access. Trident Microsystems has gone further to provide customized solutions by developing a chip set to enable digital processing of analog signals in television sets. The digital television chip set has been embraced by leading Chinese television makers such as Changhong, TCL and Konka. These domestic customers form the natural customer base for local designers as they make purchasing decisions locally.

If Chinese design companies form global alliances they will also be able to justify their initially heavy investments by serving international customers. Economics justify exporting design services from China. A design engineer with five years' experience costs between $14,000 and $30,000 a year in China compared to $80,000 and $150,000 in the U.S. This holds true at lower levels too – junior design engineers, make $9,000 to $20,000 a year in China versus $50,000 to $100,000 in the U.S. Avanti Shanghai, for example, employs over 500 employees in its first development center outside the U.S. Its development team uses the Internet to exchange data with Avanti centers around the world, provide design services and develop EDA tools for global customers.

The economics for outsourcing design services to China also work well for IDMs and design companies in the U.S., particularly when economic downturns put more pressure on U.S. companies. In fact, relatively highly-paid senior engineers account for only a small percentage of all employees in a typical fabless IC design company, providing even greater opportunities

Viva Via

Via Technologies, a leading Taiwanese design house, was founded in 1992 as an outsourced design house for IBM and started operations on the mainland in 1999 at the same time as it began to develop its own branded designs for microperipherals, CPUs and motherboards. In two years it hired 500 designers in China and now plans to expand that number to over 2000 in the next two years, a number far exceeding the current size of its design force in Taiwan. This will give it a cost advantage. At the same time, Via is building strategic alliances with leading local OEMs such as Legend and Midea while heavily investing in marketing to establish its brand position and secure high-quality distributors. With this investment, it was successful in achieving a 40% growth in sales in China and is ranked number one in the Chinese microperipheral market.

to leverage low-cost Chinese workers for administrative and production staff. This lower-risk approach to provide mainly other chip suppliers and OEMs with small pieces of ASIC or ASSP designs on a contract basis could also be available to domestic designers who need to gain skills and easier entry into difficult markets. However, the value capture is correspondingly lower than selling designs directly.

A TAIWAN CONNECTION?

Ultimately, it may be the combination of world-class global manufacturing with low-cost design that is the winning investment. Taiwan's leading-edge manufacturing technology nicely complements the emerging design strength of China. Combined, they could dominate the global industry.

Leveraging Taiwan does not mean that all fab capacity must be based outside China. In fact, all the major Taiwanese foundries are actively pursuing fab projects in China. As early as 1999, a group of Taiwanese engineers invested in Central Semiconductor Manufacturing in Jiangsu province. UMC has agreed to sell equipment to Belling while staking its claim to land outside Shanghai, as has TSMC. Thus fab investments in China will still be significant, generating revenues of over $12 billion and supplying up to 60% of non-leading edge digital and analog wafers.

However, design companies will be the main players in China. As Chinese design firms leverage their skills to introduce new products, by 2005, fabless design companies are expected to supply semiconductors of over $10 billion in value to domestic OEMs, satisfying half their needs for non-leading edge products. As Chinese design firms build their skills, they will also begin to introduce new products. For example, the design experience and IPs in nonvolatile memory needed in the short term in smart cards could lead to potential new products such as smart cards with flash memory for high density applications or ferroelectric memory for better memory performance. At 2002 multiples, design companies serving Chinese customers could have a staggering value of over $50 billion. Taiwanese fabs for their part will benefit from their alliances with Chinese design companies to support their continued investments.

Innovative and flexible alliances will be needed to make these strategies work, similar to those that enabled Taiwan's own foundry business to take off. TI's license agreement with MIPS and Altera's joint venture with TSMC for its U.S. fab are examples. Successful foundries must supply a range of skills and services to their design customers, including standard design libraries and Electronic Design Architecture (EDA) services. They do so through a network of partners including holders of IP, owners of EDA tools and providers of design implementation services. Likewise, design firms will need to partner closely with OEMs and related hardware suppliers to provide one-stop bundled solutions. For example, in smartcards, successful design firms must offer a choice of chips, card readers, system software and system integration services by managing an outsourced production chain.

✳   ✳   ✳

The semiconductor revolution is sweeping across Asia. With its robust economic growth and immense human resources China is uniquely positioned to emerge as a global industry leader. Doing so will require an innovative and design-led approach, potentially including partnerships with established manufacturing companies in Taiwan.

2.4 CORNING: RIDING RAPID GROWTH AND THE HIGH-TECH BOOM

Interview with Simon MacKinnon, President of Corning, Greater China

A high-tech leader for over 150 years, Corning is new to the China market. But its growth has been rapid and today it is one of the most successful high-tech companies in China. Simon MacKinnon, President, Greater China, has been guiding Corning's growth since 2000 and has had over 20 years' experience in China across a wide range of industries. In the following interview he shares his perspectives with Jonathan Woetzel on the opportunities and challenges of the China market.

Q **Why is Corning in China? What drives the market opportunity in your view and why did you yourself sign on?**

A Let me answer that in three parts. First, personally I have been involved in China since 1979. I lived in Shanghai in the mid-1980s and then worked for P&O, a Fortune 500 British services group in shipping, transport and real estate. This included five years in Japan before returning to China to spend five years establishing and building up P&O's construction, exhibition, ports, shipping and travel businesses in China. In 2000, I joined Corning as President, Greater China region. One way or another I have been committed to China for the better part of 20 years.

Second, what are Corning's businesses? Corning is a technology company with a portfolio of businesses which divides into two parts. The first half is telecommunications – we invented optical fiber and are the largest producer. We lead in production of optical cable and we produce a range of photonic products – the devices for managing light. The other half of our business is what we call our materials businesses. We invented and are the world-leader in manufacturing honeycomb ceramic substrates, which are at the heart of the catalytic converter for cars. We are also the world-leader in the business of manufacturing glass for information display, used in LCD displays for PCs, notebooks and now televisions. Finally, we make high-purity glass used in stepper lenses, which are part of etching lines on microchips.

In China these businesses have all grown dramatically. In 1999 our China sales were $90 million; in 2002 they will be over $380 million. In 1999 we had one manufacturing plant; in 2002 we now have nine. In 1999 we employed 80 people in what was essentially an import organization; in 2002 we employ around 1,800. In 1999 China was less than 2% of Corning's global sales and today it is over 12%.

Third, as to what drives the market opportunity for Corning in China. As a provider of high-tech products, Corning is an extraordinary barometer for the development of the Chinese economy into high-tech sectors in recent years. Five years ago, Corning's products were not of much interest to China. Today, Corning's products are very much aligned with China's needs. In telecoms, China is building its network using the latest fiber optic technologies. In automotive, along with the rapid growth of the car market there is a growing desire by the Chinese Government and people to improve their environment, leading to the introduction of automotive emissions control legislation. In computers, as the number of Internet connections rises fast and computers are more widely used in schools, China will this year become the world's second-largest PC market. In televisions, China is fast emerging as one of the largest projection TV markets, with over half a million sets sold in 2002.

In summary, Corning is now in sectors of the Chinese economy which are all growing faster than the overall economy: telecoms, automotive, information display. This decade will be one of tremendous opportunity and growth for Corning in China.

Q What's driving this growth and is it sustainable?

A Well, it's a combination of being in the early rapid-growth stages of the economy and then different dynamics for each industry. In telecoms there is the opportunity to leapfrog whole generations and install the latest technologies. In pollution control, the needs are great and China is catching up to North American and European emissions standards. In consumer products, there are long-term trends at work as penetration increases in a large-potential country. Our more consumer-related businesses in information display are partially driven by the expanding middle-class market and the ongoing cost reduction in TVs, which makes them more affordable in second- and third- tier cities.

Q How does Corning seek to position itself in this rapidly evolving market? And how important will China be for Corning's growth?

A Corning wants to be the world's low-cost manufacturer while adding unique value for each customer. This depends on the customer's specific need; whether it is quality, reliability or other product attributes for each customer. In China, Corning wants to be the leader in each of our segments as we are elsewhere in the world.

As for many foreign companies, China has become more important to Corning as it has developed as a market for our products and a location for manufacturing for export markets. How rapidly this proceeds depends on the development of the country and it will happen at different rates depending on the industry concerned.

Q How much of this growth is based on China's overall economic growth and how sustainable is this?

A It is no secret that China has been priming the pump to sustain growth and employment. How long it can continue to do so is a question. At some point the problems in the banking sector will come home to roost. Will there be a dip? Government may have to slow down a bit but for the next year or two it won't shut off the tap.

There is no such thing as straight-line economic growth. Whilst China will continue to achieve rates of growth that will be the envy of many of its competitors during this decade, we can expect both external factors and Chinese domestic issues to cause periods of slower growth and turbulence.

Q Why did you decide to put plants in China? Was this necessary to boost sales?

A Good question, and the answer is different for each of Corning's businesses. I will give you three examples. First, in environmental products (ceramic substrates that go into car catalytic converters), we projected that the business would grow in China as well as in the rest of Asia, and planned our production accordingly. A classic pattern has been foreign companies coming to China and building their plants only for China demand. Locally this became known as the "1.3 billion consumers syndrome", and many ambitious investors found that the market did not develop as quickly as they had projected and that their foreign rivals built big plants based on similar thinking. The result is that many foreign companies' plants ended up producing at well under capacity.

Corning had the advantage of learning from these earlier investors in China and we planned our Shanghai environmental products to fill the plant with China demand and also to use it as a platform for the region, supplying to Korea, Japan and other Asian markets. So this was a global or regional decision.

Second, Corning today has five joint ventures. All of these are in telecommunications. In telecoms, even today it is not easy to gain permission for a 100%-owned investment and in the 1990s a joint venture was the only ticket if you wanted to be a significant player in China. In telecoms the entry of China into the WTO will lead to tariff reductions over the next five or six years. Corning will therefore be well placed to serve our Chinese customers using both local and import channels.

A third example is Corning's display business, making flat panel glass for PCs and TVs. This one is driven by customer moves. These industries are now mainly based in Asia and in this specific case the TFT-LCD modules are now made in Japan, Korea and Taiwan. China is next as China moves rapidly up the PC and TV sales charts – this year China is set to overtake Japan and become the world's second-largest PC market after the U.S. The entry ticket is half a billion to a billion dollars for a TFT-LCD plant and the industry is new to China; two investments are now on the way and we will be working with them.

In summary, for most Corning businesses the leveraging of cheap labor resources in China is not the most important reason for investing in China. We have invested to better serve our customers and to gain the inside track that being a local manufacturer can give you if you are committed and take the long-term view.

Q **What have been the biggest challenges you have faced in building Corning's business?**

A Challenge number one is winning and then sustaining top-level commitment in the company to drive growth. Leadership must be committed to grow and dedicate the resources necessary to support growth. Corning is organized business by business and each business has its own strategies; each is responsible for driving its own sales. Each has made its own decisions on whether to have partnerships or to build up on its own. In all cases leadership has to be committed.

Challenge number two is building and deepening commercial relationships. In China, markets are typically not long-established. You need to keep developing and keep a strong grip on the customer. China is usually a spot market as well, with few of the long-term contracts more typical in older market environments in North America or Japan. It is vital not to be distracted from meeting customer needs while you are growing.

Challenge number three is in hiring and building up local Chinese leadership. Personally I believe there is already a growing gap between those foreign companies who are committed to doing this and those who are lukewarm on this subject or who are still using large numbers of expatriates, here defined as all non-PRC Chinese. This takes radical thinking and action to make it happen. It means giving trust and actively planning the careers of your best Chinese managers. It means challenging and changing the views on China and Chinese talent in wherever your Head Office is located. It means working hard to link your Chinese managers into your worldwide organization.

With Corning's rapid recent increase in investment in China, we have not had a decade to work on this local leadership challenge; for us this is a work in progress.

Q **What tools and approaches have you used to keep growth on track?**

A First of all, being an international company has helped Corning's determination to grow in China. We have made a variety of global acquisitions in recent years and we have a remarkable record in doing international joint ventures. Recent examples of acquisitions include the purchase of Siemens' and BICC's optical fiber and cable businesses. Some of these brought with them assets in China. Our environmental and display businesses were already global and China growth came in response to customer demand and to enhance existing global manufacturing strategies.

Second, using a rigorous approach. For a long time, I was known as "Mr. Homework" because I used to run the British Chamber of Commerce in China and when asked questions about the key ingredients for success in China I would invariably respond "do your homework". In China you have to be very rigorous, very demanding and put in the effort to prepare your strategy. You should not compromise the investment assessment requirements used in your company to justify making a China investment or business decision. In retrospect, some companies rushed into China in the 1990s and spent money without thinking enough about where their competitive advantage was in China – for example, in the mid-1990s many small banks and insurance companies piled in to China. So I am very strong on doing your homework and applying the same standards of rigor as you would in your home market in making big decisions in China.

In China it is also important to work at your government and industry relations – I spend a lot of my time on this to make sure we understand the local geography and make a social contribution. All this requires corporate leadership that has a vision and is able to engage from a long way away across a range of issues. Ultimately, the way you will be successful in China will be different from the way you have been in the U.S. or Europe but you won't know how it will be different until you engage.

One last key tool: your company values. Corning has a 150-year history and we have a very strong corporate culture. We also take our values seriously. As we build our businesses in China we are working hard to make sure that we bring these unique values to China and make them live in the Chinese context. It is part of what makes Corning unique, what unites us and what makes us special.

Q **What's special about government relations in China? How do you do it well?**

A There is nothing mystical about it. Is it easy? No. Is it important? Very much so! In China things do work in a different way and you have to find the right people and give them the tools to help you to win in this area. Your company seniors must be committed to regular visits. We engage with the cities where we build plants. We engage and work with the national policy makers for our industries. We contribute to the community and engage at multiple levels in order to work out issues and problems. One important element is continuity – you have to be consistent in your relations with government. As anywhere else in the world, Chinese Government bodies learn over time whether you are consistent and reliable, whether you do what you said you would do.

Q **What is the role of leadership, both global and at the business level, in driving the China business?**

A Each Corning division drives its own sales and in each division there are senior managers who make these decisions. There is also a geographic overlay in the international division, which has traditionally been the importer for countries where there is no local plant. In China our international division has helped businesses to get established. We have had strong drive from the business leaders to grow in China and strong local support from international division to help execute the business strategies.

Overall, I am a passionate advocate for a strong China local leadership which is empowered to run the businesses. I currently chair our Corning Greater China Business Council, the group of Corning China leaders which meets to share experiences, tackle issues and develop initiatives. In China we have also strengthened the regional overlay. My own position is a bit unusual in that I have geographic authority from running the international division but also I have operational responsibility for the telecommunications business and joint ventures. Companies do have to be flexible and alter their structure and leadership models to suit the needs of the market and their stage of development in China. Our structure and leadership may look very different in a few years time as Corning deepens its presence in China.

Q **Finally, anything you can share with us that you know now that you wish you had learned earlier?**

A You can never underestimate the need for patience and the capability to deal with change! Be prepared for much more change and a bigger variety of challenges than you have dealt with anywhere else. China is not a place for the faint-hearted or the short-termist.

Be prepared for tough competition. Choose the right leaders, be rigorous and, where necessary, structure organizations and strategy differently in China than elsewhere. This last is most important – you should structure and set objectives around the objectives and reality in China rather than your experience and comfort zone elsewhere. This is very demanding for many companies but does make the difference.

REFERENCES

1. In the same way, in semiconductors in the 1980s and multimedia in the 1990s, Samsung developed partnerships and increasingly invested its own money in R&D consortia and start-ups.
2. *Harvard Business Review*, "Going Global: Lessons from Late-Movers."
3. $24,160.
4. Andrew Grove, *Only the Paranoid Survive: How to Exploit the Crisis Points That Challenge Every Company*, New York: Bantam Dell, 1999; Bill Gates, *Business @ the Speed of Thought: Succeeding in the Digital Economy*, New York: Warner Books, 2000; Stan Shih, *Me-Too Is Not My Style*, Acer Publications.
5. Original-equipment manufacturer.
6. Companies that get involved in designing products and then manufacture them for branded players.
7. DRAM and foundry production are the two dominant modes of independent manufacturing, in addition to proprietary IDM plants. Another manufacturing option is analog and optical manufacturing of bipolar analog and mixed signal and optical chips. This also offers the opportunity to gain scale but is mostly controlled by IDMs, based on their proprietary technology. Moreover, CMOS is overtaking BiCMOS and bipolar processes, making this a less fruitful long-term play.
8. Both in-house and contract A&T are expected to grow at over 20% a year, with contract A&T growing slightly faster to amount to 25% of the total market by 2005. AMD Suzhou was established in 1999 and by 2001 employed over 300 people to assemble and test flash memory and communications products with an emphasis on

high-volume production requirements. In 2001, Intel announced that it would expand its A&T center in Shanghai at a cost of $200 million. Future expansion will enable Intel to assemble and test computer peripheral chips.

9. Having entered China in 1987, Motorola built its first semiconductor A&T plant in 1992 with less than $25 million. It has since expanded this investment by $200 million to serve both domestic and Asia-Pacific demand. However, its biggest investment was a fab in Tianjin, which it took five years to build, and which when completed in 2000 had a total investment of $1.7 billion.

10. It must be noted, however, that the U.S. continues to control exports of sub 0.35 micron technologies to China, particularly for key manufacturing and testing equipment such as lithographic tools for line width smaller than 0.35 micron, and testing equipment for frequencies over 333 MHz, subjecting them to lengthy clearances. Manufacturers such as Applied Materials, SVG and HP are subject to these restrictions. Other countries usually honor U.S. control policy but make certain modifications. In general, approvals are difficult for equipment of the same generation as, or two generations behind, leading-edge technology.

11. China's potential foundry demand is expected to grow from 66 million 8" wafer starts per month (WFSM) in 1997 to 120 million by 2004. China's foundry demand is a function of total CMOS production in China and the estimated market served by foundries. Total CMOS product revenue in China is assumed to have a 40% gross profit margin. Divided by average foundry price of $1,200 per wafer will reveal the total wafers required. Of these, 50% could be produced by foundries, 78% can be assumed to be non-leading edge and thus addressable by Chinese foundries.

12. A far larger number of segments will generate less than $100 million in profits in the same timeframe, reflecting the relative concentration of the industry around fast-growing segments.

3

Trouble in the Heartland

C hina's industrial heartland is on the brink of transformation. With huge demand pressures, traditional enterprises are breaking out of their hidebound state. A wave of mergers and acquisitions is set to break over the domestic environment, liberating the productive energies of the world's biggest industrial sector. In the automotive industry, as the global market remains saturated over the next five years, global OEMs will be jockeying for their share of the only national market that is likely to grow. Already the world's seventh-largest, China's domestic automotive market is projected to break into the world's top three by the end of the decade. A strategy that will help the auto giants in their quest for a share of China's market may have an even more valuable global application.

An asset-light strategy would see the major auto brands concentrate on what they are good at — product and brand development, and sales and marketing — while contracting their manufacturing, not just component supply but full production, to Chinese OEMs who are both willing and have an irresistible long-term competitive edge. A manufacturing base in China could become a global resource. The potential value to both global and Chinese players is high. But for this to work, both would need a fundamental change in mindset.

In steel, China has quickly become the world's largest market, and demand is set to soar during the next decade. Yet the country's steel producers are in poor shape to take advantage of their homeland's boom. Fragmented, uncompetitive, unprofitable, heavily in debt, and geared to the wrong products, they are losing out to imports. But all is far from lost. Given steel's strategic importance, the Chinese government is intent on remaking the industry to achieve international competitiveness. It has vigorously pushed for the industry restructuring needed to restore profitability to the main producers, which are still predominantly state-owned. Beijing is also forcing these producers to go to the private sector for the money that the industry desperately needs for growth. Foreign and local private investors, as well as regional governments, have their eye on the booming demand, but many have decided to wait for more restructuring before they act. To overcome the legacy of state planning, mills must shed their production quota mindset and focus on what their customers want. Operational improvements to boost productivity and strategic alliances are required as well. Those that move first have a chance to transform the industry, and to become tomorrow's leaders.

A restructuring of China's transportation and logistics sector is also clearly in the cards. Already, the Chinese government has designated logistics as a strategic industry and has committed to promoting investment in a number of logistics centers across the country. Seeing the emerging opportunity, newly established and incumbent service providers are moving aggressively to upgrade transportation and logistics services. Today, aspiring players in the sector include SOEs, local or joint-venture third-party logistics firms, foreign transportation and logistics groups and new domestic players emerging from domestic manufacturing and distribution. However, apart from the usual challenges of building relationships and networks, players may face policy shifts, due to social or other imperatives, or come up against local protectionism that often causes large gaps between central government policy and local practices. Victory will go only to those that move fast enough, have high tolerance for risk and build on their unique strengths.

3.1 A TUNE-UP FOR CHINA'S AUTO INDUSTRY*

by Paul Gao

Faced with the prospect of stagnant global sales over the next five years, the world's biggest carmakers are jockeying for a share of one of the few buoyant national markets. China's domestic car sales, growing at more than 10% annually, will probably account for 15% of global growth over the next five years. So far, global automakers have pursued successful joint-venture

* Originally published in *The McKinsey Quarterly*, 2002 Number 1, and at www.mckinseyquarterly.com. Copyright (c) 2002 McKinsey & Company. All rights reserved. Reprinted by permission.

strategies by investing heavily in assembly plants operated by Chinese partners. But as competition in China heats up, a new tack may be needed in the quest for profitable market share.

An asset-light strategy would have the major auto companies concentrate on what they do best – developing products and brands — while contracting out not just component supply but also the whole assembly process to Chinese automakers that can capitalize on competitive cost structures. Although scaling back capital investment in such a healthy market might seem bold, outsourcing manufacturing is neither uncommon in other industries nor entirely unprecedented in the auto industry. Moreover, the nature of the Chinese auto industry and market makes outsourcing particularly attractive. Outsourcing might also help Chinese automakers take their first steps to becoming a global manufacturing resource. But if the strategy is to work, global carmakers must build up the skills of these Chinese partners, which in turn must embrace contract manufacturing as a more profitable path to creating a globally competitive industry than launching their own brands.

THE COMPETITION IS ABOUT TO HEAT UP

With sales of 2.1 million-plus units in 2000, China buys more four-wheeled vehicles than all but six other national markets, yet its passenger car market is still in the early stages of growth (Exhibit 3.1). Indeed China, with only 600,000 car sales a year, has fewer than 10 passenger cars on the road per 1,000 people, compared with 250 in Taiwan and more than 500 in Germany and the United States. But demand – promoted by better roads, new sales and distribution channels, the deregulation of the auto market, and China's entry into the WTO – will increase as the country's economy continues to grow.

The dominant production and sales joint ventures between global and local companies have the best position for meeting that demand. Only 15 years after Volkswagen entered the market, more than half of the passenger cars sold in China roll out of VW's Changchun and Shanghai joint ventures. Other foreign joint ventures account for nearly all the rest – a further 43%. In the shadow of these foreign alliances, 20 domestic carmakers share just 3% of the market because of China's eroding policy of regional self-sufficiency as well as a protectionist policy that is quickly following suit.[1]

As global firms focus more and more on China, local manufacturers will do well to hold even that meager share; they concede too much ground in R&D, product development, and sales and marketing. In addition, DaimlerChrysler, GM and VW plan to expand; Ford has set up the

Exhibit 3.1   China's passenger car market expected to grow 23% annually, the fastest in the world

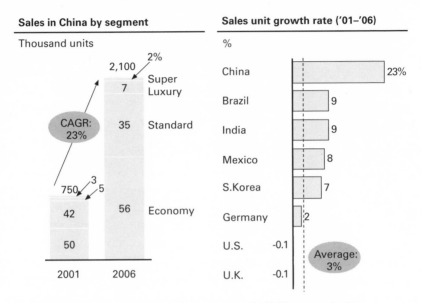

Sales in China by segment	Sales unit growth rate ('01–'06)

Thousand units

CAGR: 23%

2,100
2%
Super Luxury — 7
Standard — 35
750 — 3, 5
Economy — 56
42
50

2001   2006

%

China	23%
Brazil	9
India	9
Mexico	8
S.Korea	7
Germany	2
U.S.	-0.1
U.K.	-0.1

Average: 3%

Source: Wards Automotive; EIU; Literature search; McKinsey analysis

company's first passenger car joint venture; and BMW is planning with China Brilliance Auto for the Chinese company to assemble its 3-series and 5-series models in China. What is more, these global carmakers are planning, for the first time, to introduce new models and upgrades in China within months of their launch in more mature markets. This development will surely end the reign of the VW Santana, a 1970s-era model that has long been out of production elsewhere but, offered without even a facelift for over 15 years, is China's best-selling car. China's entry into the WTO will cut import tariffs drastically, heightening pressure on local producers. It will also allow global carmakers to own businesses focusing on operations in which they have unmatchable advantages: sales, service and distribution channels, as well as loan services to car buyers – services that are sure to be welcome in a market where personal credit is scarce.

For global brands, the strategic issue is no longer whether to enter the market or how to compete with Chinese companies but, rather, securing or consolidating profitable market share. For Chinese automakers, this means that their ambitions will increasingly depend on the strategies of those global companies.

THE NEED FOR AN ASSET-LIGHT STRATEGY

Competing in China involves big money: a capital investment of $1.5 billion for GM's Shanghai plant alone, for example, and $1.7 billion for the two facilities of VW's joint ventures. Thanks to the protection of the industry, this investment has largely paid off: with tariffs ranging from 80% to 100%, models bear price tags up to 150% higher than those in the United States and Europe, allowing successful joint ventures in China to enjoy levels of profitability not seen anywhere else. For each Honda Accord, for example, Honda's Guangzhou joint venture makes over $3,000 in net profit, three times the net profit for a comparable U.S. model.

But greater competition is already squeezing those margins. Even with technology upgrades, the list price of the standard Santana fell by 25%, to RMB115,000 ($13,850), in the five years up to October 2001. As tariffs fall, so will prices. Against this, sales and marketing costs will rise in a more competitive market, and more frequent model upgrades will mean that heavier investment will constantly be needed to retool assembly plants.

This scenario — global companies stuck on a direct-investment treadmill as financial returns become more uncertain — has played out in much of the world. China, which almost alone among new markets has its own very large auto industry, offers a point of departure. For the global carmakers, pursuing an asset-light strategy would involve contracting out the manufacture of vehicles to Chinese-owned production companies. If they can meet this demand for production, as Chinese firms have done in other industries, their global partners would reap a number of advantages.

First, the global carmakers would retain the continuing advantages of Chinese production: the ability to overcome whatever nontariff barriers to imports (such as quotas and licensing restrictions) survive China's entry into the WTO, as well as cheaper labor, reduced freight, and local-government concessions. And the global companies would gain these advantages with lower financial risk than they would bear if they tried to produce cars themselves.

Second, there are the direct benefits of contracting out. Global automakers in China could employ up to 40% less capital, which promises a corresponding 60% increase in their return on capital. Alternatively, contracting out would free up funds that could be concentrated on the higher-value skills of product development and design, and sales and marketing. It would also enable global companies to pursue those parts of China's embryonic after-sales market (retail financing, leasing, servicing, repairs, spare parts and rentals) open to them after China's WTO entry. In developed markets, these activities generate 57% of the industry's profits, yet there are few established players in China.

Finally, indirect benefits would flow to the global carmakers from the increased specialization and scale of the Chinese contractors, whose chief advantage is the ability to develop and use their expensive technology and capacity to serve more than one customer. Given the size and automation level of the relevant assembly plants in China, doubling a plant's output would translate into a 5% saving in unit costs. Ultimately, global brands may draw on this Chinese resource to supply other markets with good quality, competitively priced cars, which would in turn build the scale of Chinese factories to an optimal cost-reducing level.

In many ways, this asset-light strategy would mimic the success some global automakers have had with recent sales and distribution initiatives. Since mid-1999, dealers of Audi, GM and Honda cars have invested more than $250 million in facilities and other infrastructure in China. Before then, companies such as Beijing Jeep, without serious competition and with demand easily outstripping supply, relied on state-owned "distributors" that merely stored cars in open-air parking lots pending the cars' allocation to other state-owned enterprises. Audi, whose customers still face a three- to six-month waiting list for its A6 model, exemplified the successful implementation of this strategy when it became heavily involved in developing the sales and management skills of Chinese firms, without investing capital in the process. The company took more than a year to select its 32 dealers, seeking entrepreneurs from the auto industry and elsewhere, who were market-oriented, ambitious, and able to finance their own premises and growth. The new dealerships use showroom designs and sales strategies that are well known in developed markets but a revelation in China.

Contracting out something as fundamental as product manufacture always raises the specter of "creating your own competition", Companies that adopt the asset-light strategy naturally hope that the manufacturers they nurture won't eventually beat them at their own game. Although little is certain in business, global car brands can find much to allay their concerns. In the car industry, it is skills in design, brand marketing and distribution, as well as a very few key components, notably high-performance engines, that help companies earn their competitive position. Their profits flow from sales, service, finance and leasing. Outsourcing assembly doesn't force companies to transfer their skills in any key area, nor should it put these advantages at risk, which is why Cisco, HP and IBM feel secure in outsourcing the manufacture of most of their high-end hardware. And many of the world's auto firms have elsewhere commenced sharing facilities or outsourcing assembly.

MAKING IT HAPPEN

Contracting out production isn't altogether novel for global carmakers: Valmet, in Finland, makes the Porsche Boxster; Karmann, in Germany, makes convertibles for Jaguar, Mercedes-Benz, Renault and VW. These successes show that, even in quality markets, customers care more about the styling, performance and after-sales service of strong brands than about which company actually produced the car. Successful Chinese automakers such as SAIC (Shanghai Automotive Industry Corporation) are already all but contract-manufacturing for GM and VW, for they are totally responsible for the quality of their output, drawing on their global partners' technology and management talent as required.[2] GM and VW, however, have invested heavily in these plants as equity partners. Contracting out manufacture requires a further degree of separation.

For contracting to succeed in China, two conditions must be met. First, the local component-supply industry will have to complete its current journey of consolidation and improved quality to meet the quantity requirements and specifications of global models. Second, global companies should continue transferring technology and management skills to selected Chinese plants.

Most global firms realize that a strong local supplier base is needed to manufacture cars at competitive cost and quality. Local components escape import duties, and though they will decline under the WTO regime, the other advantages of local production remain, particularly lower freight costs and faster supply. Competition and quality in the Chinese component-supply market are already rising. Every one of the top 10 global automotive suppliers had set up shop in China by the end of 2000 – most, like Delphi, with a number of joint ventures – and many are exporting components to Europe and North America. Consolidation is being driven by China's shift to global models, by the tendency of Chinese companies to outsource their own component manufacturing, and by supportive government policies.

Yet global automakers could do more to help. One way would be to go on matching local capacity with international expertise, as Volkswagen has done so successfully with its joint-venture partner SAIC, its international first-tier suppliers, and the Shanghai local government, which aims to make autos a core local industry. Automakers might also insist that their dealer networks sell only branded, quality-assured spare parts rather than the counterfeit local products that now make up over 50% of all after-market supplies.

But a strong local component industry is only half of the picture, for if global automakers are to rely on local manufacturing, they will have to support efforts to increase the quality and scale of Chinese assembly plants.

Further capital investment, even if available, isn't required; instead, the global companies can inject technology and management expertise into plants that are already being consolidated.

BMW's developing relationship with China Brilliance Auto is a good example. Brilliance hired Giorgetto Giugiaro's firm, Italdesign, to design its proposed Zhong Hua passenger car and was building plants and training workers to manufacture it. Instead of seeing Brilliance as a competitive threat, BMW sent out its own engineers and technicians to help the Chinese company not only in building the assembly line but also in training workers, engineers and managers in processes and quality control. As Brilliance proves itself with the Zhong Hua, BMW will give it the go-ahead to assemble the company's 3-series and 5-series models for the East Asian market at its new Shenyang plant.

Toyota's relationship with Tianjin Xiali is an alternative approach to building up Chinese skills to mutual advantage. Toyota licensed Tianjin in 2000 to produce a car, marketed as a Tianjin Xiali, based on the Japanese Toyota Platz/Vitz compact (known as the Toyota Echo in the U.S.). In this way, Toyota receives revenue from the license and from car kits and components while building up Tianjin's abilities – all without risking the Toyota brand. Toyota also announced a joint venture with Tianjin to build an all-new model that will bear the Toyota brand. Although Toyota Tianjin is a joint venture, the same staged approach could be taken with wholly outsourced manufacturing.

As in all such arrangements, contracts must enhance the parties' mutual dependence: the global buyer suffers if the Chinese plant can't meet production schedules, just as the plant suffers if the global buyer doesn't order sufficient volume. Global automakers will also need to protect their intellectual property rights and product quality standards, though reputable Chinese assemblers now realize that their lucrative global manufacturing contracts will be at risk if they attempt to appropriate their partners' intellectual property or fail to meet quality standards.

THE OUTSOURCING OPTIONS

For global brands with a smaller market share or a lower level of capital investment in China, asset-light manufacturing is the most relevant, because it gives them an opportunity to leapfrog the competition by using capital more efficiently. But the bigger players in China could also work with this strategy.

First, heretical though the idea may seem, proven joint-venture facilities can offer their manufacturing capacity to other brands – a strategy that has been used successfully at the GM and Toyota joint venture, NUMMI (New United Motor Manufacturing Incorporated in California), though these two companies do compete. Modern auto plants are flexible enough to make a variety of models and to switch among them quickly. There are limits to this approach, however. The collaboration between Ford and VW at Autolatina, in Brazil, came unstuck when both carmakers used the plant to build models that competed directly with each other rather than sticking to complementary lines.

Global automakers could also turn to contract manufacturing once local demand exceeded the limits of their existing joint-venture capacity. In addition, they could reduce their equity in existing plants, allowing the Chinese partner to take on other contracts or the foreign partner to apply capital to additional value-creating slivers in the auto value chain.

In the longer term, global carmakers could develop their Chinese partners as suppliers to other markets. Global companies have already started shifting the assembly of low-end to mid-market cars to different countries with a lower cost base. Even Volkswagen, with one of the most unionized labor forces in Germany, is assembling VW and Audi models in Poland, Portugal, Slovakia and Spain. Particularly in a global downturn, pressure on manufacturing costs will inevitably force global players to think about China, where labor costs, which make up 10% of total manufacturing costs in developed markets, are about 1/30th those in Europe, Japan and North America. Low labor costs have enticed electronics companies such as Ericsson and Philips, as well as most manufacturers of PCs, to work with quality contractors in Asia.

WHAT'S IN IT FOR CHINESE AUTOMAKERS?

Contract manufacturing may seem a lackluster aspiration for a Chinese auto industry that has long seen its Japanese and South Korean counterparts as models of home-grown brands that became global leaders. But the conditions that underpinned the Japanese and South Korean economic models have long since disappeared. China would be helped neither by a 1970s-style oil shock (the fuel-efficient cars that propelled Japan to the forefront are now the norm) nor by the favorable exchange rate that helped South Korean brands break into low-end European and North American markets.

Insisting on self-reliance now carries huge financial risks in an extremely mature and competitive global industry. The development cost of a new mass-market car has risen to more than $1 billion, and the financial performance of most leading global automakers has long been poor. The miseries of Japan's once mighty Mitsubishi and Nissan and of South Korea's

Daewoo, Hyundai and Kia are forcing government officials and industry executives in China to rethink their policies. Despite two decades of determined reforms, none of China's domestic carmakers has the scale or skill to develop globally competitive new products.

By comparison, contract manufacturing can be less risky and more rewarding. Leaders in electronics manufacturing services outperform branded customers in profitability and return on investment. Auto component specialists and module suppliers around the world enjoy a higher return on capital than the leading brands they supply. Furthermore, unlike Brazil, Britain and Spain, where the auto-assembly industries are subsidiaries of global carmakers, China has protected local ownership and can thus retain the profits the industry generates.[3] As Chinese firms build up their manufacturing skills and capital, some might be tempted to launch their own global brand or even to purchase a financially distressed foreign brand and then rebuild that franchise, as Proton has done with Lotus. However, most would think twice about risking billions of dollars to launch an untested brand and, at the same time, losing their lucrative contract-manufacturing customers to other local competitors.

How would China's automakers prepare for this role? As they are preparing today; by pursuing consolidation, productivity, quality, and the global relationships that flow from them. In the long run, given the ever-increasing cost of developing new cars and the sales needed to recoup it, the Chinese market is big enough to support only five or six large automotive companies, either joint ventures with strong global partners or Chinese-owned contractors. Among those likely to succeed are companies such as First Auto Works (FAW), Guangzhou Honda, SAIC and, perhaps, Brilliance, which have the productivity and quality to deliver.

But most of China's domestic producers suffer from an inflexible manufacturing system that wastes capital investment, makes production lead times long and unreliable, and undermines the quality of products. The immediate need of these producers is to learn from the proven production practices of the country's leading plants, to adopt lean manufacturing initiatives and to avoid increasing capital investment whenever operational inefficiencies constrain capacity.[4]

✳   ✳   ✳

Since most global carmakers have had large investments in China only since 1999, it may seem odd to advocate scaling back the industry's capital investment now. But the nature and pace of structural reform and consumer demand in China require constant review of strategies. As margins become tighter, producers will need strategies that both pursue market share and manage costs. To win market share, global automakers should concentrate on their new sales and distribution networks in China and on their product and brand development around the world. To manage costs and capital, contracting out manufacturing to Chinese companies may be a leapfrog strategy for Western carmakers willing to take the first steps now.

3.2 REMAKING CHINA'S GIANT STEEL INDUSTRY*

China's steel market has quickly become the world's largest, and demand is set to soar during the next decade. Yet the country's steel producers are in poor shape to take advantage of their homeland's boom. Fragmented, uncompetitive, unprofitable, heavily in debt and geared to the wrong products, they are losing out to imports.

But all is far from lost. Given steel's strategic importance, the Chinese government is intent on remaking the industry to achieve international competitiveness. In addition to vigorously pushing for the industry restructuring that is needed to restore profitability to the main producers, which are still predominantly state owned, Beijing is forcing them to go to the private sector for the money they desperately need for growth.

Foreign and local private investors, as well as regional governments, have their eye on the booming demand, but many have decided to wait for additional restructuring before they act. To overcome the legacy of state planning, mills must shed their production-quota mindset and focus on what their customers want. Operational improvements to boost productivity and strategic alliances are required as well. Companies that move first have a chance to transform the industry and to become tomorrow's leaders.

A GROWING APPETITE FOR STEEL

On the back of surging construction and infrastructure investments, demand for steel in China has more than quadrupled since 1980 while Japan, Western Europe and the United States have experienced single-digit growth rates. China consumed more than 130 million tons of steel in 2000, surpassing the United States to become the biggest market in the world.[5] Chinese producers,

* Originally published in *The McKinsey Quarterly*, 2001 Number 4, and at www.mckinseyquarterly.com. Copyright (c) 2001 McKinsey & Company. All rights reserved. Reprinted by permission.

generating 3% of the nation's gross domestic product and employing more than three million people, supply 87% of the domestic market.

Yet China is still only in the early stages of burgeoning demand. There is a well-established relationship between a country's GDP and steel consumption (Exhibit 3.2). China uses a mere 0.12 kilograms per dollar of GDP, or 92 kilograms per head, whereas Malaysia, for example, consumes 450 kilograms per head. Partly closing that gap in the coming decade could double demand even if new technologies allowed China to bypass some of the more steel-intensive phases of economic development.

Part of the demand for steel will involve relatively cheap long products used in construction. China's steel industry concentrates on them, but stricter building codes will augment the growing demand for high-quality construction steel. Growth will be even faster in the market for higher value-added flat products, above all for world-scale customers in the automotive, appliance and assembly sectors. Markets for stainless, galvanized, coated, and other more complex processed steels are expected to grow faster still. Because China is short of the plants needed to make these products, it imports them from South Korea, Japan, Europe and the United States.

Annual demand is set to increase by 50 million tons, to more than 182 million tons, by 2005, but no more than 27 million tons of net planned expansion capacity can be identified. This implies a gap, chiefly in flat

Exhibit 3.2 A steely need as GDP rises

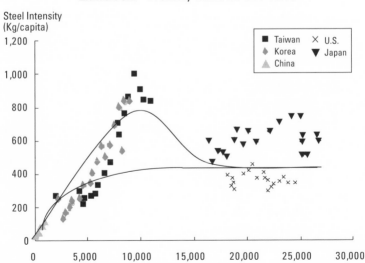

Source: IMF Yearbook, IISI Yearbooks

products, of up to 44 million tons in the supply of finished steel by 2005 – a gap that can be filled only by imports or higher productivity. The capacity shortfall is the unsurprising result of the downward spiral of profitability and investment since the early 1990s: some township and collective enterprises have built small plants with minimill technology, but only one large greenfield mill was built during the decade, and the level of investment dropped by 50% from 1995 to 1999.

If these trends continue, China's steel industry will become increasingly incapable of serving the country's needs. But steel doesn't feature as a major investment area for the central government in the tenth Five Year Plan (2000) because Beijing is gambling that continued deregulation and consolidation will be catalyst enough for improvement. And to be sure, if the industry is willing to restructure, private and foreign capital will arrive.

CONSOLIDATION: THE FIRST STEP

Many of the industry's problems are rooted in its fragmentation, a result of China's 1960s-era policy of regional self-sufficiency. Small loss-making companies abound, and even the industry's biggest must grow to become competitive on a world scale. The very largest Chinese steel company – Shanghai Baosteel Group, at 18 million tons – is dwarfed by the 40-million-ton capacity of Arcelor, in Europe, as well as the 25-million-ton capacity of both South Korea's POSCO and Japan's Nippon Steel.

Since 1997, Beijing has pushed to close obsolete and underperforming plants – just a part of its strategy to shift state industry to a more investment-friendly market footing. The consolidation program has been controversial, and the record is mixed at best. Managers of consolidated regional mills have been left with the unenviable choice of decommissioning or carrying excess capacity. In many of the merged entities, the burden of the loss makers has so far outweighed the promised benefits. The Shanghai Baosteel Group, for example, was formed in a 1997 merger of Shanghai Metallurgical, Meishan Iron & Steel, and Baoshan Iron & Steel (Baosteel). Since then, the company has absorbed seven other mills. Although it dominates demand in the greater Shanghai area, four years after its formation it still derives almost all of its profits from Baosteel.

By contrast, the Hualing Group, in Hunan, appears to have consolidated four smaller mills more successfully, thus raising profits and generating ongoing cost reductions. Encouraged by this and early relative success stories in other similarly fragmented industries, such as airlines, Beijing is persevering with its consolidation policy, as it must. Liaoning Province, in China's northeast, is proposing to merge its mills at Anshan, Benxi, Dalian and Fushun. Shougang Steel could acquire Tangshan Steel in the north, while Wuhan is slated to go on expanding along the Yangtze River.

THREE WINNING STRATEGIES

Beijing's policies and the strong demand for steel will provide an opportunity, while those mills that survive will have found a way to improve their performance dramatically – and thus to attract investment. Some investors, seeing the industry's potential, are stepping in: ThyssenKrupp's $1 billion stainless-steel venture with the Shanghai Baosteel Group, in 1999, was an extraordinary vote of confidence. And international lenders, including the U.S. firm McDonald Investments, are attempting to structure deals with local leaders such as Handan Iron & Steel.

Mills can tailor at least three winning strategies to their own needs, even as they push ahead with consolidation. These strategies may be familiar elsewhere, but they represent big steps for China, given the culture and capabilities of its steel enterprises.

Spurring Productivity

What prevents the Chinese steel industry from beating the price-cost squeeze imposed by the country's opening to world trade is low productivity. In the early 1990s, Japan and South Korea met China's growing demand for high-value steel while cheap Russian steel flooded the low-value market. Before quotas were imposed, in 1996, imports peaked at 28% of consumption. Prices, which imports were setting by then, dropped 30% from 1996 to 2000.

Meanwhile, the price of raw materials, again set by international markets, was rising. Local iron-ore mines failed to meet the increasing demand, for they, like the mills to which they were attached, suffered from low productivity. Mills looking for higher-quality inputs had to import them, since the iron content of China's ore is generally less than 40%. Imports now account for up to 30% of the iron ore consumed in China.

By 2000, the Chinese steel industry faced the same price-cost squeeze confronting the rest of the global steel industry. Its profitability had declined from 6.1% in 1990 to 0.7% in 1999, far below what is needed to attract reinvestment. As the industry's share of national investment fell from 6% in 1996 to 2% in 2000, most mills had to borrow to finance expansion and even operating expenses. The industry's debt-to-equity ratio rose from 1.26 in 1995 to 1.65 in 1999, compared with typical U.S. ratios of 0.2 to 0.6 in 1999.

In this environment, any Chinese mill that wants to survive will have to make operational improvements. The opportunities are significant; even the top-ranked mills could reduce their costs by up to 9% to match international standards if they merely targeted nonlabor areas such as energy management, product yields and maintenance.

Better performance, however, will also require layoffs, which are often impossible without government support. Shougang Steel, for instance, employs more than 100,000 people to make seven million tons of steel, though international standards suggest that the number of workers could be only 10,000 to 20,000. Shougang could in theory dismiss a majority of its employees immediately, but the local government, though supportive in principle, refuses to allow layoffs on this scale. Such enterprises have been employers of last resort, after all, and some other arrangement must be made for the full range of employee and family social services they provide.

Just as important, mills need the freedom to reward their people for individual performance. Although salaried employees – a majority of all workers – do receive a bonus, it is often the same for all of them, and when everybody gets the same bonus, it is just another part of fixed income. Meanwhile, the chairman of the largest steel company in China makes just 20% of the salary of a typical joint venture's general manager.

Handan Iron & Steel is well known as the first Chinese steel enterprise to put itself in order. Back in 1990, it produced 1.1 million tons of steel bars, wires, beams, plates and other construction steels. Of the company's 28 products, 26 were sold at a loss. Handan's response was to make use of market prices for the internal transfer of raw materials, fuel, consumables, and refractory and semifinished goods. Previously, Handan had applied the government's allocated prices, which were grossly below market levels; though the company sold its products at a loss, each of its operating units was miraculously profitable.

By knowing the market value of its end products, Handan could work backward to arrive at the cost-reduction targets needed at all stages of production to ensure a profit. Handan included all of its employees in a program to identify and capture the potential cost savings at each stage. Finally, it developed a new performance-management program to sustain the improvements. In only eight months, the company turned itself around, achieving such great success that "learn from Handan" became a nationwide slogan. From 1991 through 1997, the company's total costs fell by an average of 5% a year. Even with fierce price competition, Handan managed to increase its profits steadily until 1995. Since then, it has clearly outperformed the industry, maintaining profits while most of its peers sustained many years of losses.

The experience of leaders such as Handan shows how China's mills should pursue operational excellence. They first need to find a determined group of people willing to drive efficiency on the shop floor. To set clear quantitative targets, they must then create what in many cases will be a mill's first reliable fact base on costs. And to ensure a controlled environment, the effort should start with pilots rather than a plantwide push.

Dominating local markets with a new customer focus

Operational efficiency is a necessary first step, but it is far from enough. The industry is officially only four years removed from the days of central planning, when state enterprises lacked commercial connections to the markets they were created to serve. The needs of local governments tended to drive production planning, and executives typically had technical or administrative backgrounds and few market and business development skills.

In the recent past, Chinese mills have fought hard to get closer to their customers. They have built direct sales channels to skirt the slow delivery times and high inventory costs of layers of independent distributors. They have invested in new product and processing capabilities – in particular, hot and cold rolling, as well as galvanized and plating capacity – that their domestic end users needed. And they have explored e-commerce: 12 large mills launched a World Wide Web marketplace.

These approaches will help, but they are unlikely to yield a real breakthrough unless accompanied by a fundamental shift away from production quotas and toward efforts to find out what customers actually want. In chasing the large yet fragmented construction markets of China, its mills have consistently overestimated demand for new products and underestimated the quality and the marketing required. Chinese galvanized steel sells at a 30% discount to the imported equivalent, but customers just aren't interested in lower-quality goods. Meanwhile, the Chinese subsidiary of Australia's BHP Steel has shown how a well-researched, differentiated, and quality offer can secure both a premium and a dominant market share in China's highly competitive construction sector.

Chinese mills, particularly in flat products, should concentrate on the handful of their customers – automobile, appliance, and container companies – that place large orders, for these customers will determine their profitability in years to come. Every mill should rigorously assess the needs of its customers and draw upon all of its cross-functional expertise to work with them to generate solutions. When a mill has unique product competencies developed with its customer base, it can then attack a broader market. Here the priorities are disciplined market research; a willingness to insist on quality; smart capital design to ensure a fair return; systems and structures to ensure consistency; and a realistic investment in the brand and product launch.

Forming Alliances for an International Market

Serving the new generation of demanding customers, both multinational and Chinese, will increasingly require these disciplines. Giants like General Motors, Toyota and Volkswagen dominate the steel-reliant automotive industry, and a similar process of consolidation is occurring in packaging and other steel-intensive sectors. These customers have long sought to consolidate their suppliers across regions, and multinational steelmakers are now developing global networks to capture them.

China's mills, however, lack the scale, relationships and experience to serve the global giants: the international presence of Chinese mills is limited to information-gathering offices, and overseas investments have been unsuccessful. But Chinese steelmakers may have an opportunity to piggyback on the global moves of Chinese appliance companies, such as Haier and Kelong, that are investing in assembly plants in the United States and Europe.

Otherwise, the threat to domestic producers is clear: join the international players or be relegated to the role of second-tier supplier. China isn't new to alliances and joint ventures with foreign players. So far, the record in the steel industry is mixed, as the former partners of one of the larger investments in Shanxi would attest: a failure to assess the market, a lack of disciplined on-the-ground management, and a complete breakdown in trust between the partners contributed to the withdrawal of the foreign side.

To make joint ventures work in the long term, both sides must commit sufficient managerial and financial resources to create an independently viable business; Shanghai Automotive Industry Corporation's joint venture with Volkswagen is a good example. Less formal links through the exchange of technology, coordination among suppliers, and co-marketing to global customers may prove equally effective. Chinese mills, however, will have to become far more disciplined in developing skills than they have been to date.

✳   ✳   ✳

What is possible for Chinese steel companies a decade from now? If they make the right moves, the industry could double its current output in a range of quality products and rival its European and Japanese counterparts in productivity. As a result of consolidation, 70% of production would take place in the hubs of Shanghai, Guangdong, Hebei, Liaoning and Wuhan.

And only two groups – which might align themselves with POSCO and Nippon Steel and with NKK and Kawasaki Steel to serve global automotive and appliance customers – would manage 60% of that business. If all went well, the companies, with a set of diversified, international and well-rewarded investors, would be listed on the Chinese, London and New York stock exchanges.

What will it take for this vision to come true? Regulators must continue to play the role of the catalyst. Developing talent will also be vital because, in an increasingly capital-intensive industry, China cannot rely solely on the competitive advantage of its low-cost labor. But the mills themselves now have, in their own hands, the responsibility for winning their share of the global steel market.

3.3 CHINA'S EVOLVING LOGISTICS LANDSCAPE

by Stephen M. Shaw and Tony Perkins

Economic reforms in China have already brought far-reaching change to many sectors of its economy. Now, it's the turn of the transportation and logistics sector. Ongoing economic growth and China's entry into the World Trade Organization could very well transform this currently underdeveloped sector. While growth is stimulating demand, WTO entry promises significant spillover effects on the sector from the further expansion and opening of the economy. A rapid expansion of China's transportation and logistics sector is clearly on the cards.

Already, the Chinese government has designated logistics as a strategic industry and has committed to promoting investment in a number of logistics centers across the country. Retail channels are consolidating and modernizing in the top-tier cities, China's major consumption centers, and spreading to the next tier of cities. Express highways linking the major cities are being completed and professional truckers are emerging. Newly established and incumbent service providers are moving aggressively to upgrade transportation and logistics services. Today, aspiring players in the sector include SOEs, local or joint-venture third-party logistics firms, foreign transportation and logistics groups and new domestic players emerging from domestic manufacturing and distribution.

But capturing the emerging opportunities will not be easy. Apart from the usual challenges of building relationships and networks, players may face policy shifts, due to social or other imperatives, or come up against local protectionism that often causes large gaps between central government policy and local practices. Broadly speaking, players should look for opportunities in three main areas: efficient, networked transportation and warehousing services, value-added third-party logistics solutions and niche opportunities for technological solutions (such as tracking-and-tracing software). Those that move fast enough, have tolerance for high risk and build on their unique strengths will eventually triumph.

LOGISTICS SERVICES ARE ELEMENTARY

Until now, the Chinese market for transportation and logistics has remained fairly underdeveloped for two main reasons: (1) the dominance of SOEs and their tendency to own and operate all functions; (2) the predominance of cellular economies with limited, local distribution areas. In fact, logistics demand has remained concentrated in the central and coastal provinces, around the major cities of Guangdong, Shanghai and Beijing/Tianjin. Cargo movement and industry output are highly concentrated in this area, the country's top eight ocean ports are located here, and its cities are well connected by road networks. The populace enjoys some of the highest per capita incomes in the country. While import/export activities and some freight forwarding have traditionally been undertaken by state-owned players like Sinotrans (China National Foreign Trade Transportation Corporation) or COSCO (China Ocean Shipping Company) and some foreign players, most domestic logistics and goods transport needs have largely been met by the SOEs themselves, as they have historically owned and operated their own trucks to deliver goods downstream to distributors and wholesalers. These distributors and wholesalers in turn have bought the finished goods and moved them to consumers through a highly antiquated and fragmented retail trade, leaving manufacturers out of control of logistics.

Not surprisingly, supply of transportation and transport-related services serving domestic needs has remained limited. Shipping within and across China is suited mainly to the transport of commodities – it is very rarely a good solution for distributing finished goods mainly because of the large scale of bulk and container ships and the low frequency and inflexibility of schedules of this transport mode. Although shipping is critical for import and export of bulk goods, domestic shipping is not well developed. Neither is onward shipping – trucking is used instead. For high-value or time-sensitive finished goods, shipping cannot really compete with other transport modes.

Airfreight may have greater potential in the future, but its use can be problematic today. Airline routes in China are highly fragmented, and most airlines focus heavily on the passenger, not cargo, business. Cargo planes make up less than 20% of China's aircraft, and the belly space of passenger aircraft is poorly utilized since domestic air routes can be circuitous and infrequent. Inefficient information exchange between airlines and freight forwarders can make coordination and delivery a nightmare. But the bigger problem is the lack of an effective, ground-based, supporting network. While China does have freight forwarders, due to lack of demand or of insight they rarely provide adequate support services such as local pick-up and delivery that are commonplace in developed economies.

While parcel post alternatives are available, for example through international providers such as Fedex or TNT, they meet only a small fraction of most manufacturers' needs for delivery of time-sensitive items. Domestically, there is only one supplier, China Post, which obviously can't meet all needs.

Rail also has severe limitations as a mode of transporting finished goods. It is the lifeline for moving bulk goods such as coal, minerals and grain. In fact, more than 90% of all goods moved by rail are bulk goods. But rail is unsuited to moving most finished goods because of extensive delays, little flexibility in routes, and the lack of a genuine service orientation. There are two other constraints to moving goods by rail. First, very few manufacturing plants in China have rail sidings, and ports often lack modern and efficient rail sidings, making it impossible to load goods directly into wagons and from wagons to ships. Second, the lack of an inter-modal rail system makes it impossible to load a full truck-borne container onto a rail wagon. Since trucks must be used to get goods to and from the rail system, and since ship containers are also loaded onto trucks for onward transportation, it often makes more sense to use trucks alone. Finally, like airlines, rail services are also increasingly focused on the passenger business, leading to neglect of the higher value-added freight business.

Given the flexibility it offers, trucking is still the mode of choice for most finished-goods producers that supply domestic markets and is likely to remain so in the future. This mode of transport, however, also suffers from considerable limitations. Trucking has remained largely a cottage industry in China due to a number of structural factors. Historically, manufacturers have provided their own ground-based transportation services, a common requirement in a planned economy such as China in which the notion of hiring such services is not well developed. Since manufacturers own their trucks, utilization tends to be inefficient due to unprofessional fleet management. Trucking services for hire have remained limited to informal leasing of a few vehicles at a time to "unofficial, local operators".

But the biggest constraint to the development of modern trucking networks and effective collaboration among truckers has been local protectionism. Local governments in China consider it very important to protect their local economies by limiting the entry of trucks carrying goods from other regions. To do this, they set up complicated regulatory requirements on transport services and stringent border controls. To illustrate: many cities will not allow trucks to enter without a tedious licensing and registration process. As a result, many trucks traversing provincial borders become restricted to hauling goods only one way. While local authorities aim to control the flow of goods between provinces or regions, this has come at the expense of the development of modern trucking networks. Another issue with trucking is the heavy cost burden imposed by toll roads: tolls amount to as much as 20% of trucking costs in China.

Warehousing in China barely meets customer needs. General infrastructure is poor: most warehouses are poorly designed and equipped, and lack automated handling of goods. This hampers operations – their low ceilings cannot accommodate automated equipment, for example – and often damages goods. Most warehouses cannot cater to special requirements since they lack humidity control and cold storage and even facilities to store goods separately to avoid contamination. Inadequate management-information systems, such as the lack of information-based inventory management, is another issue. Manufacturers and distributors are faced with high discrepancies in actual and recorded inventory data, a high ratio of missing items, and a general lack of real-time product or order tracking. These deficiencies in warehousing have led manufacturers, particularly foreign ones, to build their own facilities.

Transportation and logistics services have historically been provided by a few major SOEs with government-granted monopolies (or near-monopolies) in rail, shipping and freight forwarding. Examples of these dominant, asset-intensive players are COSCO[6] (shipping), CMST[7] (warehousing and trucking), Sinotrans[8] (air freight forwarding, shipping), China Post (mail and parcel post) and China Rail. A few new local companies or foreign-local joint ventures have tried to offer very limited solutions to specific industries, with some IT services and coordination of basic transport services. Examples are ST-Anda (serving beverages and packaged foods companies), PG Logistics (fast-moving consumer goods), and EAS (electronics). Foreign logistics players have for the most part been thwarted by the tough policies barring foreign ownership of distribution and transportation assets, their low ability to gain true operating control of critical assets (for instance, in trucking), and significant barriers in local economies.

The situation began improving, even if marginally, when multinational companies with operations in China started to seek logistics solutions to manage domestic distribution and imports/exports. Third-party logistics contracts of two main types resulted. On the one hand, import/export-oriented contracts in complex assembly industries such as electronics and automobiles often emerged as part of global arrangements with foreign logistics players. On the other, local contracts to handle domestic distribution from plants to city-level distributors or major retail points also developed.

All logistics customers, however, continue to face a number of frustrations in moving their goods to distributors and retailers. They cite five major drawbacks:

- High logistics costs: The lack of effective transport networks increases distribution costs, thus decreasing profit margins. In China, transportation and warehouse costs can amount to 30% to 40% of the total costs for manufactured goods, more than 60% for food and livestock, and around 70% to 80% for certain chemical products. On average, both inventory and delivery times exceed 30 days, a striking divergence from the most advanced practices. The problems are particularly acute for many overcrowded sectors in China, such as consumer electronics and home appliances. Facing white-hot competition and continuous price wars, they are in desperate need of more efficient logistics.

- A lack of reliability in pick-up and delivery time.

- A lack of transparency in the shipment process: In China, until goods show up at their destination, manufacturers have almost no information about their whereabouts.

- Loss, damage or pilferage of goods: Both rail and trucking involve a lot of human handling. In the process, goods are misplaced, damaged or stolen. The use of covered trucks is easing the problem but about 60% of all trucks in China are still open-bed trucks.

- Lack of control in marketing/sales: Manufacturers relying on arms-length distributors generally have no idea how and when an end sale occurs. With strong competition between distributors, goods can end up at unintended destinations or be sold at unfavorable prices, despite attempts by manufacturers to curb cross-regional sales and to develop and maintain brand positioning.

For these and other players, however, relief may be at hand. Like nature, markets hate a vacuum and gathering market forces are now compelling many players (with the government's encouragement) to fill the gaps in China's transportation and logistics market.

STRONG FORCES ARE RESHAPING THE MARKET

The recent acceleration of economic reforms has proved a strong force for change in China. Its direct outcomes, economic development and market growth, are increasing demand for transportation and logistics services. In addition, by changing regulation and encouraging investments in infrastructure, the government is playing a key role in further stimulating demand for transportation and logistics. Given increasing demand, annual growth of China's third-party logistics market is likely to reach 20% to 30% over the next several years.

Increased economic development and income growth in China have expanded the market for consumer goods to secondary and even tertiary cities. The geographic market has thus progressively expanded from around five cities to 30 to 40 cities. While some of these cities are located further inland and to the northeast, most are still concentrated along China's east and south coasts. Given the large populations and increasing spending power of these regions, manufacturers are now looking for practical solutions to reliably move their goods to these attractive markets, without losing control of goods transported.

Furthermore, a strong trend towards consolidation in many of China's industries is creating larger and more complex players who need logistics solutions for moving goods between several manufacturing plants in China or for distributing their products across China. In air conditioners, the number of players fell from over 400 in 1996 to 90 by 2000 and in refrigerators from almost 200 to less than 40, over the same timeframe. In color televisions, the top six players have increased their market share from 35% in 1994 to nearly 70% recently. Consolidation is also starting to affect the beer industry, as the hectic acquisition activity of the top four breweries shows. This consolidation has led to the emergence of many national brands, which require national (or at least, multi-regional) distribution coverage, with all the transportation and logistics complexity that this entails.

The emergence of new retail channels is also creating demand for transportation and logistics solutions. Large chain stores and hypermarkets are growing rapidly, reflecting the preference of consumers for larger, more appealing stores offering choice assortments, low prices and trusted brands. Just one consumer-appliance chain store, Guomei, more than quadrupled its stores from seven to 30 in just two years (1998 to 2000), and is projected to expand to some 80 stores by 2002. In the process, it will expand its presence from Beijing to Shanghai and several second-tier cities, including a number in northeast and southwest China. Growing sales from such large chain stores, including Guomei, will likely make up about 20% to 30% of the total retail sales of home electric appliances in China by 2003. In other words, while the traditional trade in China still cannot be ignored, today, modern retailers are making real inroads in the first-, second- and even third-tier cities, creating a greater need for specialized logistics solutions to serve these outlets and an ability to bypass trade distributors, that is, wholesalers.

All these factors are reshaping demand for more extensive, reliable distribution solutions. Faced with increasing competition and falling margins, manufacturers are paying a lot more attention to optimizing distribution and their overall supply chains. Their need for sophisticated solutions is making them more and more open to third-party transportation and logistics services. The response by traditional players and emerging providers has intensified competition and led to a rapid evolution of the sector.

Actions by the Chinese government are stimulating the development of the transportation and logistics sector. The agreements the government has made as part of the conditions for entry into the World Trade Organization (WTO) will open the sector to foreign participation over a three-to-four-year timeframe. Further, the government is itself investing in infrastructure and encouraging change in industry structure that will enable faster acceptance and development of third-party logistics.

China's entry into the WTO will stimulate the development of transportation and logistics services in two ways. First, it will pave the way for new, often foreign, investors to collaborate with incumbents, who own most of the hard assets. Recognizing the antiquated state of the sector, the Chinese government has given it priority for development. As a result, asset-heavy incumbent companies are now actively looking for technical and operational know-how, opening up opportunities for foreign companies to work with them.

Second, as noted above, WTO entry will open up several transportation and logistics sectors to direct foreign participation. Within four years of WTO entry, foreign companies will be allowed to own 100% of Chinese freight forwarding, third-party logistics and customs brokerage firms, as opposed to roughly 50% now. They will be allowed to fully own trucking companies within three years of WTO entry and rail services within six years. Domestic express and air parcel services, which are currently government monopolies, will also be opened to 100% foreign ownership within four years of WTO entry. Areas that will remain restricted are maritime trade and shipping, in which only minority foreign ownership will be allowed, and air cargo, on which there is currently no draft agreement we are aware of.

Importantly, opportunities will arise as SOEs accelerate their restructuring, which many embarked on aggressively in the late 1990s. As they shed non-core interests and assets to focus resources on their core businesses, many will spin off their in-house transportation departments and outsource these requirements.

China's transportation and logistics sector will also benefit from government policy and investment aimed at developing the sector. The government aims to increase outsourced logistics in SOEs' manufacturing and distribution functions, create sophisticated logistics centers and networks by promoting the consolidation of, and collaboration among, logistics companies, actively encourage manufacturers to adopt supply-chain management through third-party logistics firms, and reduce logistics costs. Government will also promote the formation of a group of third-party logistics providers, establish several nationwide multi-modal transportation networks, some large-scale, modernized logistics and distribution centers, and several core logistics bases (which might then become centers for Asia-wide logistics), and approve around 30 modernized product distribution and logistics centers as spearhead projects. Another noteworthy transportation initiative is the construction of a national trunk highway linking the major consumption centers, all cities with populations over one million and most cities with populations over 500,000. To be constructed in stages, the project will be completed by 2010.

Clearly, opportunities in transportation and logistics in China are likely to increase in the next five years. But all players seeking to capture these opportunities will have to contend with existing providers who are now rapidly ramping up their aspirations and initiatives. Broadly, there are four types of such service providers in China today. In their own way, they all seek to become logistics leaders in China.

As mentioned above, large SOEs such as Sinotrans, COSCO, China Rail and China Post have massive assets and strong relationships with traditional SOE manufacturers and other local enterprises. All have initiated plans to transform themselves from purveyors of basic services to providers of value-added third-party solutions. Their existing advantages make them formidable competitors. But their ability to offer value-added services in a cost-effective and efficient way on their own is very limited, making them receptive to partnerships and other cooperative arrangements with leading foreign third-party logistics companies who have real technical, operational and solutions know-how. They may also view potential foreign partners as sources of capital and, in fact, many are hoping to make public offerings.

Local players or joint ventures between local and foreign companies, such as ST-Anda, EAS and PG Logistics, are other sound players with a fairly strong, albeit relatively small, market presence. These local or "semi-local" companies have often been started by managers who have left SOEs.

They have no asset base of trucks but are trying to piece together transportation and logistics solutions for specific industries such as fast-moving consumer goods or certain consumer durables. Joint-venture firms typically offer superior services compared to local entrepreneurial players, and are often involved in assisting the growth of the modern retail trade in China's top cities. But very few of these companies have the ability to handle direct distribution to the highly fragmented traditional retail trade across China's cities, and many are struggling to keep up with ever-increasing demands for better solutions across a broader business and geographic scope. For these companies, the future lies in providing superior solutions that meet customer needs, accessing superior talent, and attracting investment so they can continue to grow.

Non-Chinese logistics players, such as Danzas, APL Logistics, Exel and Inchcape serve primarily multinational companies, generally in export- and import-related logistics. A few have tried to set up specialized services extending from their core business; for example, OOCL's specialized bonded rail links from ports to a few selected inland cities. This type of player primarily offers port-based consolidation or de-consolidation with customs brokerage. They pose a threat to other types of competitors through their greater capabilities, strong overseas networks and international customer relationships and, for the time being at least, a superior ability to attract top Chinese talent seeking work experience and development opportunities in leading multinational organizations.

Increasingly, non-Chinese players are trying to expand on two fronts: (1) extending their export-import services further into China using several transport modes and linking these services into their already strong global supply-chain networks; and (2) developing workable domestic solutions for their largely multinational clients. They are also trying hard to develop total supply-chain solutions for the most advanced Chinese manufacturers. However, this has met with very limited success to date due to their weak relationships with local customers and limited outsourcing by local companies. These players might have the skills to succeed but face at least two constraints. First, bringing their expatriate managers into China will make their costs prohibitive. Second, new entrants will lack knowledge of and relationships with local transporters. They may be able to build piecemeal solutions with the help of small truckers but may have difficulty approaching large players.

Finally, a number of new players are entering the logistics sector from China's manufacturing and distribution sectors. An example is Haier Logistics, which has transformed its in-house distribution division into an independent logistics services company and formed an alliance with China

Post. The emergence of such new players stems from the frustration felt by better local manufacturers with the constraints on their own transportation and logistics activities in China. But they are also emerging because they see the opportunity for outsourced, high-quality national distribution services and feel they have the capability to provide effective services. The questions are "In how many more industries will this be the case?" and "How will they acquire the expertise to make their businesses work well?"

CHANGES UNDER WAY NOT FOR THE FAINT-HEARTED

The changes ahead certainly promise to make a backward and embryonic sector of the Chinese economy much more appealing for new investment and modernization. True, the sector has well-established local incumbents with entrenched asset positions and customer relationships, as do many other industry sectors in China. But these incumbents lack sophisticated operational know-how, investment funds to modernize, and the ability to attract, develop and retain top talent. Many appear to be massive SOEs but, in reality, are generally loose confederations of locally run organizations that may not embrace a new, top-down strategy. While these companies struggle to reinvent themselves, new entrants, local and foreign, have a significant window of opportunity. As always, there are obstacles to success. But companies that approach the market in the right ways should be able to overcome them.

Three broad areas of opportunity deserve careful attention over the next two to four years, as the WTO agreements kick in.

The first is to create effective domestic transportation networks in China, or at least in key parts of the country. For example, companies that can navigate the many local barriers and assemble the skills, IT capabilities etc., to create a dependable, flexible less-than-truck-load (LTL) or full-truck-load (FTL) domestic trucking service should have no trouble finding customers. Compared to the very poor service standards of current operators, such a company could charge a premium price. A truly networked, efficient and transparent LTL service to a large number of retailers, covering numerous major cities in China, would meet retailers' need for a "last mile" service. As such, it would be a unique offering, with little real competition. Numerous distributors and manufacturers are likely to flock to such a service. Other opportunities are domestic parcel services, as an alternative to China Post, and inter-modal rail services by foreign players (as in OOCL's bonded rail links).

The second opportunity is in offering true supply-chain optimization services to major Chinese manufacturers, distributors and retailers. To be sure, not all these companies in China are ready to outsource supply-chain management. But an increasing number are prepared to try out well-equipped service providers, given the competitive pressures they face in their own marketplaces. Even the best local manufacturers and assemblers run highly sub-optimal supply chains today, and significant cost savings can be squeezed out in a number of high-value industries such as computers and peripherals, consumer electronics, and appliances. A full supply-chain perspective is needed, and the solution provided would need to incorporate excellent control of information flows and deliver high-quality basic transport services. Clearly, the major local players who control transportation assets do not have the capability to optimize customers' supply chains. This presents a unique opportunity for creative and adventurous players to build world-class businesses in China and beyond by forging alliances with foreign or local players.

Finally, for more specialized players there may be niche opportunities to provide technological solutions, in the form of tracking-and-tracing hardware and software, tools that allow visibility into factory processes, specialized network optimization software, and financial services related to distribution management, among others. The size and scope of China's market could allow these more specialized plays to develop into big businesses themselves before long.

The prospects are promising, no doubt. But players should remember that they could fade, if government policies and agreements turn out to be short-lived or don't materialize as expected.

And no matter how exciting the future may be, several daunting challenges must still be tackled in building a transportation and logistics business in China. Success will hinge on judicious decisions that take into account regulatory uncertainties and unfavorable aspects of economic policy, current limitations in the transportation and logistics sector, and players' own capabilities.

In China, as in most emerging markets, government policy may need to shift direction, sometimes suddenly, if economic reform entails too much social dislocation. Best-intended policy can also be rendered ineffective by a lack of compliance at the local level: local authorities can be slow to abide by central policies or agreements. At the company level, national Chinese companies can have trouble getting their local branches to fall in line with strategy. Furthermore, contracts between service providers and customers are not always upheld, which could imperil the much-needed trust in third-party logistics providers.

Another problem in China is that the rule of law is uneven at best, and thus business investments often need to be protected by building numerous relationships, perhaps at many levels of government. For a major foreign investor, the risk here is that business fortunes can change along with political ones. And on the economic front, since China's currency remains unconvertible, a sudden devaluation if the economy falters could severely affect investment returns.

Breaking into the market for transportation and logistics solutions is very difficult in China. Solutions providers have to work hard to convert customers, who are very skeptical about these services and tough negotiators. Operating within the logistics sector is made more difficult by the scarcity of professional managers and talented operators. As noted before, bringing in foreign talent could make costs go out of control. At the same time, the market for experienced local technical and managerial talent is getting tighter every day. As in other emerging markets, standards of service and professionalism have remained low, especially beyond the top-tier cities.

It goes without saying that every company must view its future position in China against its specific aspirations, strengths and capabilities. Another major consideration is its risk tolerance and timeframe for investments with positive returns. None of these will be easy judgments to make. Even with the opening of China's transport and logistics sector as articulated in the WTO accession terms, players cannot take it for granted that things will work out as promised.

In general, players with serious aspirations in China's transportation and logistics sector would have better chances of success if they approached the market in the following ways:

Think local/multi-local before thinking regional or national: Right now, setting up nationwide distribution capabilities is much too difficult in China since economic activity is concentrated in specific pockets of the country and widely differing local barriers must be tackled on an ad hoc basis. Even companies that would normally operate on a national scale should consider developing comprehensive coverage of one part of the country before spreading out to the rest. The rewards of this kind of focus can be great: thanks to the scale of the Chinese market, a successful business in just one part of China can easily become as big and attractive as one covering an entire Asian country.

Focus on information and coordination in developing logistics "solutions" rather than asset ownership: Many of the hard assets in the transport and logistics sector are controlled by domestic companies and may not be considered high quality by international standards. These assets need to be deployed more efficiently and in a networked fashion to achieve higher coordination, utilization and other operating synergies. Using these assets, solutions that add value to logistics customers need to be crafted. The smarter players will develop and apply the know-how to create and sell solutions based on agreements that bind and control basic transport assets, rather than fully owning them. If they succeed, they will surely enjoy much higher returns and lower financial exposure.

Pursue alliances aggressively: Alliances will be critical to manage potential competition and build the transport networks and relationships needed. Early movers could lock in some promising collaborations. Local companies with strong asset positions but low skills seeking global stature and investment would make a good match for sophisticated international players with global networks, ample investment funds and high China aspirations. Senior management in major Chinese companies is growing in sophistication, and negotiating agreements with them is more straightforward than in the early years of China's economic reforms.

More importantly, there could be a strong first-mover advantage in successfully developing strong transport networks. This makes it essential to actively manage competition as the network is built out over time. Similarly, the market for supply-chain solutions will be relatively narrow at first, and concentrated in a handful of industry sectors. Again, managing competition between potential head-to-head competitors could make the difference between profit and loss.

Focus on organization building as much as strategy or operations: While transportation and logistics is necessarily a highly operational undertaking, in the long run, any logistics service business will be defined by the quality of its solutions, and, therefore, the skill and will of its people. Their drive, innovation and commitment will make the essential difference to service quality and the impact of solutions. This is doubly important in China – any winning business cannot grow without a strong contingent of talented people that understands how to work within the constraints of the Chinese market. Furthermore, as most winning logistics businesses will depend on alliances, setting up the right incentives, deal structures and management processes is essential for proper coordination and delivery of the targeted services of the desired quality.

※　　※　　※

To be sure, the opportunities for developing modern transportation and logistics offerings in China are much greater now than before. This is a pivotal supporting industry that will enable China's sustained economic advance. But many players are eyeing China's enormous potential and the landscape is getting crowded. Those seeking a major position in China in this sector will need to act fast.

3.4 ORIENT OVERSEAS: WINNING IN ASIAN SHIPPING

Interview with C.C. Tung, Chairman of Orient Overseas Container Lines

Orient Overseas Container Lines is the leading international container line serving China and Asia. Founded in 1969, it is one of the world's most advanced lines, with over 50 vessels under its operation and a leading-edge reputation for IT, logistics and customer service. Its chairman, C.C. Tung is an MIT graduate born in Shanghai but now resident in Hong Kong. A former chairman of the Hong Kong General Chamber of Commerce, leading local philanthropist and board member for some of China's most significant companies, he shared his views on the shipping industry, logistics and the challenges facing both Hong Kong and China.

Q Could we start by talking about the origin of OOCL?

A We started the containerized transportation business in 1969. During the early years of containerization we were actually more experimenting than running a full-scale business. At that time, we used war-built cargo vessels and converted them to make them suitable for containers. I remember the first vessel's capacity was 300 Twenty-foot Equivalent Units (TEU) and I remember distinctly the first ship sailed with only 30 TEU. Those were the humble beginnings and now today you have vessels larger than 7,000 TEU and people are talking about even 10,000 TEU. So that gives you an idea of the changes over the years.

Q How would you characterize the current business?

A Most people look at containerized transportation as shipping but it has really now gone beyond shipping. Most of what the company does involves land transportation, managing terminals and, to the extent that we have to satisfy many of our customer requirements, we are involved in warehousing and distribution through consolidation. More and more it is actually a logistics business and our scope of activities continues to grow.

But even if the business is now closer to logistics, it is still the shipping market that drives the price of container capacity from Asia to Europe and North America. Vessel building (shipyards) has reached overcapacity and this will continue to drive the economic situation.

Q On what basis does OOCL compete?

A OOCL seeks to do three things. First, to be close to our customer. We define our products accordingly and our organization structure reflects this. Second, we try to understand the needs of the buying country [i.e. the shipper]. This is a positive factor for us because of our knowledge of manufacturing in China. China already has over 50% of Asian consumer goods exported to North America and Europe. We understand the way business is done in China and we have been a first-mover in onshore logistics. Third, we try to cater to the customer's way of doing business. By helping the customer to control their own business we need to provide full transparency over their logistic and supply chain. That's why seven to eight years ago we made a decision to invest in IT. We feel that the IT structure we have developed gives us two benefits: internal efficiencies through an integrated decision-making enterprise system; and, through Internet and EDI linkages, the ability to provide our customer with complete transparency over the entire logistic pipeline.

Q What role does China play in the OOCL shipping business?

A China is the manufacturing center of Asia. Other emerging markets are starting to trade with China. Intra-Asia trade is again growing rapidly; Eastern Europe and Russia are buying more consumer goods and for us the Baltic Sea market has been growing. Although OOCL is not the biggest player this is because shipping is a very capital-intensive business. Instead, we aim to be a premier player in China and Asia.

Q What is the state of logistics in China? Are the new investments in infrastructure starting to make a difference?

A Chinese logistics still has substantial potential for development. First, trucking is still the dominant mode for long-distance transport rather than rail. Cargo sometimes has conflicts with national priorities for rail – people, food and energy are the rail's priorities. But cargo carried by rail could be more economical. Second, hardware is easy to build and there are already a number of big players and local governments who are investing substantially. The difficulty lies in putting the pieces together; avoiding insufficiencies and inefficiencies in the service. There is still a great deal to be done in this area.

Q **Is OOCL investing in Chinese logistics infrastructure? Are there interesting growth opportunities?**

A OOCL is primarily serving the needs of multinationals in China logistics. Through our IT capability, we can provide better management of delivery, both domestic and export, for our customers. There are good opportunities to work with multinationals to create a one-stop shop. Logistics for us is beginning to show signs of being a stand-alone business. But we have to be capable in all elements of logistics – trucking, delivery, warehousing and shipping. It's easy to convince shippers if you own the assets but logistics is supposed to be an asset-light business. The question is can we manage a business through partnerships and alliances with local trucking and warehousing companies? We need to make some adjustments to the model to make it work in China. For example, we already have some joint ventures (in trucking operations) in Shanghai and Guangdong and we have a nationwide operating license. In warehousing, we have taken over the management of warehouse operations of some overseas Chinese companies who need distribution services over some 30-plus locations in China. This gives us a tremendous platform for growth.

Q **So can OOCL be a logistics leader in China?**

A Successful logistics providers tend to have long histories. We will continue to develop our logistics business. We must be distinctive in what we do. Right now, the synergies in logistics needs for our domestic and international business are quite substantial. We won't take a hardware-driven approach – we want to have a flexible and adaptive approach to grow the business in this vast market and, with the support of our IT capability, I believe OOCL will be an important player.

Q **OOCL is known as a leader in the IT area. Is this a competitive advantage in Asia? How so?**

A Increasingly, we are living in a real-time economy. Without IT it is difficult to compete. As I said, IT engenders efficiency. Costs are lower, particularly as you grow. Automation allows you to grow without adding overheads. Second, working with the customer directly via an efficient IT system allows you to generate more volume, because it is easier for the customers to work with you than with others. Having an efficient IT system allows our customers to manage their logistics pipeline more efficiently by cutting their business costs. But marrying IT to a business is not easy. IT people are different from business people. We have to be careful not to over-invest in technology.

Q Do you see Asia as a leading source of IT capability in the future?

A IT capability has yet to be fully embraced by the SMEs in Asia and therefore has not quite become a tool to enhance customer loyalty. This is different from in the U.S. and I have to say Asia is somewhat behind in this regard. But this is changing. Even with the tech bubble bursting, basic education about IT is quite strong. Almost every meeting I go to, especially in Hong Kong and China, there is something about IT. And in the current business environment people now expect IT to enhance the bottom line or see it as a necessary feature to compete in this global market.

Q Turning to local matters, what is the outlook for the Hong Kong economy? Do you see strengths that will sustain growth?

A Hong Kong's opportunity lies with China and specifically the Pearl River Delta. Hong Kong is a gateway to China. In the old days, when China was closed, Hong Kong might have been a little bit spoiled by its unique position. With China opening, Hong Kong is still the gateway to the Pearl River Delta because of its proximity, infrastructure – our port is still the largest container port in the world – strength of financial market, communications, abundance of professionals, rule of law and way of doing business.

Q Will Hong Kong compete with Shanghai?

A How to integrate with the Pearl River Delta is Hong Kong's challenge – integrate cargo, people and capital flows across the physical boundary. In some ways capital is the easiest of these, despite capital account controls, as Hong Kong is a point for international capital access, a genuine stepping stone. Shanghai is still somewhat behind Hong Kong on the soft side of infrastructure and because of capital account controls.

There is plenty of hinterland, though, for Shanghai to tap for different purposes. For logistics and shipping, Hong Kong and Shanghai have different hinterlands. I do see the Pearl River Delta competing for foreign investment with the Yangtze River Delta. But it may be easier for Guangdong to work with Pearl River Delta cities than Shanghai with other cities in the Yangtze River Delta, particularly in terms of developing collective measures to attract foreign investment. Shanghai and the Yangtze River Delta may have an advantage in terms of total population and market size.

In the battle for FDI, Taiwan investment will be the next tussle. Taiwan's government cannot hold back its companies from investing in China. Taiwan investors today will be investing in higher technology than in the past, when most were investments in consumer-goods manufacturing. Then Japan will come next with even higher technology.

Q So should Hong Kong go back to the role of a middleman?

A Hong Kong needs to be a middleman but under a different definition. It must add value. Logistics and sourcing are possible ways to do this. Li and Fung is a case in point. Small- and medium-sized companies in North America and Europe may feel more comfortable working through a Hong Kong company than going direct to China. Multinationals will go direct, as they have the resources.

Q Which mainland cities do you see as having the greatest growth potential? What is driving this?

A Hong Kong's immediate concern is the Pearl River Delta. Of course, the Chinese government will continue to press ahead in the interior of the country. They are building the physical infrastructure and they hope that direct investment will follow. Particularly as the coastal provinces move up the value chain, the labor-intensive light-manufacturing industry could well move into the Western region. But logistics might be the key bottleneck and Hong Kong can be an international gateway for the Western region of China.

Q How do you see trends in Asia-wide manufacturing? Is China benefiting at the expense of other areas?

A Multinationals are moving their facilities to China. The combination of a large domestic market and the potential to serve the international market makes an attractive opportunity. There is a shift from Southeast Asia going on. But as China develops, it will become an increasingly important market. The Southeast Asian economies will develop more trade with China. There will be a shift in the regional trade pattern.

Q **Is this shift welcomed by Chinese companies?**

A I think so. The goods being moved in are not being manufactured in China today. So it creates new opportunities. Chinese companies have opportunities in parts supply – for example, to Sony. Chinese products are at the lower-end in value but they will climb the value and quality ladder in future. Sizable Chinese companies could either start as an OEM operation for a foreign buyer or try directly to serve overseas markets. The potential for scale to serve both domestic and international markets must be attractive. Questions remain about the ability to execute this. Sony and Canon think of China as one piece of their global supply network. But local companies like Haier take a more local focus – they build a plant in the U.S. to serve the U.S. market. Maybe there is something to be said for a Chinese company making its products for the U.S. in the U.S.

Q **Do Chinese companies have the potential to be global winners?**

A Bigger companies are more internationally oriented. Their management wants to compete with their international peers. They still need a little more time to become more acclimated to global practices. But it is easy for them to catch up because they start so far behind. Better management can help them make big improvements fast in productivity and efficiency. I think this is true for both state and private companies. They all recognize they have to compete and their goal is to compete with their international peers.

Q **Finally, where do you see OOCL in 10 years?**

A We like to say that we want OOCL to be the company whose quality of products adds value to business in a way that no other company can.

REFERENCES

1. At the start of the 1990s, China had over 600 registered makers of automotive vehicles (supported by an even larger army of small captive component suppliers) that produced in all only 500,000 vehicles a year.
2. In Honda's 2001 annual survey of its overseas plants, the quality of Guangzhou Honda's product came out on top.
3. Employment would also benefit from global integration. Spain, despite the foreign ownership of its auto industry, has increased its automotive output from two million to over three million units a year in just a decade, thereby creating thousands of manufacturing jobs and building up a competitive local auto-supplier industry.

4. Chinese automotive companies are not strangers to the Toyota manufacturing system. In fact, Eiji Toyoda himself came to China in the early 1980s, at the invitation of the Chinese government, to instruct Chinese manufacturers and component suppliers in his ideas.

5. Metric tons: 1016.15 kilograms, or 2,240 pounds.

6. China Ocean Shipping Company.

7. China Material Storage and Transportation Company.

8. China National Foreign Trade Transportation Corporation.

4

Energizing Energy

C hina's voracious economic growth has made it one of the world's largest energy consumers. At the same time, China's energy policy has shifted from maximizing domestic self-sufficiency to a more balanced set of objectives including increasing the efficiency of its energy sector, minimizing energy waste and environmental costs and maintaining a secure supply. This change in turn will create dramatic restructuring in a sector of the economy that amounts to over 10% of GDP.

Rapid depletion of domestic petroleum reserves and increasing environmental pressures have now forced a look at the alternatives; in particular, gas. While the market looks attractive, investments required are huge and the supply environment is uncertain. Building an integrated gas chain in China will be one of the 21st century's greatest energy investment challenges.

On the other hand, the petrochemicals industry has already attracted billions of dollars of investment that will go to build a series of petrochemicals hubs. These in turn will precipitate a wave of consolidation to transform the industry into a world-class business.

And even China's once moribund coal industry has spawned four super-groups who are already gobbling up market share in Asia. These groups could potentially change the balance of world trade. Global coal majors should seize the opportunity today to work together with these emerging giants to develop the industry.

4.1 THE GREAT GAS GAME

With rapid economic growth and limited fuel choices, China has begun to invest in developing its gas industry. However, the risks are huge – massive investments in transmission and distribution are needed, the market must be developed ahead of demand and regional overcapacity is putting downward pressure on prices. Government's ability to define a new regulatory framework acceptable to investors, and companies' commitment to developing the local market will determine if the government's ambitious plans can be realized.

A BIG NEW INDUSTRY

China is already one of the world's largest energy markets. With over 750 million tons-oil-equivalent (TOE) of annual primary energy consumption, China ranks second in the world in energy consumption behind the U.S. Energy consumption appears to have a significant upside as China is at the low end of the international development curve. China consumes only 0.7 TOE per capita compared to the global average of 1.5, Europe's at 3.1 and the profligate U.S., at 7.9 tons. As China is fast industrializing, attaining global consumption levels implies a doubling of energy demand.

At the same time, the costs to China of rapid economic growth and intensified energy usage are becoming more apparent. Environmental damage has made China's cities some of the dirtiest in the world. Eight of the 10 most polluted cities in the world are in China. The U.N. estimates pollution of all types costs China 8% of GDP annually. High growth has also encouraged energy waste as small-scale power plants and inefficient local producers take advantage of temporary supply bottlenecks. Chinese pollution is also creating an international problem – China is the world's second-largest emitter of carbon dioxide (after the U.S.). Sulfur pollution in China is causing substantial acid rain in Korea and Japan.

Most of current Chinese primary energy demand is met by coal, which accounts for over 70% of primary energy consumption. While China's coal reserves are enormous, coal's impact on pollution and carbon dioxide emissions will constrain its growth. Transportation bottlenecks also limit the potential to further develop coal as a primary energy use. During the winter months, coal transport already uses over 50% of China's available national rail capacity. China is in fact actively engaged in rationalizing its coal industry. Since 1990 over 500 small coal mines have been shut down and investment has been concentrated in a few major world-scale facilities.

The balance of today's energy demand is met by oil. Oil is also unlikely to take up the slack as China is facing critical resource constraints. With 20% of the world's population, China's petroleum reserves are no more than 2.3% of the world's total. China became a net crude oil importer in 1993 after China National Petroleum Corporation (CNPC) discovered that the long-heralded Tarim basin would not in fact be a second Daqing, itself in decline for decades. By 2000, China imported over 23% of its crude oil consumption, primarily from the Middle East, a situation that will only accelerate in the coming decades given demand growth. By some estimates, China's oil imports will be second only to those of the U.S. and Japan by 2010.

Of the alternative fuels, gas, hydropower and others account for less than 7% of consumption. Hydropower's growth is centered on controversial mega-projects such as the Three Gorges. Even with these projects, industry observers believe hydropower will amount to no more than 5% of China's primary energy mix by 2015. Nuclear energy has been stalled since the completion of Daya Bay near Hong Kong. Solar and other fuels are insignificant.

Accordingly, China's government has decided to go for gas. China has significant local gas reserves, particularly in the far west and north of the country. Domestic gas development was initiated in Sichuan 50 years ago. With markets largely devoted to fertilizer production, development there was and is relatively high-cost due to the difficulty of penetrating extensive granite structures in the area. This picture began to change with China's first gas development, the South China Sea gas, discovered by Arco in the 1980s, followed by the smaller Pinghu and Bohai finds near Shanghai and Tianjin respectively. However, the largest discoveries came onshore in the mid-1990s. The Ordos Basin near Beijing and the Tarim Basin in the West were found to have significant reserves for development. Premier Zhu Rongji was quick to identify these as important drivers of economic growth for the interior. And unlike coal, gas will contribute significantly to a reduction in China's carbon emissions.

China has also begun to explore the options that offshore LNG might provide, potentially in competition with the domestic supply industry. CNOOC conducted a bid round in 2001 for an initial LNG terminal in Shenzhen, which was ultimately won by BP. The supply contract was then awarded to Australia's Northwest Shelf Consortium in 2002 after a bidding process notable for its sophistication. BP was awarded the consolation prize of a second smaller contract in Fujian. More terminals are now under discussion in Shanghai and Qingdao, with both Sinopec and PetroChina mentioned as potential players. Other coastal markets are likely to develop quickly as LNG is an attractive investment for local governments looking for big-ticket items to boost local industry.

BUT RISKS ARE IMMENSE

However, developing the industry will be challenging. Massive infrastructure investments are needed. The market must be developed ahead of demand. And looming regional overcapacity could create price and profit pressure.

China's major onshore reserves lie far from the major coastal markets. Capital requirements for transmission and distribution infrastructure to bring China's gas to market will be massive (Exhibit 4.1). Current plans for the East-West pipeline alone propose a project costing over $5 billion in investment, spanning 4,000 km and with a carrying capacity of 12 billion cubic meters by 2007.

Downstream investment requirements will be at least as significant as the transmission infrastructure. Historically, almost no power generation was gas-based and very few Chinese cities had a natural gas-based residential network although most had some form of coal gas usage. Local governments, which own distribution networks, are now raising cash to invest in upgrading aging equipment – local distribution company investments for East-West gas are estimated to top $10 billion, twice that of the pipeline itself. Power generators have likewise been investing in gas-fired peaking capacity. And industrial plants along the route of the East-West pipeline are investigating gas-based fuel burners.

The government intends the cash for these projects to come from the private sector, both domestic and international. As the primary owner of China's major onshore gas reserves, PetroChina, the internationally listed vehicle of China National Petroleum Corporation, has been held responsible by the government for the development of nationwide gas transmission infrastructure. This is a huge bet for the company – gas-related expenditures accounted for over 9% of total capital expenditures in 2001.

Even when the gas arrives, the market will also require pump priming. The Chinese market has had a track record of being unready to take up large-scale gas supply. Without incentives to these downstream consumers, gas market development is likely to go slowly. South China Sea gas had to wait almost a decade before finding its way first to Hong Kong and China Light and Power, and then to Hainan Island for use in power and fertilizer production. Likewise, the development of the Pinghu field off Shanghai required a decade of negotiations before it was finally undertaken by a consortium formed with the direct participation of the government of Shanghai, which guaranteed offtake by the city's residential gas system and power stations. More recently, Ordos gas had to wait for a year at the Beijing city-gate as city distribution networks had to be refurbished to take the higher pressures. And with the State Council dictating the split up of the State Power

Exhibit 4.1   National gas pipeline network will be built by year 2010

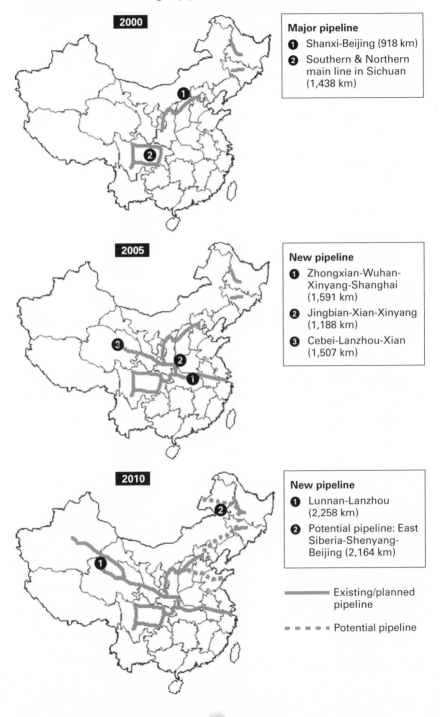

Corporation and the separation of generating assets, state influence on these generators to take gas at high prices will be much reduced.

Finally, the regional gas environment is uncertain as price pressure from oversupply grows. In the Asia-Pacific region there are enough proven gas reserves to last for decades of production. This kind of overhang in the long term could mean that gas will look like refining – an industry where incremental margins drive prices.

The Asian gas market has long been a relatively stable affair. Initiated in the wake of the Arab oil embargo of the 1970s, the market has catered to buyers motivated more by security than economic concerns. Japan has from its infancy been the dominant marketplace, signing 20- to 30-year contracts with its suppliers in Australia and Southeast Asia. Suppliers agreed to take the risk of supplying for the long-term in exchange for a "take or pay" arrangement with the buyers. In this cozy environment, producers reaped very attractive returns.

However, the game is changing dramatically. Over 120 billion cubic meters (bcm) of capacity is coming on line in Asia, as are new producers in the Middle East. Total new gas demand in Asia, however, will amount to no more than 55 bcm by 2010. China and India are the largest sources of new demand, both being rapidly growing economies looking to diversify their energy mix away from declining petroleum reserves. But reality is that LNG imports from both countries will be limited by infrastructure constraints at least in the medium term. Thus over 50 bcm of capacity from international pipelines and LNG must find their own markets in what promises to be a very competitive environment (Exhibit 4.2).[1]

Adding uncertainty is the expiration of much of the current LNG contracts in the period from 2000 to 2010. In total, over 40% of Korea's LNG supply will be up for negotiation, while Japan will renegotiate 50%. If Asian gas overcapacity does materialize, gas prices region wide and eventually in China could decline significantly. Estimates show that the Middle East provides a huge reservoir of gas supply to meet Asia's needs and is likely to be the marginal LNG supplier to the region. The marginal price of this supply is on average 40% below current contract prices, implying the potential for a significant drop.

On the other hand, reserves are being developed by a small number of major oil companies, in cooperation with host governments. Shell, for example, holds 15% stakes in more than seven projects across the region, making it a player in almost any LNG deal. For a regional spot market to emerge, ownership would have to fragment and a substantial new logistics infrastructure would have to emerge. In Asia, the average contract size is orders of magnitude larger than those in Europe and North America –

Exhibit 4.2   Pipeline and LNG projects will compete for the same markets

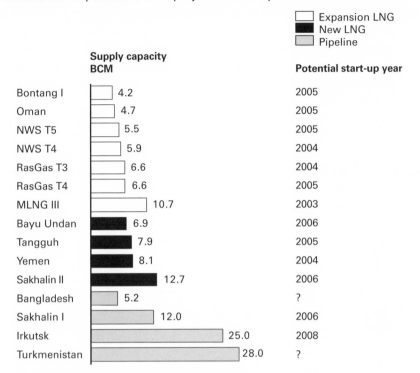

☐ Expansion LNG
■ New LNG
▨ Pipeline

	Supply capacity BCM	Potential start-up year
Bontang I	4.2	2005
Oman	4.7	2005
NWS T5	5.5	2005
NWS T4	5.9	2004
RasGas T3	6.6	2004
RasGas T4	6.6	2005
MLNG III	10.7	2003
Bayu Undan	6.9	2006
Tangguh	7.9	2005
Yemen	8.1	2004
Sakhalin II	12.7	2006
Bangladesh	5.2	?
Sakhalin I	12.0	2006
Irkutsk	25.0	2008
Turkmenistan	28.0	?

Source: DRI; EIA International Energy Outlook; FACTs; Press research

leading to a less liquid market. Thus the ability of the leading players to hold the line will determine how quickly Asian LNG prices decline.

NEEDED: A NEW REGULATORY FRAMEWORK

To mitigate these risks and attract investment, China needs to put in place a regulatory framework that both incentivizes investors and rewards the most efficient. Domestic pipelines may create large externalities from the government's perspective. Investors need more tangible guarantees. Such a framework needs to have three key elements: transparent supply pricing, security for transmission investments, and an improved contractual environment.

Offshore, the principle of market-based pricing for supply is already well-established. The Chinese government requires all players to compete for the right to obtain its support in LNG negotiations. In the 2002 bid rounds, the process took over a year and multiple bids, first for the LNG terminal and then for the supply contract. In the end, industry observers believe that China achieved all it could have wanted with the winning bid from the Northwest Shelf Consortium coming in at a very favorable price and including equity ownership.

China now needs to ensure that, in a future state where its oil companies are increasingly the owners of offshore equity fields, this level of transparency and market-based pricing is maintained. This may conflict with another government objective – China's government is greatly concerned about security of supply and is actively seeking to manage its exposure to the volatile Middle East, particularly given its rising oil requirements. CNOOC has obtained 25% equity positions in the offshore gas fields that will supply the LNG. While the exact prices have not been disclosed, both stakes are worth hundreds of millions of dollars. These investments should not be allowed to bias the pricing negotiations of future LNG supply contracts.

Onshore, regulation has yet to be formally proposed. Returns on downstream assets are driven primarily by local regulation as they are often natural monopolies. While gas pricing is officially centrally controlled, the State Planning Commission has expressed the view that energy users need significant incentives to switch. As a result, local governments have considerable flexibility to vary city-gate gas prices both by geography and end-use markets. These governments have in many cases indicated initial willingness to provide incentives for new investments. However, experiences in power, pharmaceuticals and other industries show that government reserves the right to raise taxation if profits are seen as "too high".

Resolving these regulatory issues is essential to finance large downstream projects. China lacks the kind of deep liquid markets that would allow commercial players to hedge the enormous bets on their own. International financing for local gas projects is already relatively limited. And government cannot expect to continue to rely on the state banks for financing given the large amounts involved.

Finally, government needs to support investors when there are conflicts with local authorities. Establishment of take-or-pay contracts is needed. The power industry has already shown that provincial and local governments cannot be trusted to keep to agreements they perceive as inequitable in the light of changing circumstances. Beijing will have to intervene to prevent Enron-like situations from developing in China.[2]

With this framework in place, investors need to develop a strong local execution capability. With the requirement of being a utility supplier go concomitant responsibilities to ensure responsible development and long-term presence in the local market. Gas contracts and markets are controlled by geographic politics. The same mayor or provincial governor who signs the

Towngas's play

Asian companies that are more comfortable with China risk may have an advantage here. Hong Kong China Gas (Towngas) has actively pursued local investment opportunities in Guangdong, Shandong and the Yangtze River Delta. Most recently, Towngas established a company in Yixing, Jiangsu, and owns 80% of the equity. The company is expected to spend about $30 million on the construction of a gas network in Yixing and adjacent cities up to 2010. Similar investments in other areas planned by Towngas are also in the neighborhood of $15 million to $20 million.

supply contract deal may also be responsible for the local gas network, power company and industrial park. Only local construction and operating talent can ensure projects come in on time and on budget. Developing local gas markets, moreover, requires a deep knowledge of and integration into the local community. PetroChina has spent the past four years signing letters of intent with over 50 power and industrial companies along the route of the pipeline.

Taking this perspective will likely require an internal reorganization to put the market in front of the asset. Many oil companies think primarily from the asset forward. As a result they are unprepared to invest and execute against the downstream requirements of their customers. Adopting an integrated perspective would find companies putting development, power, residential distribution, and transmission specialists in one group to prioritize integrated projects, as opposed to analyzing only a portfolio of supply exploration options.

REWARDS TO THE EARLY MOVERS

Those who get into the Chinese gas industry early are likely to be the best rewarded. As upstream prices decline and value shifts downstream, lower upstream prices will create substantial incentives to accelerate the use of gas and the build-out of a nationwide gas grid. Terminal and pipeline companies will have great opportunities to invest and grow the network. Local distribution companies could see windfall profits but will also be pressured to find and acquire new customers. There could likely also be a significant LPG opportunity as a transitional fuel. Already, downstream opportunities seem sufficiently attractive to invest in. PetroChina has been able to attract Shell, ExxonMobil and Gazprom as partners in the East-West pipeline.

Those who stay offshore for their part will find their margins under pressure, as buyers will take the opportunity to redefine the rules of the game through aggressive auction processes for new supply contracts. With declining prices, only the most competitive sources of supply will be able to access the market. This would tend to favor those with Middle East reserves like ExxonMobil in Qatar. With lower wellhead gas prices, the government will likely not push hard to develop significant new tranches of domestic gas reserves. International pipelines from Sakhalin and east Siberia will face even tougher negotiating pressure.

For those players without low-cost LNG positions or unwilling to commit to local market development, selling out existing upstream positions to Chinese buyers may be the only option to participate in the growth of the Chinese market. Even if not the absolute lowest cost, offshore developers may be able to participate in the market through these equity deals. If the equity is accompanied by a long-term contract, say for more than 10 years, it will also provide a measure of security against the inevitability of further LNG market price declines.

⁂   ⁂   ⁂

China's gas industry is on a steep upswing. Official forecasts show gas doubling from 3% of national energy supply in 2000 to 7% by 2010 and as much as 13% by the year 2025. China and the world's energy companies have also been enthused over the prospect of gas-driven growth. But making the dream come true will require both new transparent regulation and a real commitment by companies to developing the Chinese market. Winners will manage the risks by building strong local organizations that integrate market and supply capabilities. The rest are likely to face commoditization as China's gas market emerges.

4.2 BP: INVESTING WITH ENERGY

Interview with Gary Dirks, Group Vice President BP

BP, one of the world's energy super-majors has been one of the most significant investors in China for the last two decades. With major positions across the energy chain, it is also one of the most successful. Gary Dirks, Group Vice President for China, shared his perspectives on the energy sector, BP's strategies and key success factors in China.

Q **What has driven BP's interest in China? How did the group get started in the country?**

A China has been an evolving piece. In addition to BP's own interests, there have been a number of predecessor companies – Amoco, Arco, Burmah Castrol – all of whom were involved in China to one degree or another since the 1970s. In the early days, the main interest was in the licensing of technology. For BP this was acrylonitrile and acetic acid in basic chemicals. For Amoco it was PP and PTA. That phase took some time – well into the 1980s when the upstream opened up, mainly offshore but to some extent onshore as well. At that time, all of our predecessor companies looked at China as potentially an interesting resource base. The upstream focus continued into the early 1990s. By then it was increasingly clear that China was not going to be a huge upstream opportunity for foreign oil companies. We all did some drilling, and Amoco and Arco found commercial resources but nothing proved to be an exciting, world-class opportunity. However, by then we had developed partnerships and some experience and we started to think of China as a potential market. Chemicals again led the way though lubricants and aviation also came in the early 90s. By the mid-90s we stopped exploration and became more downstream and chemicals focused. For example, BP did YARACO with Sinopec [an acetic acid venture in Chongqing], while Amoco explored a PTA project in Zhuhai.

That's about it for the early history. The amount of money spent was not insignificant. By the time I arrived in 1995 the predecessor companies had spent in the range of $20 billion mainly in upstream. But the story now is the market. This can be served from the outside and increasingly from the inside. We believe the market has the potential to grow at around 7% per annum through 2010, though not without risks. This growth for us translates into 150 million new households who can buy our products. So in China we are investing in the full range of our market-facing businesses – chemicals, downstream in lubes, LPG and, increasingly, retail. In gas and power we will facilitate the development of an international industry, through, for example, LNG. Externally, chemicals are the bulk of what we have coming in – this will phase out with growth in our domestic production. But China will still be important for the marketing of hydrocarbons from Russia and Indonesia. In the upstream (exploration and production), we will work what we have and may participate in some niche opportunities. However, we are not expecting to have large-scale participation, as our upstream strategy focuses heavily on lead positions in best basins – and we do not expect this to be available to us in China.

Q What are the drivers of this growth and do you believe it is sustainable?

A China is like other high-growth developing countries. Its large population sustains a growing workforce. Its government has done a good job in basic education so this workforce is well-trained. It is politically stable and, while the commercial environment has its problems, it is attractive overall. This translates into a large number of people passing the magic $5,000 per annum income market that makes them potential customers.

There is of course a substantial list of risks, of which I see four intertwined ones as among the most significant: the banking system, in particular the non-performing loan problem; state enterprise reform, which puts pressure on employment; government's fiscal capability – its ability to debt finance and deficit spend, which is particularly important as the tax system really needs work; and social security reform and the ability to provide a social safety net. In addition to these there is the agricultural issue. China has 800 million farmers and its agricultural sector is not globally competitive. WTO will put substantial pressure on the sector, so there is the problem of how to manage the population that leaves the land and tries to move to urban areas. In the extreme, all this could potentially lead to civil unrest and political turmoil. The good news is that the leadership is well aware of the issues, is not fooled by the magnitude of the challenge, and is showing every sign of making the difficult choices it needs for the country to progress.

Q So for BP, where do your own current initiatives lie? Which geographies and segments do you see as most attractive?

A Our belief is that for most of the rest of the decade, the market opportunities will be primarily in the developed coastal areas. There may be some isolated opportunities in well-developed parts of the interior; for example, Chongqing and the surrounding area in Sichuan, or the area around Wuhan. But mainly the areas that are now receiving the bulk of the investment will still be the ones where the greatest opportunities lie.

Upstream, we will continue with our projects in Yacheng and at Liuhua with CNOOC as our partner. In chemicals, we have the acetic acid project in Chongqing with Sinopec; PTA in Zhuhai; in Shanghai with Sinopec we are building a 900,000 ton ethylene cracker complex. In gas, we have invested in an LNG terminal in Guangdong, again with CNOOC. In aviation, we are across South China, and in lubes we are basically nationwide under the Castrol and BP brands. In retail, we are just getting started in Guangdong with PetroChina and in Zhejiang with Sinopec. We are also looking for opportunities for gas in Fujian – LNG terminals. We expect there will also be additional chemical developments and we want to grow retail. We are looking for a full range of growth opportunities.

Q **BP is certainly one of the most significant investors in China. Do you consider yourself as successful?**

A We are certainly significant. We have now spent (and I emphasize spent as not all was on capital or projects) $4 billion. We will spend a further $1.5 billion to complete the projects we have initiated. I think overall it could be called a successful start but still only a start. Four billion dollars is not a material business to BP nor is it significant to China if we stop there. Neither is $5.5 billion for either the group or the country. It's a start. What we have to do is ensure that the investments we have made and are making meet the expectations that executive management and the shareholders had when they approved them. In other words, we have to deliver. We also have to identify further growth options and we have to make them material. Finally, we have to ensure that we have done what is necessary to create conditions where the business is sustainable for the long term. So four things: delivering returns, growth opportunities, getting material, and ensuring sustainability over the long term.

Q **How do you ensure the last? What tools or approaches does BP employ?**

A We ensure we have sound partnerships and that the business is aligned for all partners. This means making sure ventures are meaningful and successful in the near term and attractive longer term. You also have to look at the competitive environment and identify what generates sources of competitive advantage. Then see what you can do to capture that advantage. The joint venture has to be able to influence or control those elements that are critical to success.

For example, I am increasingly comfortable with our YARACO joint venture in acetic acid in Chongqing. The venture has long-term access to an advantaged raw material supply. It uses world-class technology. It has deep local government support, which perceives a chemical industry based on natural gas as key to growth. Our partner is deeply committed to profitability in the short term and to long term growth. That said, it is missing a few things. While there are Western markets, it is a long way from the main Eastern markets so there are logistics issues. But the key elements you would want are there. It is operating and has a history of delivery. We have made one additional investment in it, have just approved a second and could consider a third if the case were correct.

Q **How does this model work with larger partners such as Sinopec or PetroChina? Is it any different?**

A I believe this can also work with larger deals. YARACO is a Sinopec company. There is a judgment to be made about how tightly controlled the sources of advantage need to be at the outset. Our competitors have different strategies in this regard. ExxonMobil has been very cautious about the sources of competitive advantage and are waiting until they can be absolutely sure before they invest. Shell, on the other hand, we would characterize as being more venturesome in getting the chips on the table first and then thinking about how to put it together later. I would say we are in the middle.

Q **How important are government relationships and how do they differ from relationships with partners?**

A Government relationships are extremely important at both the local and national level. Through the planning system, governments set targets for the industry and they give guidance on projects and ultimately approve them. Government is separate from partners, though for major partners there tends to be a strong alignment of government goals and the goals of the partner. Thus we need separate relationship management for government and partners, but not completely unrelated. We manage government relationships in a connected but separate fashion. We need to establish in the minds of both what our strategic interests are. We have to be clear and open. And particularly with partners, and local government we have to understand their strategic intent and do what we can to reconcile various interests while still holding to our overall high-level business goals. BP employees need to be able to handle these interactions at local and national levels.

Q **That brings us to the topic of organization. How does BP organize to deliver results in China?**

A We operate a matrix but it is much deeper in China than elsewhere in the world. I am the CEO for all businesses in China and as such am accountable for their performance. This would not be the case anywhere else in the world. But we also have powerful business streams, and each division in China is responsible upwards to their stream head. There is an important dialogue between myself as Group Vice President for China and the stream Group Vice Presidents on how to align national aspirations with stream aspirations. This challenges us to keep the processes neat and tidy. We need to maximize the value of being one entity in China while not losing the specialized expertise of the streams.

Practically, in China we have an executive team that meets regularly and we have biweekly telephone conference calls to deal with day-to-day issues. We also have a performance contract for China, functional contracts for China-related staff, stream-based processes and contracts, and management processes. These all allow us to be very clear on performance expectations and to act in concert. Day to day we keep it informal – the formal processes are there to assure alignment, clarity and rigor.

Q **How about people? What is the people agenda for BP in China?**

A The top four things for our team in China are: to deliver profits; generate growth opportunities; the people agenda; and to mature relationships with government and partners to take advantage of our early start. In terms of people, our simple goal is by 2010 to have all of our executive management be PRC nationals. This is not to say we would actually operate that way. Nowhere in the world are we 100% local – we always have a mix of expat and local. But we would aim that for each expat in China we want a Chinese national posted internationally. This means an aggressive program to get the right people into the company and develop them. We have an offshore-posting program starting with 20 nationals now and we expect by the end of 2003 to have 30. We expect to stabilize around 50 postings in the second half of the decade. The majority of the overseas postings are from 18 months to three years and typically two years. Aggressive development also includes in-country programs – training and regular job movement. Over the long term if things go well, China could export their talent to the group but this is not the intent in the first instance. Right now we have about 1,300 people who would say they are BP, of whom there are about 200 expats. If you add in the joint ventures and service station staff, that would be about 2,500; so a total of around 4,000. This will grow some but we are more a capital- than labor-intensive organization.

Q **Coming back to a specific topic, you said the strategy was to facilitate gas development. Does that mean you do not see investment in gas development itself as an opportunity? What needs to happen to realize this opportunity?**

A We believe the production and sale of gas inside and outside of China will be attractive. But the reticulation and direct sale of gas is not our core business. It is potentially attractive but we would consider it only on a case-by-case basis. Overall, the prospects are good. We see that gas will increase as a percentage of the energy portfolio mix. Demand could grow at 12% per annum well into the next decade. China has made commitments to import and to develop its gas, particularly through concerted effort to supply the coastal areas. The Guangdong and Fujian LNG terminals are significant undertakings, as is the East-West pipeline. And the interest in Russian gas is real. The challenge is to provide gas affordably to Chinese citizens and to ensure that there is a balance of alternative sources to provide diversity of supply.

There are, however, issues around regulation. Historically, gas has been point-to-point, matching sources of supply with destination. This works with relatively isolated developments. But when you link up developments and start to create a national grid with a potentially more substantial and liquid market, you need more comprehensive regulation. You need to define the roles of various entities, access rights and so forth. But the government knows this and events will drive the regulatory agenda. The markets require it. In Shanghai, the arrival of East-West gas and East China Sea gas will require sharing of facilities so the roles will have to be clarified. It's a small beginning but it will get bigger. Guangdong may be where it happens next and then Beijing and the rest of the country in due course.

Q **BP was also one of the first global majors to invest in the IPO of a Chinese company – that of PetroChina. Are you happy with the results of this investment?**

A We were the first global major to invest in an IPO of a Chinese oil company, and we were very happy to do so. With regard to the results of the investment, it is still work-in-progress. It hasn't yet fully met our expectations in terms of new business opportunities. On the other hand, the right things are happening and we can still fulfill those expectations. I remain optimistic that the investment will do what was expected of it.

Q **What do you know now that you wish you had known when you started in China?**

A China is a complex place. I tried hard to prepare but it was still more complex and subtle than I expected. Everything involves relationships, which have taken more effort and have been more difficult to nurture than I expected. There is a need to constantly refresh relationships and to refine the strategic aims of the business you have put in place. I did not fully appreciate the importance of keeping things alive in this regard. In China, people talk about how signing a contract is a new beginning. It is difficult to portray how deeply this really runs. There is a constant state of negotiation. Thus, ultimately sustaining an understanding and a strategy is quite a challenge.

Another insight I didn't have when I arrived is the importance of national staff and how subtle a role they play. People said yes they play a role but it wasn't conveyed to me just how important. You absolutely have to have high-quality staff and you must involve them and trust their judgment. This took some time to fully realize.

Finally, it is easy to underestimate how ferocious the competition in China is and how determined the Chinese system is to ensure no one company gets too far ahead or that any Chinese company gets too disadvantaged. This puts great pressure on your strategic thinking. Sometimes the environment is clearly not in your favor. Looking forward, there are a lot of niche players plus six major companies – three Western super-majors and three Chinese companies – competing in China. There is not space for all to be successful. The broad-based competition among the super-majors, among the Chinese as a group and between the groups and the niche players in one-off situations creates a very difficult competitive landscape.

I see the intensity of competition as the flip side of growth. It is easy to believe growth will enable you to recover from a poorly conceived start, But the reality is opposite. It is difficult to recover because it is difficult to claw anything and the ferocious competition means that if anything is unclear and not nailed down, you can be overwhelmed by competitive forces.

Q So overall, where does that put China in the global priorities for BP?

A China remains one of the more attractive organic growth plays in the portfolio. We intend to keep building. Fierce competition is nothing new to us. We have a good base and a set of opportunities and relationships. We intend to keep on making investments as long as they fit our strategy and deliver the returns we expect.

4.3 RESHAPING PETROCHEMICALS

With double-digit demand growth, and a need for high-quality products, China's petrochemicals sector has already attracted significant investment. These new investments are likely to precipitate a wave of consolidation in what is still a fragmented, under-performing industry. Players must decide whether they have what it takes to play the consolidation game or exit.

THE PETROCHEMICALS DILEMMA

China is an attractive petrochemicals market, benefiting from strong consumer and industrial demand. China's emerging middle class wants quality materials in key end-user industries such as construction, home furnishings and white goods. The country's industrial growth is creating new markets for more sophisticated applications in automotive, process and other industrial applications. Over the past decade, demand has grown at more than 12%, and at even higher rates in value-added products.

China's petrochemical industry, however, has not kept pace with demand growth, in particular in higher-value products. China is the largest importer of petrochemicals in Asia. Over 50% of domestic consumption of key chemicals such as polyethylene (PE) and polypropylene (PP) is met through imports. Most of these imports are from nearby Korea and Japan, with the balance from Singapore.

What industry there is, is highly unprofitable. Margins have declined steadily since the mid-1990s at most chemical plants. PetroChina's downstream sector, including both petrochemicals and refining, lost more than $1 billion in 2000, while Sinopec, the owner of most of China's upstream petrochemicals capacity, has consistently missed its operating targets. Much of the industry is already operating in the red and debt levels are increasing rapidly.

Part of this is certainly due to the depressed state of regional petrochemicals prices. With the 1997-98 Asia crisis, the petrochemicals sector went into sharp decline as demand dropped by up to 40% for some commodity chemicals. Supply on the other hand continued to rise as many projects reached completion in the next two years. As a result, regionwide utilization fell from the high 80s into the low 60s. This in turn had a precipitous impact on prices, which fell dramatically and have yet to fully recover, particularly in China which has historically acted as the region's clearing market. The prices found in China are often the lowest around.

Also at fault are hugely inefficient operations. Domestic petrochemical producers suffer from outdated equipment with low utilizations, high energy costs, low yields and quality, and inefficient labor. Chinese refineries typically employ more than 10 times the staff that their international counterparts do.

More fundamentally, the industry is too fragmented to compete with imports. Most current facilities are relatively high on the global cost curve. Lack of competitive feedstock, the small size of local markets, and the fact that local governments have been the primary source of funding for the industry have historically driven only small-scale production investments. Over 75% of capacity would be judged at risk due to small scale by international standards. Processing complexes in the northeast face especially difficult market conditions at home and disadvantages in selling beyond as the historical legacy of building refineries on top of oil fields has led to huge surpluses in the northeast and deficits in the south. Basic technologies are also weak. Seventy-five percent of China's coking equipment was catalytic (as opposed to coking or hydrogenation cracking), which generates high gasoline yields. In China, though, demand for diesel is greater than for gasoline. Cat cracking also creates quality problems for both gas and diesel.

COST-CUTTING A FIRST STEP

Faced with the challenge of new investment needs and growing international competition, Sinopec and PetroChina, the owners of much of today's industry, committed in the late 1990s to reduce their costs to internationally competitive levels. For the two giants, reducing costs is a must as a high-cost production structure creates vulnerability to oil price swings and reduces their ability to invest. In doing so they are following international examples. Internal restructuring to reduce costs and improve efficiency was the watchword of the global oil industry in the 1980s and 1990s. Companies such as BP made huge strides in productivity by adopting decentralized, performance-driven strategies. Dupont and other leading chemical companies have shown that even in China, differentiation in compensation based on performance, and a transparent and rigorous system of performance evaluation can make a huge difference to the bottom line.

Much progress has been made to improve performance in the last two years. PetroChina in particular has emerged as an early winner in meeting investor expectations, having achieved a 15% reduction in total cost from 1997 levels by 2001. In petrochemicals, PetroChina focused on commodities such as PP where technology was available and there was already a substantial local industry. Introducing competitive management in this industry created up to 15% in net margin at some plants. Most of this was related to cost reductions through higher yields, better energy management and reduced overheads.

Upstream Success Paved the Way

By December 31, 2001, PetroChina's Exploration and Production division achieved 75% of the RMB6 billion ($725 million) cost reductions set for the four years up to the end of 2002. Analysts report that the company is on track to achieve a targeted $4 per barrel lifting cost by 2003. Doing so has not been easy — over 30,000 employees were fired in 2000 alone. But year-on-year profits were up in 2002, even after over RMB1 billion (over $120 million) was earmarked to pay for restructuring costs.

One important reason for its success is that PetroChina went through the painful effort of restructuring to create a genuine nationwide strategy in each of its business streams. Sinopec by contrast is still a collection of regional fiefdoms, each with its own local strategy, often competing with other Sinopec areas. In lubricants, for example, Sinopec offers over 10 different brands with overlapping or identical product qualities and customer foci. PetroChina by contrast has a national planning process that sets a consistent brand strategy, market positioning and investment priority. Likewise in manufacturing, PetroChina again has been more aggressive than Sinopec by adopting a three-pronged strategy. Along the coast, PetroChina is investing in building its wholesale infrastructure. In the northeast, it is rationalizing capacity to create a niche market. In the interior of the country, it is restructuring to reduce capacity aggressively.

Another key element of PetroChina's new process is a performance-management system with three major components. Key Performance Indicators (KPIs) have been developed for all senior and middle managers to ensure a focus on cashflow and improved return on capital invested, and away from the traditional supply and production-oriented measures. The actual KPIs were then driven down to the specific tasks required of each manager. In addition to purely financial measures, at lower levels of the organization, operational KPIs such as energy usage and equipment reliability were linked to the financial measures. The second tool was the Performance Contract, signed by every regional manager and the senior management of PetroChina. This contract specified the targets to be achieved in the year, and targets were based on annual top-down expectations. For managers without direct line responsibility, qualitative measures were developed. Typical Performance Contracts included six to 10 measures and both expected and "stretch" targets.

Finally, PetroChina has also moved to create business units, still largely on a regional basis, to enhance accountability at lower levels of the organization. The old organization relied on central functional units to manage a loose coordination across assets. The key change envisioned was creating strong business unit leaders around sets of like assets (for example, manufacturing, exploration, new production, mature production). This would create real accountability at lower levels of the organization to improve performance and share knowledge across like assets.

However, it is already clear that cost-cutting alone will not be enough to provide sustainable earnings for China's petrochemicals players. In an environment of ongoing tariff reductions and very competitive regional pricing, breakeven profitability is all that can be expected at most of today's facilities. If China's producers want to continue to serve their market with new products, they will need new world-class facilities to produce them.

NEW HUBS WILL DRIVE THE INDUSTRY

To provide a stable basis for the industry's development, China's government has now decided to invest in building major petrochemicals hubs. Newly built world-class facilities will provide the feedstock, cost structure and market access needed to compete against regional players. As long as China's market was too small to justify world-scale investments, particularly in a context of regional overcapacity, there were good reasons not to consider petrochemicals investments. Market growth has now mitigated this concern to the point where investing in a local production base makes economic sense.

Four major new petrochemicals facilities are expected to provide the foundation for a modern industry in China. All are located along China's prosperous coastal region – Shanghai, Nanjing, Fujian, and Guangdong – with good harbor facilities, easy access to nearby markets, and greenfield locations. The north has lost out due both to its distance from key markets and Middle East crudes, and to the difficulty in adapting its existing older facilities to the new product requirements. Instead, Shanghai and the Yangtze River Delta in particular boast a concentration of the new investment. Nanjing Chemical Park is already host to one of the largest refineries in China (Yangtze Petrochemical). With its new facilities, the Yangtze River Delta could produce over 20% of China's total petrochemicals slate.

Some of the world's largest multinationals – Shell, BP, BASF and ExxonMobil – are investing in these projects. They see participation as critical to gaining access to the domestic market, and as complementary to their existing offshore hubs. With WTO the Chinese government has proved willing to grant these players 50% stakes in the projects. In exchange, the government expects them to contribute a portfolio of technologies and to play an active role in management of the venture.

On the Chinese side, the government has designated Sinopec as the lead Chinese company in three of the four projects (CNOOC being the lead in the Shell Guangdong venture). This position is largely a legacy of Sinopec's historical role as the principal counterparty for foreign companies interested in China's downstream industry. These complexes are an integral part of its strategy as they are all in geographies it dominates and it lacks alternative upstream growth opportunities. Lacking the marketing know-how or operating skills of a multinational, they still bring substantial government support and the ability to shape local industry conduct.

CONSOLIDATION LIKELY TO ENSUE

The new hubs are likely to precipitate a reshaping of the industry. While simply producing to meet new demand can create some value, even greater opportunities lie in forcing the currently fragmented industry to consolidate, and by leveraging domestic bases to go overseas.

With hubs in place, China will be able to meet and profit from the increased demand from the domestic market. Hubs will be more than just simple ethylene crackers. All have significant associated downstream petrochemicals facilities. All the new hubs are being built to world scale and are expected to use largely imported Middle East crudes. This will ensure a substantial cost advantage versus both imports and today's domestic industry. Being newer facilities, they should also have better operating

What is a Petrochemicals Hub?

The concept of a petrochemicals hub was born out of observing developments in Europe and North America where Rotterdam and the U.S. Gulf Coast have received a disproportionate share of investments. These hubs have advantages over alternative investment locations in environmental management, feedstock costs, flexibility of offtake arrangements, and access to financial and human capital. Greater availability of feedstock sources reduces risk and increases the ability of companies to place extra capacity. Integration synergies from sharing streams between refineries and petrochemical complexes can be worth three to four points of return on investment. And information flows can be optimized through proximity, allowing producers to react quicker to changes and to use feedstock not available in commercial markets (e.g. offspec quality). As a result, in North America, the U.S. Gulf Coast remains the preferred location for new petrochemicals investments. Originally, an outgrowth of the Spindletop discovery in 1901, today the Gulf Coast accounts for 35% of U.S. refining capacity and 80% of the capacity of the top 25 petrochemicals produced in the U.S. Of this, the Houston area alone accounts for more than a third.

economics and labor productivity, not being burdened with the social costs of traditional SOEs. Local governments are already investing in industrial parks and infrastructure around the hubs to support their expansion.

Marketing capabilities within China, however, will be an important success factor. In the old, supply-constrained environment, simply having the product would be enough to make the sale. New entrants, even those with modern scale facilities, need to build their sales network both to serve existing and to capture new customers for value-added products. This will be a challenge as distribution is generally quite fragmented, with local distributors achieving at most 10% to 20% share of a given geographic market.

Successful players must establish strong shadow management relationships to ensure consistency of service and product quality. Typical arrangements require local distributors to stay within geographic boundaries and to assign dedicated sales staff to the company's products. In exchange, the company provides marketing and sales support, as well as a guaranteed supply of the product in specified qualities and amounts. Annual contracts are reviewed and monitored for performance, both in terms of volume and for adherence to contract terms, on the basis of which bonuses are paid at year-end.

As world-scale facilities have a substantial cost advantage compared to the current Chinese industry, the even larger opportunity is to leverage the hubs to shut down existing uneconomic capacity. For example, PP demand is expected to increase by almost 60% between 2000 and 2005 (Exhibit 4.3). This translates into 1.6 million new tons of capacity, or approximately eight new world-scale plants, if the industry targets achieving a 90% utilization. But of 2.8 million tons of capacity in the industry in 2000, almost two-thirds could be considered closeable by international standards, thus creating additional investment opportunity for nine new world-scale plants.

In addition, international experience shows that consolidation can drive higher industry profitability in commodity petrochemicals. When industry utilizations reach above 80%, industry prices can rise to beyond marginal costs to allow for capital recovery. Industry utilization in turn is driven by the investment conduct of players and the fewer the players, the better. The most profitable sectors typically have no more than five players accounting for over 80% of the market. Yet in China in industries like styrene, PTP and

Exhibit 4.3   Chinese PP cash cost curve – 2000 & 2005

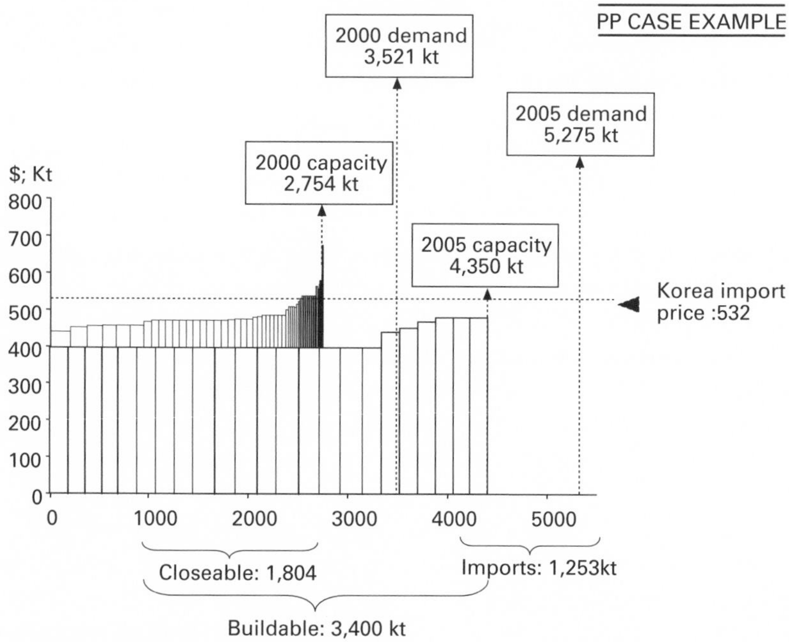

Source: McKinsey analysis

the like, as well as more local commodities like PP, industry concentration in China is far lower than it is globally. As the petrochemicals hubs expand and drive out smaller players, concentration could rise and with it industry utilization and pricing.

Key to making the consolidation strategy work will be the ability to manage industry conduct. Unless old capacity is consolidated as new modern technologies are introduced, potential restructuring will lead only to a bloody free-for-all as demand will be insufficient to cover all the new capacity. To ensure that value is retained, investors must discipline capacity additions with the closure of substantial local capacity. For example, multinational investors have to date sought explicit commitments from the Chinese government to close local capacity as part of the investment deal. An example is BP's highly successful acetic acid plant in Sichuan, which has replaced the equivalent of 40% of the competing local industry.

Even in industries where local players are not significant, restructurers will need to be excellent and creative deal-makers to avoid the risk of overcapacity. For example, in one intermediate product, an alliance between Japanese and European players was precipitated by the recognition that demand drops following the Asia crisis made it impossible to establish two world-scale plants in China. As a result the parties agreed to jointly invest in a shared upstream facility while both reserved the right to their own downstream blending and marketing operations. The alliance then accounted for over 60% of the market supply. This provided an efficient way to ensure stable industry conduct while preserving the premiums each valued from their proprietary products.

Finally, restructuring and consolidation potential is not limited to China alone. Winning domestic players have the opportunity to leverage their domestic scale to go global and restructure downstream industries in the developed markets. For example, Haixin, a Shanghai textile fibers producer, has acquired U.S. producer Glenoit's textile fabric assets to develop a global footprint. Glenoit used to be a dominant U.S. producer but after the Asia crisis was driven into bankruptcy by lower-priced Asian imports. Haixin's investment will boost its global market share to 25% and allow it to offer a full range of textile products to its global customers.

✳   ✳   ✳

China's petrochemicals industry is headed for change. With rising demand and major investments on the way, the only certainty is that today's players will have a dramatically more competitive environment. Winning players will set high aspirations to not only meet rising demand but also consolidate the industry.

4.4 BHPB: Building a Rock-Solid Business

Interview with Clinton Dines, President of BHPB China

BHPB is the world's largest minerals group and a company with over 100 years of history in China. More than many, it has experienced trials and tribulations in building its China business in the new China. Clinton Dines, the President of BHPB China and resident in China since 1988, shares his perspectives on the industry, the challenges for building a business and lessons learned.

Q Let's start with the history of BHPB in China. When did you get started in the country?

A Actually it goes back to 1891, the first business from Australia. But the first real beginning of the business was BHP's steel business in the 60s. Then the iron ore business kicked off in the early 70s with Australia-China recognition. And that kind of built up. And then through the 80s a variety of the businesses got up – manganese was quite strong; we actually had a little bit of coking coal business here; we had the oil business, selling crude oil to China. Then various parts of the company had different projects – BHP Engineering built a cement plant in Fujian. It was a bit of a mixed bag of different things. On the Billiton side, essentially the business came in as a trading business in the 1990s with chrome and nickel and alumina. Then Billiton bought a manganese business from BHP, so there are some commonalities.

But essentially it is a sales business, a trading business. We have been selling them stuff for a long time. And then there has been the odd minor investment. The steel business went from the 60s, a supply business of semi-finished steel, into where in the early 90s they put in a couple of small value-added processing plants of high-end steel products – Colorbond, galvanized steels, painted steels, coated steels. But we're out of that business now [due to spinoff of BHP Steel].

Q Your own role – you have been with BHP almost all of that time?

A It's funny – 14 years in the role means I've been everywhere. It starts off with me and a secretary and a driver in Beijing in the Minzu Hotel in 1988. BHP's business volume at the time was only about $20 million. That was actually an uncharacteristically low year. When we peaked out with steel we had 350 people and 23 offices all over the country.

During that period of time my job and my role has changed a lot. I was the first country executive that the company chose on the basis of country skills as opposed to company skills. All of my BHP counterparts around the world were company guys. It was a bit of an experiment – not subsequently repeated except in South America. There is always that debate but over time, as you get a bit of longevity in the company and networks, the definition of the role changes. You can then be seen both as a company and a country guy but that takes time. Fourteen years later and you're still working on it. That's unusual to be in the position that long.

And the position itself has changed as well. There is a representational role, a lobbying role, a business development role, an active involvement in terms of administering initiatives and helping set up businesses, and when we make decisions to pull out of businesses there's a very active role in tidying up. There's always a lot left behind that has to be dealt with to preserve the company's reputation and good order.

The role at the moment is in another evolution. Probably for the first time we are going to be managing China more holistically than we ever have. We have had China very fragmented by business group – that's been the history. Also to some extent by geography – big office in Hong Kong for a long time, office in Beijing, office in Shanghai, then even subdivided within those offices by businesses. Quite driven by the strategic business unit (SBU) approach. Now that doesn't change in essence. The SBUs still own businesses and people but organizationally we put China under one roof and try to get more consistency on how things are done, starting from basic things like HR and administration, but also moving to business practices and making sure that we are more whole as a company so that our ability to share skills and experiences between business groups is much more emphasized.

Q **Why is this happening now?**

A Well the merger [between BHP and Billiton] has a lot to do with it. Changing management philosophies has a lot to do with it. It doesn't take much except the recognition of the fact that we weren't doing as well as we could do to get that to happen. I think it has been self-evident that the way we were was suboptimal. Recognizing that takes decisiveness and some drive from management. It probably also takes the fact that five years ago China mattered less than it does now. There is a bit more attention and willingness to ask the question "How do we do better?" and address the answer to that question.

Q **How much does China matter now?**

A China is quite a small part of our total global business. Percentage-wise, it's in the mid-single figures but with relatively high growth. Obviously China matters globally in almost all of the commodity businesses we are in. And that is grabbing attention. In virtually every commodity we are in, China is a major customer of ours, with high growth or a major influence on the way that commodity is performing globally. So you have to be knowledgeable about China; you have to be involved. And I think we may be stepping from an arms-length involvement where we sat offshore and sold them stuff to being a bit more onshore, a bit more knowledgeable because China's importance is becoming more evident.

Q **Is China's growth sustainable?**

A Clearly I think it's going to stay that way but there'll be some bubbles along the way. China has had a pretty sustained growth record and that has to give you some degree of confidence that things will keep going on. But some of that growth has been achieved by postponing some fundamental reforms. So the question is, how long can these fundamental reforms be postponed? Can they grow their way out of their current issues? Are the ancillary issues beyond the structure, like corruption, going to be overwhelming to the ability to generate and sustain reform?

Given their track record, particularly in the last 10 years, you would have to say that there is a pretty savvy government leadership that is economically literate and relatively adept at political, social and economic problem-solving. This also of course equals continued tenure of the Communist Party. So their sustainability as a governing elite really depends on them solving these problems. And they have been relatively good at it so far. The empirical evidence you can observe and the data shows they are aware of the issues; but they have some pretty significant political hurdles to overcome, particularly in terms of political philosophy, to allow them to deal with the next phase of reforms. But it's as good a bet as there is on the planet.

Q **How about in the minerals sector – is there a new agenda here?**

A The mineral sector has suffered from possibly some neglect and some failures of reform. There are some sectors where there has been active reform and a lot of progress has been made, painful as it may have been. The minerals industry is not terribly attractive; second, it has not been well-developed in China in any event, with some exceptions like coal; and third, China is apparently not naturally well-endowed, so those things contribute to why the sector has been a bit neglected.

The minerals sector is also pretty strategic – meaning resource nationalism, resource sensitivity. And it's very hard to reform. The resource and processing associated with it are both geographically disparate – very, very widespread. There is a lot of local ownership in these sectors and so a lot of local sensitivity, which we experience in all countries. You can just look at the state sensitivity in the U.S. or Australia to understand that.

There's probably also a cost-benefit aspect. China is a large producer but not necessarily an economically viable one, so to go ahead and reform an industry that is in that sort of state is painful. What you are doing is destroying an industry, creating a political and social problem and your outcome is no industry because it is not economically viable in the beginning. That would apply to China's iron ore industry, which has a big part in sustaining China's steel industry now. On economic fundamentals, very little of that iron ore should be coming out of the ground. So you would not want to actively reform that industry – the endgame is no domestic industry and lots of imports. Instead, you would want it to gradually wither away over the next 15 or 20 years. So you can see Beijing, if they think about these things, hesitating to lurch forward with reform in these areas.

You can begin to see also some recognition that there are economic burdens that go with not addressing the problem. But it's very hard to get reform to happen without attention of very senior people. If Wen Jiabao becomes premier you never know. He is a geologist and knows a little about it. But the various agencies in Beijing responsible for the sector – the Ministry of Land and Resources – are relatively impotent in driving any reform agenda. So I wouldn't be overoptimistic about the capacity and will to drive reform in the mining sector.

There may be more reform in the oil and gas sector because that is strategically so much more important. In 1993 when they went from net exporter to importer because of economic growth, that became an imperative to drive reform in that area. As they see steel developing and iron ore imports also going that way, that might drive reform in that area, but probably it makes sense to let the iron ore industry manage itself gradually on economic fundamentals. The owners of iron ore resources in China are mostly steel plants anyway, which are increasingly market-driven, so they will manage their way out of the problem over time.

Q Do you see these pressures affecting state enterprises' behavior?

A Well in some instances you wonder if they have even heard if there is a market economy out there. But let's be fair – in the majority of instances, the behavior is very self-evident just in dialogue you have across the table. The motive for making money – not necessarily the profit motive, more cashflow or income – seems to have displaced other motives. The other motives are not entirely diminished, as some senior people are still thinking of a political career and of the political consequences of their decisions. You still see senior officials go in and out of government and commercial situations; for example, the ex-Jiangsu province governor who became the head of Shenhua Coal.

But it's impressive how commercial and savvy are the guys who are not the chairman – the VPs. When you get upcountry and middle-sized SOEs, it's very variable. There are some who are very entrepreneurial and some who are still in the dark ages. But by and large it's a pretty good 60/40 bet that when you walk into a Chinese SOE that the guy on the other side will have a vague idea of cash flow, profit and loss and a balance sheet, and his motivation is around buy low, sell high and "I've got to make a good profit on this". That creates an alignment in terms of the conversation and moves you to quicker outcomes. It used to be more of a ritual mating dance where you tried to work out what the other guy was thinking and while he tried to work out what you were. You can move to outcomes faster now – that doesn't necessarily mean deals of course.

Q Why are Chinese players diversifying and buying overseas assets such as gas, oil and mining?

A China in general appears to be relatively resource-poor. It's a big piece of dirt – the third-largest geopolitical entity in the world and to some extent not thoroughly exploited – so you have to say "apparently". Some situations though are clear – iron ore, manganese. In oil and gas, there is a bit more to be found but because of its scale and the rapidity of its growth China is an energy importer for the foreseeable future. In these commodities it's those fundamentals – they haven't got it, they buy a lot of it, why shouldn't they own a bit of it.

Companies are getting a bit more focused with individual corporations coming out and looking for opportunities. In steel and copper there is agglomeration into vehicles with intent to get equity position. That's about security of supply and recognition that we are going to be buying this stuff for forever and a day so why not own it? As companies have to produce a better quality product at a more competitive price, the imperative drives back into their business. They have to think more strategically. They realize they have to import. So first things first is security of supply. The next part is reflective of mercantilist culture – let's try to own a bit of it.

It's not quite the same as the Japanese approach. The Japan approach was very much Japan Inc., MITI-driven, where the Japanese government provided low-interest loans to create resource availability for the benefit of the Japanese economy. The Chinese model will be slightly different. No doubt government support and facilitation will play a role but probably more Chinese corporations will front the policy. CNPC, CNOOC and Sinopec will be the aggressive people articulating the strategy and buying the assets. The Chinese government will be a background facilitator but with a clear strategic intent. You can see this happening over time. The 1980s Channar joint venture in iron ore with Hamersley was very much government to government. The later ones like Baosteel to Hamersley are very much company to company. Not much government involvement – just rudimentary approvals to facilitate the transaction going forward.

Q **What is the BHPB strategy in this context?**

A For some sectors its clear that, in order to capture the market share, companies like ours will have to accommodate the needs and intentions of the users in China. We will have to be willing to engage in discussions about equity in certain sectors. In LNG it was never explicit, but implicitly equity had to be on the table. In iron ore it is not as clear and Chinese steel companies vary widely in ambitions and stages of development and scale. Some, like Baosteel, have clear ambitions; others are interested but lack the wherewithal.

In other sectors in doesn't matter so much. Where you have a terminal market like in the copper business, for instance, it probably doesn't matter so much. Chinese players have a strong intent [to acquire resources] and have a large, fast-growing market but basically it's a LME type of product. Some products are in the middle, like aluminium and alumina. Aluminium is a LME product but alumina isn't. You can have a quite active debate.

There's no doubt that in all of these sectors you get approached. There has always been a mercantilist impulse in China. The strategic drivers have really kicked in the second half of the 1990s. That's a function of the economy growing so fast. They became a trillion-dollar economy and now they have had these wake-up calls that they will have to be massive importers.

Q What's the reaction of the competitors to this?

A Hard to say. Some are very willing to be accommodating – others are more standoffish. By and large that probably reflects the degree to which they have thought about it and also reflects the degree of China's importance to those companies. Company by company it varies.

Q How do you organize in China to deliver against this?

A We are now beginning to evolve it. Our model is about marketing to China. Key in doing that is to optimize our capabilities to be good marketers. First of all, get the organization unified and focused. Second, build the skill sets and optimize the capacity to sell and market well. This includes better collection and analysis of information. Also building back into the organization more comfort and information flow about China leading to good quality decisions. We need to get a bit ahead of the curve. Our decision-making has tended to be reactive.

The strategy will also entail taking advantage of regulatory relaxation in China to move our capacities further along the supply chain. Traditionally, iron ore goes on the boat Freight-on-Board in Australia but there is a lot of value between there and when it goes into the blast furnace in China that we have not participated in. We have done this in Japan and elsewhere, so our ambition is to push along the supply chain not only for profit but also to better service customers and capture and hold market share.

Q That would imply a lot more local capabilities then?

A Yes, we are now trying to unify and consolidate. We then need to move into a phase of capacity building. Finding and growing the right capabilities is our biggest challenge. Even offshore talent is hard to find. If you find them offshore and bring them onshore then you have the interface between imported capability and local environment to deal with. Capability building will require patience and tenacity and probably a lot of investment in either buying in skills or developing the skills. Finding good senior local capabilities is also very difficult. The industry is not terribly complex but the mechanics of the supply chain are difficult. Attracting high talent to our industry is hard – we are beginning to overcome that in terms of how we think about compensation but it will continue to be difficult. We also need to build our brand name and knowledge that people have of the company so that it becomes a better-known company and we are able to attract people in China.

In terms of retention, a big part is the extent to which you put investment into developing people's skills. Development is a great retention tool and we also have to think about career paths. We have to signal to high-caliber local staff that if you come to work with us, you will get investment in your personal development, you will have a career path, and that we are a good company to work for. Those things have to be thought through and then we have to sustain our commitment to them over a period of time to develop credibility. There is no more cynical a group of people on the planet than a group of Chinese employees because they come from a cynical environment. Convincing them that you are real and that what you have to offer them is real is a real HR challenge.

Q **What do you know now that you wish you had known earlier?**

A Organizational things for me. After you have done your first joint venture you know a bit. When you have done your second you begin to see the pattern. When you are on the third you are convinced there is a pattern. In China there is something to learn every day. But you become comfortable with the patterns. The real issue is that you are a bit remote from the organization. The things I am still learning are how to interact with the organization, how to build consensus around ideas for China, how to persuade people of the value of opportunities, how to support people in dealing with issues of risk, how to work across a large multi-divisional complex organization. I've done a lot of that and had varying degrees of effectiveness at different periods of time depending on qualities of relationships and ability to influence.

One of my learnings might be, you can be very effective in China but if you are not effective in the organization, don't bother. You can be very effective in the organization but if you are not effective in China, don't bother. In all major organizations you'll see that – the guy who gets parachuted in and has no chance or by the time he has worked his way up the learning curve it's time to go home. Conversely, a character like me who has the China side but is a new guy in the company who has to build networks over time – that's the conundrum. Do you end up with the perfect creature, both organizational and country? That's hard to do. And should it be personified in a single person? Probably not. What you should be doing is building an organization in China that has credibility with the parent organization and also have people in the parent organization who have comfort and experience in China. That all takes time.

4.5 COALESCING AROUND COAL

Coal is big in China – both in demand and reserves, much of which are internationally competitive in quality. But an inefficient, small-scale and downright unsafe industry has long wasted this potential. Now the government has decided to invest – four large corporations will control up to 50% of domestic demand. New ports, rail links and washing facilities will link China to the rest of the world. This wave of investment in turn will spark off regionwide competition. As China's capacity comes to market, regional suppliers will lose market share and prices globally could suffer if conduct degenerates. Instead, leading regional players should work together with their Chinese counterparts to develop and market China's resources. By moving away from the old dig-and-deliver to a truly global mindset, the whole industry can benefit.

AN INEFFICIENT GIANT

Coal today accounts for about 58% of China's primary energy demand. This is expected to remain constant as China seeks to manage its overall energy supply within global environmental and economic constraints. Thus, as total energy demand in China grows, so too will demand for coal – from 1.2 billion metric tons (MT) in 2000 to 1.45 billion by 2005.

One reason China is sticking with coal is that it is largely self-sufficient. Over 800 billion tons of probable resources have been identified, of which over 400 billion are proven, enough to account for centuries of production. Coal imports in 2000 totaled less than two million tons, mainly of metallurgical coal supplied by Australia. Metallurgical plants demand consistent and stable quality coking coal, which is in limited supply in China. Coal is also a huge source of employment, particularly for impoverished rural areas. In 1998 the industry employed over six million workers in over 70,000 mines. In these coal towns, mines are also often the only providers of hospitals, schools and other social services.

However, the industry is not in good shape. Most of China's mining industry is small-scale and lacks the wherewithal to develop substantial new resources. Township and private mines (over 30,000) average output of only 10,000 tons. Local state-controlled mines (that is, those owned and controlled by city and county governments) produce about 500,000 tons per annum output on average and are in even worse economic shape. Many do not have the cashflow to pay workers as their customers pay late and operations are loss-making, yet they still have to maintain social support. Even worse are their abysmal safety records. Most of the 5,000 recorded deaths in the industry in each year occur in these small-scale mines.

As in oil, a lot of investment is needed to get China's coal to market. China's main coal supplies are relatively concentrated in and around Shanxi province (Exhibit 4.4). This is mostly mountainous area, suitable for drift mining, but is still relatively far from the main coastal markets in the East and South. Areas requiring more difficult shaft mining (for example, Yanzhou) have the advantage of being close to the coast. Areas in the West are too far from the action. Although there are good-quality reserves with low ash and sulfur levels and a high calorific value, they are too far from the coast to ever be competitive.

Exhibit 4.4   The coal reserves in and around Shanxi province will remain China's main source of domestic and export coal

Too far from the action
- Proven: 5.9 BT
- Probable: 12.3 BT
- Good-quality reserves, with low ash and sulfur levels and a high calorific value
- However, too far from coast to ever be competitive for exports

Supply Yangtze River cities and exports to South East Asia
- Proven: 3 BT
- Probable: 40 BT
- Still fairly undeveloped
- Yangtze River as main inland transportation method
- Rail links to South East Asia have been developed to allow exports

China's main domestic and export coal supply
- Proven: 403 BT
- Probable: 800 BT
- Mostly in mountainous areas, suitable for drift mining
- Areas requiring shaft mining, e.g. Yanzhou, Zibo,have advantage of being close to coast

Source: China Coal Industry Development and Research Center, Interviews

And China's transport and marketing infrastructure is already stretched. Thirty percent of port capacity is already used for domestic seaborne coal transport and exports. Transporting coal every year puts a tremendous burden on China's rail system – approximately 45% of current rail capacity is devoted to coal transport and much of the small-mine coal is transported by truck. And only 20% of China's coal is washed to allow for transport and delivery directly to end-users. Significant infrastructure needs to be built if these inland resources are to be further developed.

Seeing these challenges, to fund the development of resources and infrastructure, China's government in the late 1990s decided to restructure the industry. It encouraged the creation of 30-odd larger mining groups, to be further merged over time into four super-groups, most reporting directly to the central government. The State Development and Planning Commission directly controls Shenhua. The China National Coal Import-Export Corporation (CNCIEC) owns Pingshuo. Yanzhou is listed on both the Hong Kong and New York stock exchanges.

The super-groups were so called as they have each over 100 million tons of production, enough to take up a sizable portion of China's domestic demand. The mines to be included in the super-groups were chosen largely from the 500 or so state-owned mines with average annual output of one million MT previously controlled by the Ministry of Coal and now devolved to the provinces. The groups were then given authority to begin developing the market.

SUPER-GROUPS WILL GO GLOBAL

With the new super-groups, the picture of coal in China is changing. While the small-scale local mines are likely to continue to produce for domestic markets, the super-groups are well on their way to being strong regional competitors. This in turn will increase foreign company interest in Chinese resources and companies. Simply cutting price will only devastate margins for all. Instead, Chinese and foreign coal companies working together to improve the efficiency of the Chinese coal industry can be a win-win solution for all parties.

Small mines are likely to continue to play an important role in the domestic market despite an inconsistent government policy. In the late 1990s, government made an effort to rationalize the small-mine sector. Although coal is a hugely important source of rural employment, thousands of mines were closed. However, with continued demand growth in the early 2000s, small mines are re-emerging. The government has turned a blind eye to this development. To quote one vice president of CNCIEC: "Domestic coal demand will increase by 200 MT between 2000 and 2005, which can be met by 300 MT extra capacity from small mines."

The super-groups for their part are more focused on export than domestic customers. Exported coal delivers foreign currency, payment is guaranteed, usually within 50 days, and there is a significant tax exemption. Domestic sales on the other hand are in RMB, payment is unreliable, and often takes 90 to 180 days. Thus exports are often more attractive, even at lower or negative margins compared to domestic sales.

The super-groups also have the wherewithal to compete globally. The uncompetitiveness of China's coal for export has been driven by high run of mine costs and long inland transport to the coast. Datong in Shanxi province is typical of large state mines with $32 per ton FOB costs. Direct labor accounts for 30% of this, driven by a large workforce which the mine cannot reduce under the current political climate. Utilities account for another 20%, which is largely dictated by the type of mining needed and the location of the mine. Significant depreciation charges per ton are caused by low capital productivity, including substantial down time because of equipment failure. Finally, overheads of up to 20% of total cost will be incurred, including the ownership of hospitals and schools.

However, newer mines like Yanzhou that are relatively efficient and close to the coast, or inland world-scale facilities like Pingshuo and Shenhua, can produce much closer to $20 per ton FOB, equivalent to South African levels. These mines have relatively lean workforces (less than 20% of the equivalent of their older state-enterprise peers) and much higher capital productivity. They have also invested in their own infrastructure to get to market. For example, Shenhua's cost has dropped as new, dedicated rail infrastructure has halved inland transportation costs.

Government investments in transport infrastructure will also remove many previous constraints to export. The current 170 million MT of port capacity is expected to grow to 230 million MT by 2005. Huanghua port alone is expected to add 30 million MT in 2005. New rail lines will add 350 MT of capacity in 2002. The total amount of washing capacity is expected to grow, amounting to perhaps 375 million MT by 2005, largely due to investment by larger mines as much of today's washing capacity is concentrated at mines that are not cost-competitive for exports.

As a result, large mines have already begun to export in significant quantities. China's exports doubled in 2001, stealing market share from incumbent Australian, Indonesian and South African producers. South Korea, for example, bought 47% of its imported thermal coal from Australia and 18% from China in 1998. By 2000, China had reversed the balance, supplying 44% of the total and leaving Australia trailing with just 27%.[3]

Longer-term, total Chinese exports from the three major mines of Yanzhou, Pingshuo and Shenhua could conceivably grow to over 150 million metric tons (MT) by 2005, given current production plans. All three groups have significant expansion plans, in particular Shenhua which plans an additional 60 million MT. This would be enough to occupy almost 50% of the traded Asian coal market.

Regional competitors all face significant loss of market share as China emerges (Exhibit 4.5). Australia is best positioned given its efficient production and geographic proximity. But erosion of share of exports to Japan/Korea will increase as China's production methods improve and overheads are reduced. South Africans will find it most difficult to compete given geographic disadvantages, even if their production costs were reduced. Only Indonesia is likely to be able to expand its production given its low costs and high-quality coal resources.

However, responding to market share threats with price cuts is not a wise idea. If the region's coal companies slug it out in the market, delivered prices that today lie around $33 to $35 per ton could drop quickly to the level of marginal costs – i.e. closer to $20 to $25. At these prices, fully 60% or 85 million tons of current Australian capacity could be uneconomic. Likewise, almost all South African capacity would be uneconomic.

FINDING A PROFITABLE SEAM

Instead, leading players should consider a more cooperative approach to develop Chinese assets, potentially in partnership with Chinese players, and

Exhibit 4.5 China's increasing share of Asian coal imports

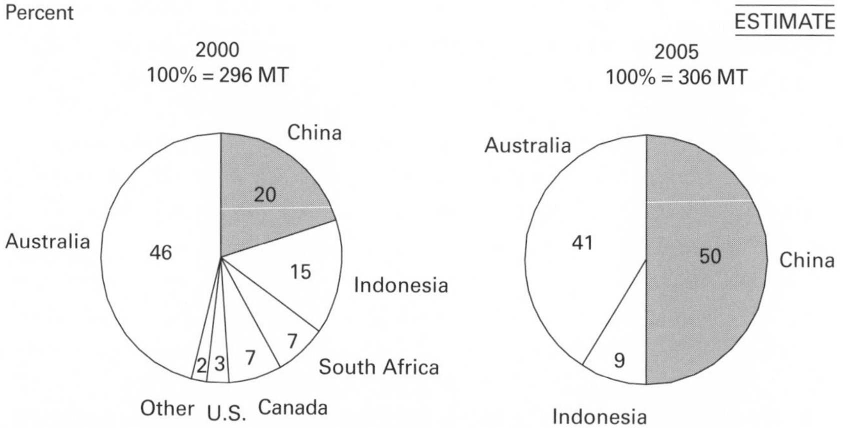

Percent

ESTIMATE

2000
100% = 296 MT

2005
100% = 306 MT

Source: EIA International Energy Outlook 2000; AME Outlook 02/00, McKinsey analysis

thereby take advantage of China's new competitive position. Opportunities exist throughout the business, from mining to processing to market development. Taking advantage of these opportunities to move into China can both preserve market conduct and help global companies realize profitable growth in the sector. Global coal companies are not restricted in their investment options in China's coal industry. Assets, marketing and customer development are all potential opportunities to consider for investors in domestic coal.

Develop Existing Mines

There are still plenty of assets to develop in China. The government plans only limited major new mine development over the next five years. Large, high-quality deposits remain to be explored. However, new mine development is an uncertain proposition. While new mines can be developed with much lower overheads and higher efficiency than existing mines, investment requirements are high ($100 million). Construction in remote areas is difficult and dedicated transport may be needed. And for foreigners, while current regulations do allow foreign funding of new mine development, local authorities may create significant delays.

Dr. Hammer's Mistake

The debacle of Occidental Coal's investment in Antaibao has scared away most foreigners from developing new mines on their own for the past two decades. Antaibao goes down as perhaps the biggest failure in foreign investment in China. Initially signed by Deng Xiaoping and Dr. Armand Hammer of Occidental Petroleum, this $200 million investment was massively unsuccessful due to very high labor costs, high expenditure on capital equipment (the largest fleet of 190T trucks in the world at the time), lack of rail links to the East and inaccurate market and price forecasts. The week after Dr. Hammer died, the Board of Occidental voted to sell back its share to Bank Of China for a small fee.

Reforming a current producer may seem an attractive alternative. But execution will be challenging. Without question, a modern producer could have a significant impact on efficiency and cost. Startup time would be faster for this opportunity than for a new mine development and investments would be relatively low. However, the large workforce at a typical mine and attendant social overheads drive up costs. Experienced investors also know that buying a whole company often brings unexpected baggage that can later prove hard to get rid of.

Developing new seams and panels at existing mines appears to be the most attractive and possible investment alternative. Mine costs are much more compressible if focused on only a piece of the mine (for instance, expansion) than on a purchase or joint venture with a complete mine. This

---

Asian American's Approach

In Jincheng, Asian American has two investments under development. In the first, it is investing $100 million to develop a new eight million MT/year drift mine with two long-wall sections, two room and pillar sections for development, preparation plant and stock pining and load-outs. Asian American is providing cash, management and one MT of exports. The Jincheng City government is intended to provide mining rights and land. The joint venture was signed and operations were planned for late 2001. However, the venture has been delayed as it has become apparent that the Jincheng City government did not actually have all the relevant mining rights. At the same time, Asian American is also investing $60 million to develop two four million MT sections in an existing Sihe mine, including two long-wall sections and four room and pillar sections mostly for development. Again, Asian American is providing cash, management and one million MT of exports. This deal has not been concluded given disagreements over the value of contributions.

---

path also entails less investment than new mine development. As for labor and overhead cost initiatives, this deal structure also allows the investor to hire only the labor required. A negotiation to allocate a portion of overhead is expected.

The mining organization itself should be set up using best practices – Australians could consider investigating whether efficient Australian production methods can be employed in China. Traditional industries like coal mining are often burdened by inefficient workforces, lack of incentives and bureaucratic organizations. However, given a strong performance push, there is no reason why dramatic increases in productivity cannot be realized.

By implication, investors in these traditional industries need to have a clear agreement with the local government on the rules of the game, and to be careful to only invest in those assets over which they can exercise management control. For foreign players in particular, partnering with a domestic third party, potentially a financial investor, could prove an attractive way both to access opportunities and to ensure efficient management once the deal is secured.

Build Marketing Infrastructure

An alternative to asset development is investing in China's coal marketing and transport infrastructure. In particular, investments in washing and processing can be an attractive standalone opportunity. Doing so in cooperation with Chinese producers can also build the basis for a cooperative marketing arrangement.

Coal washing appears to be the most attractive and accessible part of the logistics chain for global coal companies. Transport investments appear only selectively attractive – while inland rail and port capacity appears sufficient for now, some provincial routes have very high costs and thus could warrant additional dedicated investment. However, gaining relevant approvals, particularly for right of way, appears very difficult. Investment in port facilities is possible but current and planned capacity appears sufficient.

Coal washing however, is typically a small investment (amounting to $20 million, for example) that enables coal to be sold both in domestic and export markets. The government is encouraging such investments and there is a healthy supply of opportunities. Total washing capacity today amounts to 250 million MT or 20% of production, but only 70 million of this is at export-competitive mines like Shenhua, Pingshuo and Yanzhou. This amount would have to double to meet total expected export potential.

Coal washing plants make money based on favorable locations and infrastructure. A typical plant requires up to $30 million investment to wash five million MT/year ($20 million for three million MT/year). Costs are RMB50 (around $6) to RMB80 (around $10) per ton to buy from local mines, which run at low cost and lack washing supply. Modern efficient preparation plants can process coal for RMB16 (around $2) per ton. This plant can then sell its coal typically at up to RMB100 (around $12) per ton more than its ex-factor cost before running into market limits.

Washing plants should be located at coal rail depots for transportation convenience. Datong and Yangchuan are two particularly attractive areas for washing-plant development given their abundant supply of quality coal and limited current washing capacity. Coal from smaller mines is transported to coal depots such as Datong for nationwide distribution. Existing transportation infrastructure and abundant supply make these ideal locations for coal preparation. CNCIEC has already built two three million MT/year plants in Datong.

Developing a coal washing business requires six key capabilities: reliable supply of coal; operational skills, including the ability to maintain coal quality; on-time delivery and low-cost operations; an export license; cash for investment; and customer relationships, both internationally and domestically. These capabilities must be acquired through partnership or joint ventures with local parties, including provinces, particularly Shanxi, national corporations such as CNCIEC, and cities and county governments.

Invest in Energy Generation

A final set of opportunities is around development of the domestic energy market. By developing domestic power, gas and oil-based customers, global coal companies may participate without risking their international markets. However, the investment timeframes for this are long and the capital risks are high.

Coal-linked energy generation – that is, development of mine-mouth power stations and associated transmission – is a challenging proposition. There is potentially a large cost advantage for supplying power to coastal areas, especially if combined with new efficient mine development. This is, however, an enormous investment and there are significant risks; for example, connecting to regional power grids is not guaranteed. Coalbed methane extraction and sale is a slightly less expensive investment opportunity but with a long payback expectation. The government is encouraging the development and Shell, for one, is participating.

Coal-oil conversion is an even higher investment, though margins can be attractive based on South African experience. However, the scale required for such a plant would require an enormous coal supply. To date only one investment has been announced: Shenhua is planning a 2.5 million ton plant in Inner Mongolia. While technology has been obtained, the total expected investment will be more than $1.9 billion for the first phase alone.

✳   ✳   ✳

China's coal industry is already a business of global scale. Now it is on the way to becoming globally competitive. Regional competitors should take this chance to work together with emerging local companies in order to capture the value inherent in the market's growth.

REFERENCES

1. Discoveries, rapid depletion of Asia's petroleum reserves and increasing environmental pressures spurred significant investment in Asian gas projects in the 1990s. Two types of reserves are being developed: landlocked onshore basins in Central Asia and Siberia, and LNG projects in Southeast Asia, Australia and the Middle East. The former require long-term pipeline investments. The latter must take a punt on developing LNG infrastructure around the region.

2. Enron's Dabhol power project in India has been a multibillion-dollar failure, as the local government reneged on what appeared to be a badly negotiated deal.

3. EIU Newswire, August 5, 2002.

5

Reviving Retail

Retail has always been one of the mainstays of the service sector in China. But in the planned economy, it became less a shopping ground than a distribution point for scarce and ill-assorted goods. Now with rising consumer expectations there is both a need and an opportunity for retail to change.

For example, while demand for oil in China has matched the country's healthy economic growth, the infrastructure to deliver it remains woefully inadequate. Regulation and local protectionism have left a distribution and retail network that is fragmented, inefficient and wasteful. Now, investors are set to completely rebuild this infrastructure to an international standard. However, with a wave of new entrants and a backdrop of monopolistic local governments, much of this value could wind up in the pockets of the consumer and the government rather than the investor. Successful players must be able to define their own unique niche while delivering world-class skills. Otherwise, the black gold of a billion consumers may become just another drop in the Chinese sea of red ink.

In the early 1900s China's department stores operated as the centers of not only commercial but also social and cultural activities. Now the format has lost its way – despite steady growth in overall spending, department stores are rapidly losing ground to newer formats. Yet there are still opportunities. Returning to their original social purpose by leveraging their real estate and traffic flow is still an opportunity for many stores to restore profit. And by refocusing department store operations around a core customer segment, revenue and market share declines can be halted. For those players who do not succeed in making the transition, it is likely that they will be forced to exit. But the value of their underlying assets is simply too high to allow traditional state enterprise management to destroy it.

5.1 ROADSIDE RETAIL*

China's automotive market is predicted to be the third-largest in the world by 2008. Only the United States and Japan will have larger markets for gasoline. China's market is growing by 4% a year, about double the rate of the developed world. The accompanying growth in demand for gasoline and related car fuel products – combined with government plans to deregulate the sector and the need to address the chronic inefficiency of current distribution – should create a juicy opportunity for multinational oil companies as well as for China's two domestic giants, PetroChina and Sinopec.

Certainly there is a need for investment. Gasoline reaches the huge Chinese market through a fragmented retail and distribution network of about 90,000 stations, almost all state owned. Many are run more as sinecures than as businesses, often with a staff four to five times larger than the international norm but with less than a quarter of the average gasoline throughput of U.S. stations. The Chinese government, which is well aware of the problem, has resolved not to allow the country's energy infrastructure to burden the whole economy: it is fast deregulating the sector, which will be fully opened up to foreign companies in 2004 under the commitments attending the country's membership in the World Trade Organization (WTO). Foreign oil companies hitherto have been restricted to one-off local deals in special economic zones or tied to investments in toll-road construction.

Although the stage should thus be set for canny corporations to move into the market, it remains unclear how they will make money from it. Competition is already driving down retail margins on gasoline, while prices for the best station sites have soared as China's large domestic oil companies have rushed to buy them. Oil companies in the West facing similar margin pressures know that most gasoline stations are viable only if they offer general retail facilities at least as large as a convenience store, in addition to gasoline. This is true in China as well. The highest-volume sites might be made to pay on their fuel revenues alone, but the rest need substantial non-fuel revenues to make a profit.

The strategic implications are clear. In China as elsewhere, the first decision for an oil company is whether to own and operate sites or merely to supply them with gasoline. If the company opts for ownership, it has a choice: to adopt a retail strategy and pursue non-fuel revenues from a portfolio of retail sites or to target only the highest-volume sites, using them

* Originally published in *The McKinsey Quarterly*, 2002 Number 3, and at www.mckinseyquarterly.com. Copyright (c) 2002 McKinsey & Company. All rights reserved. Reprinted by permission.

to build a high-quality gasoline brand that can also be offered through independent retailers. At present, the Chinese oil majors are pursuing neither strategy; they have simply rushed to grab any available site, where they sell as much petroleum-based product as possible while ignoring the retail potential. The multinationals have been more judicious in selecting sites for their initial joint ventures, but they too have neglected the strategic choice. Unless all of these companies, domestic and international alike, change tack, their investments in expensive Chinese real estate may unravel.

THE MARKET AND SITE ECONOMICS

China's dominant oil companies are Sinopec, in the south and east, and Petrochina, which has the more comprehensive refinery and distribution network, in the north and west. The two companies aim to capture, between them, 70% of China's gasoline sales volume by 2005. Since their IPOs, in 2000, they have invested heavily in petroleum-related infrastructure and brand building. They see this as one of the few opportunities they have to grow in their core business.[1] Having already raised their share of sales to more than 40% and secured most of the prime sites in the biggest cities, they are on track to meet their target.

Until 2004, multinational companies will be allowed to own outright only the 300 or so sites they now possess through local deals struck prior to government deregulation of foreign investment in the sector in the mid-1990s, but they can build up their holdings through joint ventures with Chinese companies. BP, ExxonMobil and Shell are establishing joint ventures with PetroChina and Sinopec by contributing capital for the purchase of sites and by supplying higher-margin premium fuels; BP and PetroChina, for example, aim to boost their holdings to 950 stations by acquiring 670 stations from local companies in Fujian and Guangdong. Such joint ventures bind the partners only in specific provinces and have so far been formed in just four out of 27 of them. For the remainder, the options of both parties remain open.

The 60% of sales not controlled by the two Chinese leaders are currently held by various quasi-government entities, including local and provincial authorities and state-owned enterprises. City governments, for example, have started their own retailing groups, often built around local highway construction projects. Some private operators are also emerging: for example, China Resources, a holding company based in Hong Kong, has 23 stations and is thinking about opening more. But, in general, smaller companies, daunted by the bidding power of PetroChina and Sinopec, are holding back.

Both of the giants hope that their spending will create a profitable structure for China's gasoline-retailing industry after the market opens up in 2004. International experience shows that gasoline retailing tends to be relatively profitable wherever the top three participants control 80% of the market, growth is strong, and the supply of gasoline is short. China should meet these conditions. Sinopec and PetroChina are consolidating the market by buying out their independent rivals and, given their head start over the multinationals, should gain a leading position in the market. Growth in demand is forecast to remain high, especially for quality gasoline. And although supply is in balance with demand at a national level, it runs short in the coastal regions, where demand and growth are greatest.

Retail margins are tightening fast, however. As in almost every deregulated Chinese industry, domestic price competition will probably be severe as the market opens up. Sinopec and PetroChina fought several damaging price wars from 1997 until they were restrained in 1999 by state-imposed price controls that are now being removed in tandem with China's entry into the WTO. The resumed price competition will intensify when new foreign and domestic companies are permitted to purchase sites, in 2004. All companies in the market will also gain greater access to gasoline as import tariffs for refined products are reduced to 5%, from 9%. Where comparable reforms have taken place – in Australia, France, Israel, Japan and New Zealand – retail margins have fallen by up to half.

In anticipation of this fiercely competitive environment, Sinopec, PetroChina and new entrants willing to take them on are ratcheting up spending on locations, brands and marketing. Good locations – the 20% of urban gas stations that generate 60% of the revenues – are scarce, and zoning regulations and the high cost of land limit new entrants. These prime sites, which move more than 1,500 tons in volume and generate over RMB 900,000 ($108,700) in fuel-related gross margins a year, currently sell for up to RMB20 million, three to six times the price of a station with equivalent turnover in the United States or Europe. The inflated costs at the high end of the market are also dragging up the price of smaller stations: RMB5 million to RMB10 million. The cost of promotional campaigns, including television advertising, is also about as steep as it is in developed markets.

MAKING SITES PAY

Selling gasoline and diesel through retail outlets is a costly business and therefore a risky one. Unless Sinopec, PetroChina, and their foreign joint-venture partners reconsider their indiscriminate buying of sites, they could find that their station portfolios hold more balance sheet liabilities than assets.

It is vital to make the sites pay, but how? There is little scope to cut operating costs, which are already low by global standards; labor, for example, is relatively cheap if inefficient. Capital costs are largely fixed once a station has been bought. And wholesale margins, on which the Chinese majors have usually relied to subsidize their retail outlets, will probably dwindle to the cost of transport and storage as WTO commitments and other reforms take effect. The truth is that the economics of most sites won't work unless there are significant non-fuel sales, for they improve site margins by lifting revenues without raising costs in a comparable way (Exhibit 5.1). Petroleum companies thus have three possibilities: they can focus on the retail opportunity of their sites, concentrate on a high-quality fuel service through the highest-volume sites, or ignore retail altogether and be wholesalers of commodity fuels.

The Retail Strategy

Elsewhere in the world, multinational oil companies have compensated for tight margins on gasoline by investing in additional revenue streams. This kind of strategic behavior takes place in the context of a global retail sector moving from ownership of product categories to ownership of retail "occasions" – the way-to-work or weekend stop for gasoline and incidentals, routine Saturday shopping, the less frequent household stock-up. Gasoline stations are designed to attract customers who want more than just fuel for their cars, and in Europe and the United States these formats now generate as much revenue from extras as from gas.

Exhibit 5.1   Most Sites Require Non-Fuel Revenues to Achieve 8% ROIC*

		Tons of fuel per day						
		250	500	750	1,000	1,250	1,500	1,750
% of	20%	1%	2%	3%	4%	5%	6%	7%
revenues	40%	1%	2%	3%	5%	6%	7%	8%
from	60%	1%	3%	4%	5%	7%	8%	9%
non-fuel	80%	2%	3%	5%	6%	8%	9%	11%
	100%	2%	4%	5%	7%	9%	10%	12%
	120%	2%	4%	6%	8%	10%	12%	13%

ROIC > WACC

* 80% of stations are less than 1,500 tons per day. Assumes average cost to acquire station of RMB5 million. Retail margin of RMB410 per ton. 10% WC as % sales. RMB259 operating cost per ton. 50% margin on non-fuel revenues.
Source: McKinsey analysis

In developed economies, this model has been adopted slowly because it takes time to convert or dismantle the legacy assets of a long-established gasoline-only strategy. Chinese players have an opportunity to go straight from the basic gasoline model to integrated retailing. Yet, so far, PetroChina, Sinopec and even the multinationals have been reluctant to pursue non-fuel retail strategies on their current sites, for they have been persuaded that, in China, the ubiquity of local mom-and-pop stores means that convenience stores at gasoline stations are redundant and that margins on non-fuel items are too thin. The marketing efforts of these companies have thus been confined to gasoline, and their sites offer no more than a limited selection of low-cost additional goods and services such as cigarettes, lubes and snacks.

Nonetheless, the integrated retail model for gasoline stations can succeed in China. As working hours and prosperity increase, the Chinese are more and more willing to pay for convenience and brands. Of course, car drivers, who are generally among the most affluent people in the country, are beginning to demand offerings not available at mom-and-pop stores, such as foreign brands and technology-based services. And the economics should work, since even small non-fuel items often have profit margins of more than 50%.

The key is to start with an attractive retail site – perhaps incorporated into an entertainment or commercial development that could also draw pedestrians – as opposed to a pure gasoline stop. Owning a network of sites improves margins for individual locations by delivering scale benefits for overhead costs such as marketing and administration as well as purchasing scale for both fuel and non-fuel items.

Chinese consumers are already familiar with novel retailing concepts such as hypermarket chains, specialty stores, and greatly improved supermarkets and department stores, which have all emerged over the past 10 to 15 years. Most of these formats have been successful, though convenience stores have fallen prey to oversupply and margin pressures. Their experience indicates profitability will depend on three factors.

The first is early entry into the market. Only companies that have been quick to introduce innovative formats and to gain national scale have made their retail ventures pay. Carrefour led the way with hypermarkets, thereby securing a leading share and leaving local and foreign competitors with less attractive locations. Yet the need to build scale quickly shouldn't persuade companies to overpay; instead they should look for opportunities in midsize cities, which represent up to 40% of national demand for gasoline and where retail demand is now growing fastest. Here, there is still a chance to enter the market early and to establish a strong brand presence without overpaying.

Developing the right retail proposition is the second factor. China's newly affluent consumers are driving change throughout the country's retail sector by seeking convenience and branded quality. For a retail gambit to work, gasoline stations must appeal to prosperous consumers such as people who drive their own private cars (accounting for upward of 40% of new car purchases in 2000) as well as the young motorcycle riders who still dominate station forecourts and are more likely to try out new and foreign brands. To serve these categories of consumers, gasoline retailers will need to offer not only high-quality goods – such as prepared and packaged foods, including a substantial number of foreign brands – but also services such as DVD rentals, photographic processing, a pick-up location for Internet orders, laundry, mail, and pharmacy counters. The precise mix and the design of the site will depend on the market segment the retailer aims to serve: affluent but more traditional car drivers or younger motorbike riders. But retailers must also bear in mind the needs of taxi drivers, who still account for most gasoline consumption in China and look mainly for high-quality gasoline and good service.

The third ingredient is the development of retail skills beyond the usual level of basic expertise. Managing a network of retail sites involves the continuous development of a portfolio of options from which each site can draw – a task that requires skills in concept design, partnering and venture capital. The state-owned Chinese oil companies will need to develop these skills both organically and through joint ventures.

The Gasoline-Specialist Strategy

Given the high cost of owning a large network of retail sites, and the accompanying pitfalls, oil companies might decide instead to become gasoline specialists. Pursuing this strategy would involve buying only those high-volume sites that have sufficient sales of gasoline and auto-related services to make a profit. Elsewhere, the company's branded gasoline and oil products would be sold through a network of retail partners.

The rationale of the gasoline-specialist route is that auto fuel is a technically differentiated product and that branded, quality products can command a premium. China, with its shortages in domestic supply and its increasingly discerning consumers, is thus promising ground for the gasoline specialist. In the case of auto lubricants, for example, the quality segment of the market accounts for only 7% of the volume but for more than 30% of the value; margins are up to three times those for the commodity lubes sold by local suppliers. The push to quality is already being assisted by government crackdowns on fake and counterfeit products and by WTO-inspired moves to promote the use of high-quality gasoline with cleaner emissions. Since China's refineries operate far below international benchmarks, and domestically generated high-quality gasoline is scarce, multinational companies have a clear opportunity. About 20% of all gasoline sold in Guangdong, for instance, is imported, and industry forecasts suggest that this amount will rise slowly over the medium term.

For multinationals not bound by existing joint ventures with the leading Chinese players, the gasoline specialization strategy makes particular sense, for the foreign companies have access to supplies of good gasoline and an established reputation for product quality and brand strength. A typical foreign-owned gasoline-station in China sells as much as two times more premium gasoline than do locally owned stations, and its prices can be 5% to 10% higher than theirs even on basic products. Multinationals that haven't spent heavily to acquire large numbers of low-volume stations can cherry-pick the best of the new sites and then focus on supplying high-quality gasoline to any independent retailers that emerge.

The gasoline specialization strategy relies on three key elements. First, such a specialist should buy only high-traffic sites and perhaps divest itself of sites with smaller volumes. Sites that sell more than 1,250 tons a year are not just the only ones that make a profit without significant non-fuel sales but can also create brand preferences within their areas.

Second, the specialist will need strong retail partners – foreign and local – to get the necessary scale for its products. Wal-Mart and Carrefour, which are building networks of retail sites in China, are obvious partners, but Jet, Quiktrip, Tesco and even McDonald's might also be suitable. Since China's retail sector is strongly regional in character, multinationals will also need to build relationships with a number of local retail partners.

Finally, a gasoline specialist should differentiate itself on products and services, not price. In addition to high-quality gasoline, it must offer quick and friendly assistance, convenient layouts, links to company- or card-payment schemes, and services such as repairs and car washes. To reinforce the message that quality is paramount, prices shouldn't be visible from the street.

Can China's oil companies realistically pursue the gasoline specialization strategy? There are certainly problems. Although these companies may decide to scale down their investment in retail sites, the quality of their gasoline and service is still relatively poor, and their brands, though well known, are perceived as being of lower quality than those of the multinationals. China's petroleum companies are just starting to try to make the quality of their products, channels, and marketing more consistent by building, for example, high-quality lubricant brands such as Great Wall (Sinopec) and Kunlun (PetroChina).

Sticking to Wholesale

Local and Asia-Pacific producers or merchant refiners, such as CNOOC, that can't invest in a substantial retail position could steer clear of retailing altogether and focus on supplying independent retailers. Once the industry has consolidated, the remaining ones will be looking for a secure source of local gasoline under their own or franchised brands. For Chinese companies that have already invested heavily in their own sites, this might not be an acceptable path. But for many regional refiners – at least if the costs of distribution aren't prohibitive – it could prove a safe way to operate as competition intensifies.

✳   ✳   ✳

Chinese and multinational oil companies, building on their established supply positions and brands, are investing heavily to sell gasoline in the fast-growing Chinese market. But with falling margins, aggressive competition, and ever more demanding consumers, selling gasoline in China isn't a simple game. The size of the country, the abundance of distinct regional markets, and the number of independent sites still available give all interested parties the ability to map out profitable strategies. But unless these companies get it right – and to do so, many of them will have to realize the full potential of retail operations – the black gold of a billion consumers could turn to dust.

5.2 LVMH: Defining Luxury

An interview with Hugues Witvoet, LVMH Fashion Group

LVMH is the world's leading luxury group selling premier and premium cosmetic, wine and spirit, and fashion brands. Hugues Witvoet of LVMH Fashion Group has been living in Asia since 1996. Formerly a consultant with McKinsey & Co., he developed hypermarkets in Korea prior to joining LVMH as President, Asia-Pacific of the Fashion Group in 2000. Areas stretching from Korea to New Zealand, China and Hong Kong are his direct responsibility. In this interview he shares his perspectives on the opportunities and challenges for LVMH, the world's premier fashion and accessories house, in developing the Chinese luxury market.

Q **How did LVMH get started in China? What were some of the key milestones?**

A China has been on the radar for a long-time. In fact, our Wine and Spirits division has been importing premium liquors in China for about 100 years – the Chinese have been drinking cognac for a long time and Asia has always been a significant market. Eighty percent of cognac volume is sold outside of Europe, and Asia is a major part of that. So China has been a potentially large market on the screen for a long time.

Perfumes Christian Dior started in China 10 years ago. We established a production line in China for a local brand, which was then transformed into a packaging line. As in most emerging markets, cosmetics is the first step in for high-end fashion. Women buy makeup and, in particular, lipstick as the first product when they are looking to be trendy.

In 1992 we opened the first Vuitton store in the Palace Hotel in Beijing. In these early years, China was just opening up to fashion. It was the place for Japanese tourists to go. In the mid-1990s Louis Vuitton opened a store in the Ritz Carlton in Shanghai. Our stores were only in high-end hotels. That was the only place where our counter parties had an understanding of high-end branding.

From 1996, we grew strongly from two to seven stores, opening in Dalian, Shenzhen and Guangzhou. The business grew at 50% annually into a solid base. And after the handover in Hong Kong we saw a continuous growth in China. China accounted for a few percentage points of the total Asia Pacific sales.

At that point we began benchmarking our competitors to understand what the leaders had done in order to identify best business practices. We decided to take a more structured approach, as opposed to the piloting that we had been doing before. When I arrived in 2000, it was clear that China was quickly becoming one of the top issues for the Group in Asia.

Q **What is the Group doing in China now? How large is the presence?**

A Louis Vuitton has seven stores in China. Total volume is still small when compared to a large Asia-Pacific market like Hong Kong or Korea. But 20% of our Hong Kong business comes from Chinese customers. In fact, a TV program in Paris said that over 20% of the sales of Galleries Lafayette and Printemps main Paris stores were from Chinese customers. So the impact of China can be measured both in China and abroad.

For the other brands, Fendi has four stores and good potential. Celine, with its easy-to-wear style and "reasonably" priced high-end fashion, has taken some time but is doing very well now. Loewe is at a higher price point and, despite low awareness, doubling its business. There is a segment, in the North of China, where customers, particularly men, appreciate very high-quality items. They are prepared to pay high prices if quality is demonstrable. Givenchy has also very quickly developed its franchise network, starting even before Vuitton, with two lines of products. We now have 45 stores in different cities in China.

Q **Your collection of stores in Plaza 66 in Shanghai is one of the most recent initiatives. How are they doing?**

A Plaza 66 was one of the first high-end malls in China. It was a challenge to generate traffic there without a traditional anchor tenant like a department store and sales picked up slowly for the first six months. Now it is above budget and we are already considering expanding the Louis Vuitton store into a global store. It is one of the few markets in the world where we could go from a 280m^2 space to 600m^2 in less than 18 months. In fact, we believe we could open three or four new Vuitton stores per year.

Why? We see the potential in China and our market research tells us we have to make a statement; and in fashion big is beautiful. When tiptoeing into the market, it is okay to avoid losing your shirt. But when you have a hunch and enough evidence, then you have to go big and customers have to see you. In fashion, you have to go big in stores to communicate.

Stores are a way to get in the mind of affluent people, even those who come from other cities. It is important to invest in your brands when mindsets are formed and the image of what is luxury is being established. Chinese people travel – 80 million travel domestically for holidays and more than 15 million travel abroad. Opening stores in new cities allows your brand to both attract city resident customers and tap into the travelers market. Chinese will travel more often and in larger numbers over the next 10 years. It is becoming easier and cheaper for urban Chinese to travel, and the government is encouraging this to foster domestic consumption.

Q **How else do you get into consumers' minds besides the stores? How about communications and media?**

A Well, we have been expanding coverage in fashion magazines in the traditional way. China has a chaotic but creative media scene.

There are international magazines of which *Elle* is the most professional today. There are local fashion magazines as well. And recently we've witnessed the launch of lifestyle magazines for specific segments. *Tatler* has launched in Shanghai as well. All these magazines are trying to define the canons of beauty and success for their readers.

But magazines are not enough to maximize points of contact. People also read quality newspapers, which traditionally do not have many luxury advertisements. For example, 80% of white-collar workers read *Beijing Youth Daily* in the capital.

Finally, outdoors provides good opportunities to reach large crowds in Chinese cities. Airports are much more interesting in China than in traditional markets. Those who travel are more affluent and brand-conscious, as all surveys from CAAC have demonstrated. They have a much higher propensity to purchase luxury or high-price items. In the Shanghai airport, Lancome and L'Oreal have large advertisements in the baggage pickup area!

Q **With all of these efforts, how do you get your message across?**

A What you need is clear simple messages to make sure people understand. It should build the basics of the brand. We go back to the roots of the brand — what it is, why are we a fashion brand. A lot of people in China don't know the Louis Vuitton heritage in luggage making. European customers have probably heard their mothers talking about Louis Vuitton or seen something somewhere. In China, the mothers don't know and the young people haven't been educated about brands. Remember that 30 years ago women didn't even use makeup in China. In the 1960s and 1970s, luxury brands were forbidden. In the 1980s, product offer was extremely limited and the focus on getting richer, not on distributing or enjoying wealth yet.

Q **So are you running separate marketing campaigns in China?**

A Not yet, but we are considering adding a layer on the global advertising campaign. This layer would focus on the history, tradition and roots of the brand, as well as explain the products themselves. We are, you could say, a supply-driven company. But to be successful as a supply-driven company in China we have to assess the level of customer sophistication through market research and to learn how to communicate the product attributes. Communicating the intangible benefits of our products is a motivating challenge for our marketing teams.

Q Stepping back, how do you see the market developing? What are the key trends that you watch?

A We are in the very first stages of the development of the industry. There are still very few people who buy our products. Even if you take the 300 million people in the educated, affluent coastal markets, our customers account for possibly less than one percent. But when you look at the socio-demographics, the fast-growing number of young people earning real money above RMB 6,000 a month [US$1 = RMB8.3], the increasing level of education and the overall economic growth, you see there are all the underlying elements of durable market growth. Even if there are only 50 million Chinese with high disposable income, this category is growing 8% or 10% a year. These people want to be seen as successful and are looking for brands to identify themselves with.

Q Who drives the market – men or women? How is this changing?

A The upper end of the market has traditionally been men. In the early 1990s men were buying for themselves; typically travel items, leather products, suits, watches. They bought to exchange gifts in business dealings. They also bought for their wives and girlfriends. So when you look at total sales, companies like Dunhill and Zegna did quite well, early on.

In the second half of the 1990s we started to see more women in the shop. These were either affluent housewives or young executives. Similar to Japan, they live at home so they have a large part of their disposable income available for their personal conspicuous consumption. These ladies are the ones who read the magazines and are excited about the latest trends. There are now some incredible articles in the Chinese press, things you would not have seen five years ago such as relationships and sex with your partner, career advice for women, etc. It is happening in Shanghai but also starting to permeate other cities.

Q Speaking of geography, where do you see the market? Is it primarily confined to the big cities or are there more opportunities than that?

A My answer is driven by the opening of our Louis Vuitton shop in Chengdu. We had a great debate on whether it was too early. Eventually, we decided to open in a 5-star hotel, a small store. For the first four or five months, there were few transactions, though with high amounts. We realized then that we had not communicated enough about our point of sale and people simply didn't know we were there. When we corrected the situation, sales took off and we are now above budget. So even in Chengdu where awareness was initially low, as soon as the trendsetters get interested, word-of-mouth means that sales grow double digit.

There is a lot of money in these cities. You can see Mercedes and BMWs in the streets. In these secondary cities, people who have set up joint ventures, own a business or have bought back state enterprises, have money. They are rich, eager to discover new international brands and are not afraid of heavy premiums. Besides, the cost of living in these cities is relatively affordable.

Q **What is the meaning of the LVMH brand to these people? What are you selling?**

A Louis Vuitton is a sign of success linked to international fashion and timeless craftsmanship. By showing their top international brands, they say, "I have access to brands that other famous people in the U.S. and Europe have." Most think it is a good investment and it shows you are leading in the fashion trend, the same as in Hong Kong. It is not about showing off though; more a sign of belonging to a group of forward-thinking, leading society members.

Q **Is this similar to other markets in Asia?**

A For example, Korea is similar but Koreans are less interested in things outside Korea. So brands that have lost some appeal in fashion markets worldwide can still remain strong in Korea. A brand delivering value over time can become part of the local heritage. In Japan, Chanel, Hermes and Vuitton show that the enduring quality element is more important. They are very well informed, which is not the case of China, and more rational in their purchasing. Japanese are also very demanding customers and will argue about quality. For sure, 25 years of establishing durability, quality and timelessness make Vuitton the supreme brand of the luxury market, a case apart in its own league. China is just discovering the brands. Maybe it will be different in 10 to 15 years. Everybody's brands are coming in now and the battle of wallet and mind shares has started.

Q **How do you organize to deliver in China? What are the biggest challenges?**

A We started to operate from Hong Kong. Now most companies have people on the ground and operations in China. Our people must live and breathe China – they must have the same experience as the customer. For us in fashion there is also the need to fight counterfeiting and copying.

We have set up an importation company in Shanghai to control our logistics and distribute to our stores in China. We can provide marketing, purchasing, budgeting and merchandising services directly to the stores. LVMH Fashion Group human resources, retail, logistics, and financial functions are located in Shanghai.

The biggest challenge is recruiting and training the right set of people. They have to understand fashion, and be able to explain why people should pay a premium. A lot of documentation and explanation is required to train our staff.

Q **Last question – what do you know now that you wish you had known when you started out?**

A I think we have taken a pragmatic approach to China. We made manageable investments; so, while we made a lot of little mistakes, we could quickly learn and adjust. I'm not sure there is one thing I would have done differently. This is probably because we went cautiously but with some determination and with no real preconceptions. We could have built and structured our local management team and systems earlier.

5.3 SAVING CHINA'S DEPARTMENT STORES

In the early 1900s, China's department stores operated as the centers of not only commercial but also social and cultural activities. With rooftop cafes, Chinese opera houses and a wide range of spectacular entertainments, Chinese department stores dominated the retail landscape and foreign players found they had nothing to offer. Now the format has lost its way – despite steady growth in overall spending, department stores are rapidly losing ground to newer formats. And with the hard times in the sector, local governments are increasingly willing to sell their local retail assets for a fraction of book value, and with them access to attractive local sites and partners.

Yet there are still opportunities. Returning to their original social purpose by leveraging their real estate and traffic flow is still an opportunity for many stores to restore profit. And by refocusing department store operations around a core customer segment, revenue and market share declines can be halted. For those players who do not succeed in making the transition, it is likely that they will be forced to exit. But the value of their underlying assets is simply too high to allow traditional state enterprise management to destroy it.

A TRADITIONAL FAVORITE UNDER THREAT

China's retail market is growing fast but department stores are missing out. Challenged by modern specialty and hypermarket formats, department stores are losing share fast. Unless they shape up, many could be sold off or driven into bankruptcy.

China's retail market is one of the largest and fastest growing in the world. In the 1990s, China's retail sales grew at 7%, on average, compared to 4% for the U.K. or 2% for Mexico. By 2000, it was larger than the retail markets of Germany, the U.K. or all Latin American countries combined. Now projected to continue to grow at the rate of 7% a year, by 2010 the retail market could top $650 billion in size, amounting to 80% of retail sales in Japan today. Furthermore, new market development since 2000 will account for almost half of this figure.

The department store, defined as a store with a sales area of at least 2,500 square meters, selling mainly non-food merchandise and having at least five product lines in different departments, has long been a mainstay of the market. Department stores were introduced in the early 1900s – they were hubs of commerce and entertainment, providing goods and services to the urban elite. During the era of central planning, their role expanded to include serving as the main point of distribution for manufactured consumer goods in urban areas. Today the country has about 7,000. Most are very small, averaging only $3.7 million (RMB31 million), one-tenth the sales of the average hypermarket in China.

Although they are generally chaotic, muddled environments, these stores still enjoy customer loyalty and are perceived as convenient, one-stop shops that ensure a degree of quality. Before the expansion of entertainment choices, department stores were a popular destination for family weekend outings, a tradition that persists today. Even in affluent markets such as Beijing, Shanghai and Guangzhou, comparatively sophisticated consumers still frequent department stores for much of their important shopping. Department stores have in particular retained their traditional attractiveness in apparel, shoes, accessories and cosmetics. They still account for the sale of approximately 35% of durable goods and clothing in China. Thanks to the high traffic, Chinese department stores achieve one of the highest rates of space productivity for department stores in the world, even though prices of the goods sold are moderate. This translates directly into a higher-than-expected return on investment.

On the other hand, few department stores have modern operations. Mainly owned by state-owned retail conglomerates, which control a portfolio of formats, department stores have not made significant changes in their operations since the days of state planning. Most employ a concession-based model. As a result, department store floor managers act more as landlords to collect rent than as true merchandisers. Product selection is spotty, service is poor and merchandising and category management is weak to non-existent. Promotional and market research is limited and there is little understanding of the needs of the end-customer. Corruption is also rife in companies that still employ traditional state-enterprise compensation systems with limited incentives. Managers benefit from their positions as opposed to their performance – for example, in kickbacks from concessionaires. Finally, few local retailers have invested in large-scale renovation to keep the shopping atmosphere up to date. Says the chairman of one Shanghai retailer: "Traditional department stores have an edge in terms of location and knowledge of the local market. But they have to adjust their management and operation concepts."

Thus, while still popular, department stores in China face a plateau in growth due to competition. Hypermarkets, supermarkets, discounters, convenience stores and specialty stores are all growing faster than traditional formats.[2] The development of these new formats has been extraordinarily rapid – within 10 to 15 years, China has seen the emergence and rise of modern formats, creating intense format competition. Global players have seen China as a testbed for new concepts, particularly given the low level of innovation among domestic players. And the domestic market has proved open to these new trends. In the U.S., by contrast, this trend took 40 years from the advent of discount retailers to the development of category killers.

This growth has come partly at the expense of department stores, which have steadily declined in popularity over the 1990s. To quote an official of the Shanghai Commerce Commission: "Now people choose to buy a lot of daily necessities at supermarkets, which offer low prices, rather than in department stores." In 2000, department stores contributed only 25% of the country's total retail sales, compared to 40% at the beginning of the 1990s.[3]

Specialty stores in particular have risen quickly, already achieving dominance in electronic goods and home appliances in Beijing, Shanghai and Guangzhou. In a survey in Shanghai, less than 25% of respondents indicated that they were most likely to buy these goods in department stores. Specialty stores are now achieving nationwide scale. Beijing Guomei, for example, has grown at 50% annually from 1998 to 2002, and by 2002 earned revenues of over $845 million (RMB 7 billion). Hypermarkets are, however, perhaps the most serious longer-term threat to department stores. They have

Convenience Stores in China

Beginning in the late 1980s China's cities offered the right conditions for the growth of convenience stores (defined as a shop selling a wide range of goods, with extended selling hours). A growing affluent middle class sought convenience, due in part to increasingly long working hours. There was also a traditionally high population density and a large amount of foot traffic in business and shopping districts. Consequently, beginning in the early 1990s operators such as Lawson's, 7-Eleven and Basics began opening the first stores. Local competitors quickly joined, many with little prior retail experience – for example, dairy, tobacco and urban development companies. Convenience stores have been growing at 15% a year, double the growth rate of the overall market.

With rapid growth, though, has come overcapacity. Convenience stores are now challenged to adopt a very tight geographic focus and concentrate on operational details, particularly management of pricing, store design and sourcing. A distinctive positioning is needed to attract demanding urban consumers. Typically, supply management can be substantially improved. Mistakes to avoid are an over-reliance on manufacturer concessions and consignment, too broad a product range, reliance on random direct store or warehouse deliveries, and replenishment of fast-moving goods before stock runs out.

already taken significant share from China's supermarkets. Many derive over 30% of their revenues from non-food items, and in major markets are coming to dominate the household goods category.

CONSOLIDATION LIKELY TO COME

Looking forward, the picture for department stores looks bleak. Sales are expected to grow only moderately at 2% a year versus market growth of more than 6%, as are average sales per store. The environment will be even tougher as demand is likely to slow down in Tier 1 cities – only Guangzhou could potentially support new stores at current GDP levels. New store opportunities in Beijing and Shanghai will come only as GDP rises.[4]

With lower demand, urban capacity could outpace demand across all formats.[5] In Shanghai, shopping malls will add a staggering 170% of current capacity in the next three years. Real estate developers have already initiated projects without securing tenants, which is likely to lead to a plethora of nondescript retail offerings executed in a haphazard fashion. Major developments that lack anchor tenants or are situated away from major pedestrian traffic malls are already seen as white elephants.

And foreign competition is coming with the promise of retail and wholesale liberalization following WTO entry. B&Q, Europe's largest home improvement materials retailer, plans to double the number of its stores in China to 16 in 2003, on target to opening 60 stores in China by 2007. Total China sales in 2002 are expected to be about £100 million. In addition, the company's Shanghai joint venture, which manages four stores in the city, is expected to become profitable for the first time in 2002 after starting operations in 1999. Japanese specialty retailers of eyeglasses, jewelry, automotive goods and others also plan to accelerate store openings in China to capitalize on the rapid growth in local purchasing power. Paris Miki, Japan's largest specialty retailer of eyeglasses, will open 50 stores in China by 2004 on the way to 200 in 2006. Sales are expected to hit ¥6 billion when the expansion is completed. Likewise, jewelry retailer Tasaki Shinju, automotive goods retailer Yellow Hat, and home-improvement retailer Komeri have all announced aggressive expansion plans. Even the Internet may come to supplement or supplant department stores over time as catalog shopping becomes a reality.

With falling market share, department stores now face a stark choice between reform and exit. Returns are dropping as intensifying competition squeezes department store operating margins. More than a third of Shanghai's 700 department stores lost money in 2001 and average profit margin was about 2.7%. For many large department stores, returns have dropped as revenue per square meter has declined and only floor space expansions have allowed total revenues and profits to be maintained. Where market expansion opportunities have been limited, department store bankruptcies and buyouts have occurred, including one of China's first stock market delistings – Zhengzhou Baiwen after three consecutive years of losses.[6]

There is tremendous scope for industry consolidation across formats in China. The top 50 players in China's retail market account for less than 5% of the market, as opposed to 30% in the U.S. (Exhibit 5.2). Many of the top local chains are located in areas around Shanghai and Jiangsu, but local players are relatively small by global standards and have far to go before they can match the size of global companies. An example is Lianhua which in 2000 had $1.3 billion (RMB11 billion) in sales and over 1,000 stores, including its joint ventures with Carrefour. But Lianhua's total sales amount to those of only 20 Wal-Mart superstores. In another instance, Carrefour's average sales per hypermarket worldwide are more than twice that of leading local player Hualian. Also, Carrefour has over 580 hypermarkets compared to Hualian's 20.

Rolling up the industry could create mega-players able to leverage purchasing, merchandising and investment economies of scale to build competitive advantages. Scale players also find it easier to build preferred relationships with government owners to get the preferred locations, build brands cheaper, and access a pipeline of human resources ahead of the competition. These relationships are also valuable after the transaction to ensure favorable zoning, transport and other commercial support from local government that can mean life or death to a retailer.

However, local players' ability to raise new financing on their own is limited. Opening a hypermarket, for example, costs around $7.8 million (RMB 65 million); $4.2 million (RMB35 million) in capital expenditure and $3.6 million (RMB30 million) in initial inventory. But annual margins for local retail players are only 10% of that. So local players tend to borrow heavily, and barely break even after interest charges. In 2001, Chinese retailers showed low debt-servicing ability, with an Earnings Before Interest, Taxes, Depreciation and Amortization (EBITDA) to interest ratio of 2.6 compared to seven for international players: anything under three is considered risky in the international industry. Short-term debt accounts for the vast majority of Chinese retailers' liabilities, making them vulnerable to withdrawal of credit lines.

Thus, local and international financial players have become aware of this opportunity and are already teaming up with retail management groups to buy out and reshape local retailers. Carlyle Group, a global private equity

Exhibit 5.2 China's highly fragmented retail market offers opportunities for industry consolidation

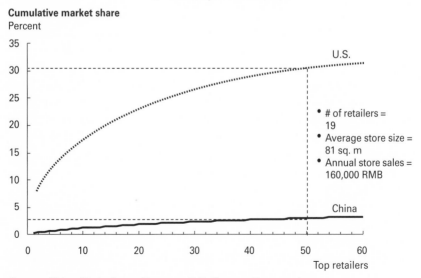

Source: China Chain Store Almanac; U.S. Census; Euromonitor

firm, bought out the Taiwanese entrepreneurs who founded Pacific Department Stores in 2000. China Retail Management, a fund owned by AIG Investment and companies designated by the State Economic and Trade Commission, has invested in supermarkets, hypermarkets, convenience stores and photograph distribution businesses. To quote its president, Allan Liu: "China's retail sector has great potential, but local companies don't have the know-how to compete effectively against the large foreign chains with significant capital and experienced management. Although many local retailers would probably prefer to raise funds on the stock market and keep their own brands, Chinese retailers are likely to fetch a better return by selling to foreign retailers than listing shares."[7]

RESTORING PROFITABILITY TO THE SECTOR

In this dire context, department stores need to move quickly to restore profitability. Two strategies can help: refocusing on the core customer, and leveraging the core locations. Those who do not get the message are likely to be snapped up by aggressive consolidators.

Refocusing on Core Customers

Internationally, only department stores that select a range of brands defined specifically for a unique target customer segment can retain customer loyalty. Today, department stores provide something for everyone. Tomorrow, they need to provide everything for someone with a truly distinctive value to survive.

A customer-driven approach has been the dominant trend in department stores globally for some time. Most mainstream department stores that have built their proposition along wide product assortments and limited brands face tough competition from specialty stores. Targeted stores that offer many brands within a smaller number of product categories are more likely to be able to defend encroachment by other formats. In China, this approach historically was not adopted as it ran fundamentally counter to the supply-driven mentality of a planned economy. In an environment where supply is scarce, tailoring an offer to a single customer segment made no sense. Instead, department stores simply stocked what the state system provided – customers were happy to get whatever was available.

The new competitive environment means that the same international lessons increasingly apply to China. Customers are no longer a homogeneous mass – entirely new segments have emerged with increased prosperity. Chinese consumers are becoming better educated and are enjoying a new lifestyle thanks to smaller family sizes. The number of affluent consumers, defined as households with annual income above US\$3,900, is growing rapidly. Only 17 million Chinese had an annual income of this amount in 2001. But this number will swell to 39 million by 2006, amounting to growth at the rate of 18% a year. This is a far higher growth rate than the market average growth of 5%, reflecting the disproportionate spending power of the affluent segment.

And, as happened in advanced markets about 20 years ago, as working hours and prosperity increase, the Chinese are more and more willing to pay for convenience and brands. For example, in one recent urban survey, Shanghai and Beijing consumers ranked fashion higher than quality when buying clothes, believed that famous brands provide better quality and said they were willing to pay a premium for products that helped them save time. Higher-income and better-educated consumers constituted up to 35% of the total shoppers in the study. These consumers like to try out new products, favor foreign brands, and can access foreign media.[8] Without a deep selection of the types of goods and services these customers want, department stores risk losing their loyal customers to the specialty stores.

Even in Tier 2 and undeveloped Tier 3 cities, which offer the remaining untapped opportunities, a customer-focused strategy will be needed to achieve sustainable economics. Break-even sales are not appreciably lower in Tier 2 or 3 cities than in Tier 1 cities. True, there will be savings in rent and wages. But these will not compensate for higher price pressure and the lower ticket size in Tier 2 and Tier 3 cities. And infrastructure is less developed, making it difficult to organize purchasing networks.[9]

Pacific Department Stores is an example of how successfully executing a core customer-focused strategy can yield success. Pacific is the most successful department store chain in Shanghai as measured by profitability. Focused largely on the high-income youth (aged 18 to 30) segment, it dominates this niche with a disproportionate share of both traffic and spending. Again to quote the Shanghai Commerce Commission: "Overseas retailers, which have brought along the latest global fashion trends as well as top brands and new management ideas, have sent the city's traditional department stores into a limbo."

To succeed in this approach, a first step for many state-owned department stores is to establish market research departments to begin to understand the customer. Extensive focus groups and quantitative research is needed to understand who is the target customer, which product categories have the greatest potential and how to rebuild the product offering. This research often reveals surprising findings when real numbers on spending are matched to actual traffic in the store.

Learning from Hypermarkets

The success of foreign hypermarkets shows how tailoring the formula to a specific customer segment can make a dramatic difference in profitability and share. Hypermarkets are the fastest-growing retail format in China with year-on-year growth of over 60%. Shanghai and Beijing both have over 50 hypermarkets; secondary cities such as Qingdao or Xian have 20 each. Hypermarkets' success has come from luring customers from supermarkets, whose growth is now projected at a meager 3%. While average ticket sizes are somewhat lower for supermarkets, at RMB50 ($6.0) versus RMB102 ($12.3) for hypermarkets, it is the far lower number of visitors per store (1.5 million versus 2.9 million) that drives the success of hypermarkets. Hypermarkets also have substantial potential to grow as the average basket size in China is relatively small. Average tickets in China are 59% less than in other parts of the world. Lower tickets make hypermarkets in China 65% to 70% less productive in terms of sales than hypermarkets in the U.S.

Foreign players have been the leaders in the development of hypermarkets and have been able to attract customers because of superior product and price offers. On high-volume items such as fresh food and dairy, foreign players have lower prices than locals. Research in Shanghai showed that overall prices are 8% to 10% lower in foreign hypermarkets than in local markets. This is true for both foreign and joint-venture products, such as Lux soap, and local products like Nongfushanquan bottled water. Meanwhile, on lower-volume items such as general merchandise and apparel, lower-volume sales for foreign players are improved through better assortment plays.

As a result, despite high capital expenditures, foreign hypermarkets at maturity enjoy attractive returns. Pretax return on invested capital is around 30% for these foreign players, compared to 9% for locals. Operating margins are 2.4 percentage points higher for foreign than local players, reflecting lower merchandise costs and better category management. Large negative working capital enhances capital turnover and reduces the burden of higher fixed costs for foreign players. And salaries are a full percentage point lower for foreign than for local players, reflecting their greater operating efficiencies. These economic positives outweigh foreign players' slightly higher operating costs for store investment-related depreciation, premium location rents, and store expenses, including store promotions at 13.7% of sales compared to 13% for local players.

For example, one store discovered that its core customer was the local Chinese housewife aged 24 to 50. These so-called traditionalists, while not as wealthy as high-income shoppers, constituted 30% to 35% of the total urban market but 60% of the spending in the store. This customer base was also relatively attractive as per-person spending was high. They were also found to be quite loyal, being skeptical about new products and preferring local offers and media. On the other hand, the store management was surprised to find that tourists, whom they had thought were the majority, accounted for less than 30% of spending and said that they were coming to the store because they saw locals there!

With greater customer insight, stores can redesign the shopping environment to be consistent with the target segment's needs and values. New initiatives should focus on how to deepen and extend this customer franchise with new products and services. The same department store, for example, found a terrific opportunity to better serve its core franchise of housewives by introducing the city's largest baby center. This would allow it to expand its space by 20% without cannibalizing revenues from other parts of the store. Meanwhile, it planned to take advantage of a new subway development by strategically locating attractive entertainment areas to pull traffic to the store from the subway entrance.

Finally, format winners know that the key to delivering operating improvements is not a system but a trained, capable cadre of managers. Winners must be able to change existing purchasing and merchandising management arrangements in order to deliver on the core, customer-focused, value proposition. Throughout the Chinese retail industry, individuals who can develop and run a commercial retail business are at a premium. Carrefour, for example, has effectively leveraged its network of Asian stores to bring in management with experience in emerging markets. In department stores, some current managers may have the potential to do the job but need greater transparency and oversight to improve performance.

Leveraging the Core Location

An alternative strategy for department stores is to leverage their under-appreciated assets. Many department stores have a central location in prime commercial areas. Leveraging this to introduce new functionality in entertainment and food and beverage could be another attractive opportunity to serve the core customer. Today, China's retail areas are often devoid of supporting functions – on many major commercial streets over 80% of revenues come from retail-related businesses. Entertainment, catering and green space per capita lag behind global comparables. And even in the new shopping malls there is a dearth of attractive F&B and cultural activities.

Even more radically, with the kind of traffic these commercial locations generate – in some cities, over a half million visitors per day on a weekend – there is also a terrific opportunity to both provide a better shopping experience and boost revenues by introducing new commercial concepts. These concepts do not necessarily have to be confined to the department store core customer segment. For example, if the store is focused on middle-aged women, a separate building could be established to serve the youth segment, which typically does not want to shop where its parents do. Likewise, entertainment concepts such as multiplexes can be located off the main drag but near enough to allow for access. Even office buildings can be co-located, as office workers enjoy access to local shopping and F&B outlets.

This development path requires developing a new real estate capability that the typical department store may not have. Letting the department store floor manager design the office building, or even a retail extension, is unlikely to succeed. While office residents may appreciate the downtown location, they may not wish to be associated with the department store's brand name. Successful examples of this kind of development model, however, do exist. For example, in Hong Kong, the Mass Transit Rail Corporation is one of the largest commercial developers in the Special Administrative Region. Its real estate group, completely independent of its rail business unit, builds and in some cases operates housing, commercial and retail projects adjacent to the mass-transit railway stations.

Where Is the Industry Going

What, then, could the department store industry look like in 10 years? Undoubtedly the shift from comprehensive to targeted stores will be well under way. The most successful ones will be part of multifunctional commercial complexes that provide a dynamic hub to urban districts. Many will also lose the shelter of the state umbrella, mostly through buyouts, some through listings. Managers who can build a strong brand will be in great demand from developers seeking proven retailing concepts to anchor otherwise speculative retail projects. Some former department store managers are already organizing themselves as management groups to take over under-performing retail assets and turn them around. Finally, foreign players will undoubtedly control many of the most attractive assets. But it is unlikely that there will not also be at least a few strong local groups. These will need to have both deep pockets and truly world-class expertise to maintain profitability in this demanding industry.

✳   ✳   ✳

With the imperative of rising competition, department store players must act now to define their role. Value inherent in today's department stores will rapidly erode without significant performance improvement. On the other hand, those who do succeed in developing a winning turnaround formula could lead a consolidation of the industry nationwide.

REFERENCES

1. The only other major opportunities in the domestic market open to the oil companies are gas, petrochemicals and diversification. In some cases, the latter is purely opportunistic — both CNPC and CNOOC have launched life-insurance businesses in partnership with global insurers who see them as "safe" but well-connected companies who are unlikely to interfere in the business. However, in others this is not so much an opportunity as a requirement in order to earn a return on traditional assets. Most of the non-listed businesses of the oil companies are in various service areas, such as drilling and machinery. These service businesses need to develop their own growth strategies to survive.

2. Hypermarkets are defined as stores with a retail sales area of over 2,500 square meters, devoting at least 35% of selling space to non-food items. Supermarkets are defined as stores with a selling area of between 400 and 2,500 square meters, selling approximately 70% of food items.

3. *Shanghai Daily*, September 16, 2002, p. 2.

4. China's retail structure has three tiers. Almost half of all retail sales – 45% – is concentrated in the top two tiers comprising 34 cities. These Tier 1 and Tier 2 cities have historically been growing at 17% to 19% a year, faster than the overall market growth of 15%. The first tier is the Big Three, the large cities of Beijing, Shanghai and Guangzhou. Tier 2 comprises three categories — the rapidly growing cities of Tianjin and Shenzhen, which are likely to match the Big Three in size by 2010; the large but slightly poorer markets like Kunming; and the niche markets like Xiamen which have wealthy consumers but a small market size.

5. Shanghai today already has almost five times the number of convenience stores per dollar of GDP as Hong Kong and over twice that in Taipei or Tokyo. In Beijing, there are three times as many supermarkets per person as in Hong Kong and over 10 times as many as in Taiwan.

6. Operating margins for supermarkets in China average around 1%, compared to 5% for those in the U.S. As a result, Chinese supermarkets do not earn a return on capital. A typical local hypermarket operates on a 0.5% margin and generates an EBITDA of around $725,000 (RMB6 million), again substantially lower than the international equivalents. Foreign companies are not immune from the impact of price competition. In convenience stores, for example, 7-Eleven in Guangdong only achieved breakeven after establishing 72 stores and nine years of investment. In Shanghai, Lawson was still operating in the red after six years, despite having 87 stores and a strong domestic partner.

7. *Asian Wall Street Journal*, 5 September 2002, p. M5.

8. In the study, adventurers constituted 10% to 15% of urban consumers and were typically fashion-conscious and trendy high-income earners, usually white collar,

often employed by foreign companies. Improvement seekers accounted for 15% to 20% of the urban market, were quality-conscious, high-income, white-collar executives, working in both foreign and Chinese private enterprises, and also had access to foreign media. The balance were traditional shoppers, more interested in local offerings of well known brands. Finally, the disadvantaged, typically medium- to low-income blue-collar workers in state enterprises or retired, comprised the low end of the market but, being extremely price-sensitive, were unlikely to be attractive to most retailers.

9. In hypermarkets, for example, only a limited number of stores could break even in Tier 3 cities where local retailers currently dominate: typically each city could support only one or two such stores on current economics.

6

Modernizing Services

The newest sectors of the Chinese economy are those that meet the expectations of a generation that suddenly has disposable income and wants to spend it. Media, entertainment and personal finances are booming in China and the party has just begun. However, those who wish to participate need to be committed for the long run as the environment is shifting and competition is already intense.

China's fund management industry has been successful in propelling the growth of China's stock markets. However, as the market matures, they will face new competitive, regulatory and customer challenges. Only a risk-based approach will provide a sustainable basis for profitability. Winning firms need to decide where and how they will develop their own risk-based portfolio – the industry of tomorrow is unlikely to look anything like that of today.

China's media industry is a paradox – it is the largest market in Asia yet the poorest performing. Years of state subsidies and control have left it peculiarly underdeveloped, with a dearth of high-quality content and a plethora of local channels. But change is knocking at the door as consumers, fresh technology and domestic and international competition are all pushing the industry into a competitive market environment. Winners in this new market will be those with distinctive content and able to find and target a programming segment. Content will be king in China and media players need to start now to capture their audience.

6.1 MANAGING CHINESE FUNDS

China's fund management industry has succeeded in propelling the growth of China's stock markets. However, as the market matures, it will face new competitive, regulatory and customer challenges. Fund managers fear both a potential market crash and increasing margin pressure, at a time when their core franchises are being eroded. Maintaining share and profitability will require hard choices around role, focus and skill set for incumbents. The winners will be those who best understand their customers rather than those who promise attractive but impossible returns.

GETTING RICH IS GLORIOUS

China needs an efficient stock market. The development of the stock market since its opening in 1990 has been a key benchmark in the country's reform. Chinese politicians, economists and academics have all been united in their opinion that China's stock market is essential to economic growth. Indeed, Jiang Zemin himself has said that public stock ownership is socialist in nature. China's macroeconomic goal is a slow but smooth transition over five to 10 years in which its capital markets integrate into the global system. A gradual lifting of capital controls will allow the government to maintain foreign investment interest while domestic investors maintain large liquid savings deposits in local banks and the stock market increases in size and depth.[1]

Today, the Chinese stock market seems well on its way towards that goal. China's stock market capitalization reached over $600 billion in value at the end of 2001, making it the largest in Asia after Japan. The number of domestic listed companies now exceeds 1,100 and there are over 66 million investor accounts. A strong legal, financial and accounting community is developing around the two stock exchanges in Shenzhen and Shanghai. Over $10 billion in new equity capital is raised domestically every year. IPOs amount to over 50% of issued equity in China, as compared to less than 30% in the U.S., even in the heyday of Internet offerings in 2000. In the late 1990s, in fact, China accounted for about 25% of Asian underwriting revenues, reflecting the dynamic growth in its IPO market.

China's asset managers and securities firms have been instrumental in the development of the market and have profited from its extraordinary growth. The largest now have both revenues and profits in the billions of dollars. Publicly reported margins at securities firms have been above 50%, and total profits topped $4 billion in 2000, an all-time high, having averaged above $2 billion annually throughout the late 1990s. The situation among fund managers is similar, if not even higher, as profits typically go unreported among these companies.

Securities firms are the largest of China's money managers. They are relatively concentrated, the top five underwriters handling 75% of the volume, compared to 54% in the U.S. and 59% in Hong Kong. Two types of underwriting licenses exist in China. Lead underwriters must have registered capital over RMB300 million ($36.3 million) and have maintained positive net income for the three years prior to application. To renew the license, a lead underwriter must have accomplished at least three deals as lead underwriter or six deals as co-underwriter in the past three years, with no deal with a subscription rate of less than 20% in the last six months. Simple underwriter's licenses have less stringent requirements but they can only participate when co-underwriting is legally required and are rarely involved in deal origination and structuring.

Trust and private funds make up another significant source of money in the market. In 2001, there were over 200 official trust funds and 3,500 private funds. These funds have predominantly corporate investors and have historically been relatively lightly regulated. Trust funds were the original entities chartered to conduct asset management by China's government. In 1987, the Bank of China, the China International Trust and Investment Corporation (CITIC) and several foreign institutions established the first trust fund. By 1993, over 70 trust funds with total assets of RMB5 billion ($604.2 million) were established and invested mostly in real estate and industrial developments. However, private funds now comprise the vast majority of fund management business with Assets Under Management (AUM) of over $55 billion. They include consulting, advisory, management and operating offices, or fund management departments of securities firms. Customers of private funds are mainly institutions such as listed companies, state enterprises and high-net-worth individual investors.

The balance of investments are held by closed-end mutual funds, initiated in 1993 when a RMB100 million (over $12 million) closed-end fund with an eight-year maturity was listed in Shanghai. The mutual fund industry in China is in its infancy with only $10 billion under management, accounting for 2% of total equity market capitalization compared to 11% in Taiwan and 50% in Hong Kong, and less than 1% of assets compared to 10% of personal financial assets in the U.S. and 6% in Hong Kong. China's closed-end mutual funds are relatively large at around RMB2 billion (over $240 million). The top five mutual funds control 80% of AUM, compared to 33% in the U.S. The shareholders of these mutual funds are primarily securities and trust firms.

BUT THE SYSTEM IS FLAWED

China's stock market is, however, deceptive. First, the market is actually quite undeveloped. Retail investors drove much of the growth in the 1990s, today making up over 80% of the investment in Chinese stock markets. These investors have lacked investment alternatives – other than the stock market only real estate offered potential for significant returns in the 1990s. Bank savings rates are fixed at low levels. And most Chinese investors are confined to the local markets due to the Renminbi's non-convertibility.

Second, there has been a shortfall in supply. A quota system administered by local governments has historically restricted annual issuance volume and has biased listing opportunities towards state enterprises. Tradable shares account for only 33% of the total market capitalization in China, rendering individual stocks highly vulnerable to manipulation. The balance is in the hands of their state owners, creating potentially significant conflicts of interest with related parties. Meanwhile, trading volume has grown at a 36% annual rate. Velocity is now comparable to Taiwan and Korea (or the NASDAQ in 2000).[2] Subscription ratios of domestic IPOs in 2000 were exceeded by 200 times and in 2001, despite a falling index (19%), the differential between primary and secondary markets was maintained, as was the over-subscription rate for new IPOs.

Third, China's securities markets are today, by almost any definition, overheated. PE ratios average 40 to 50 compared to 10 to 18 in Hong Kong for the same companies. Yet the performance of the Chinese-listed companies is generally poorer than that of their Western counterparts (Exhibit 6.1). In one study, average Return on Equity (ROE) for listed companies in China was 7.5%, versus 16.3% in the U.S. Only 5.3% of listed companies in the U.S. made a loss, as opposed to 9.1% in China. And even sales grew faster in the U.S. than China – 16% versus 13%.

Fund managers and securities firms have gotten rich in many cases by taking advantage of this overheating. Trading strategies have relied largely on regulatory advantage and the personal networks of staff as opposed to true research, fund management and stock-picking capabilities. Systems boil down to commissions and deal-making is the predominant style; internal competition is rife. Selling skills are nascent and price-focused. AUM-based performance evaluation is an illusion and funds' shareholder interests are damaged due to the large amounts of kickbacks and trading costs.

More specifically, the biggest source of revenues and profits for securities firms and fund managers has been proprietary trading – up to 60% of annual revenues in the 1990s. IPOs have been one rich source of profit for securities firms, particularly for large players who have benefited from IPOs by building preferred relationships that allowed them to receive

Exhibit 6.1 Performance comparison of listed companies in China vs U.S.

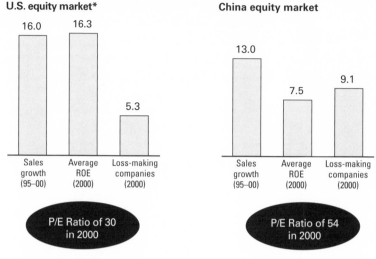

U.S. equity market*

China equity market

* NYSE listed companies

Source: Compustat; McKinsey analysis

preferential access to the IPO quotas allocated by the CSRC. Quotas in hand, securities firms have been able to negotiate favorable issuance prices, leading in turn to explosive stock price growth. In 2000, the average PE ratio on issuance stood at 31 compared to 54 in the secondary market. Same-day returns averaged 157% and 30-day returns 174%.

Likewise, in the fund industry local firms have often bought stocks at prices higher than their true value and personally split the difference, creating personal interest-driven portfolio strategies. Self-dealing is common. For stock they hold, funds sell and buy the same stock within the same day, creating artificial volume by placing buy and sell orders simultaneously. Funds may also sell shares held to other funds, sometimes run by the same fund management company, with the price (often inflated), time and, most importantly, the commission to fund manager agreed in advance. All closed-end funds have 15-year durations and, therefore, diminished short-term performance pressures. In 2000, for example, the industry averaged a 32% return compared to market index growth of 51%.

A DAY OF RECKONING AT HAND

Now, however, a change may be coming for the industry. Fund managers are caught between the Scylla of an impending market crash and the Charybdis of margin pressure. These threats in turn will force change on the fund management industry. Many funds, particularly those that have offered guaranteed returns, will be bankrupted. The remainder will have to relearn the basic principles of risk management to survive.

The short-term cause of a market crash would be a rapid increase in supply that punctures the bubble of high valuations as China is accelerating plans to sell stakes in its state-owned enterprises. At the end of 2000 only 36% of China's top 500 companies were listed. In contrast, in the U.S. 94% of the top 500 companies were listed. Within many major sectors such as banking, telecoms, airlines and utilities, less than 40% of the top 10 players ranked by revenues were listed by mid 2001. The government has now set an explicit target of reducing the percentage of non-tradable shares from 67% in 2000 to 30% in 2005. Why? China needs revenues from SOE share sales to fund its growing pension gap (Exhibit 6.2). Public pension payouts are likely to outpace contributions as early as 2004. By 2010 the deficit could be as high as $110 billion. To fund this gap, IPOs and sales of state shares in listed SOEs are needed.

Furthermore, a dramatic increase in listings of small and medium companies may occur as the IPO review process is shifted from a quota-based system to expert review. Historically, an annual IPO quota was given to each provincial government for it to allocate to companies it favored. As a result, small-to-medium-sized companies had few opportunities to list as

Exhibit 6.2   China's growing pension gap

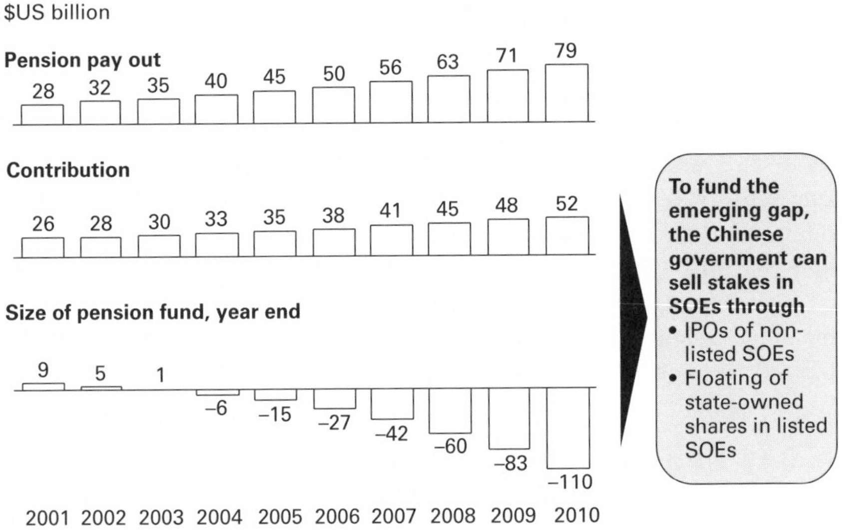

$US billion

Pension pay out

28 32 35 40 45 50 56 63 71 79

Contribution

26 28 30 33 35 38 41 45 48 52

Size of pension fund, year end

9 5 1 −6 −15 −27 −42 −60 −83 −110

2001 2002 2003 2004 2005 2006 2007 2008 2009 2010

To fund the emerging gap, the Chinese government can sell stakes in SOEs through
• IPOs of non-listed SOEs
• Floating of state-owned shares in listed SOEs

Source: Literature search; McKinsey analysis

quotas were allocated mainly to relatively large SOEs. This also made it difficult for smaller companies to attract venture capital given the risk that there would be no public market exit option. The CSRC will now directly review all listing applications and allow an expert panel to make the final decision on their listing. With the shift in the IPO allocation system to an expert review, medium-sized companies are likely to have a greater chance in the public markets. As a result, by 2005 up to 10% of mid-sized Chinese companies could be listed, generating over $140 billion in issuance from 500 to 1,000 companies.

Potential RMB convertibility on the capital account could make the situation even worse. At current PE ratios, allowing Chinese investors to invest abroad would result in large net capital outflows and lead to an immediate market crash. And even at "rational" PE levels following such a crash there will be only moderate foreign participation given the low level of transparency around Chinese companies.

In fact there has already been a warning of how the market crash could unfold. Government announced an initial experimental plan in June 2001, under which 10% of the total capital raised through IPOs and secondary issuance of state-owned companies was to be used to buy out state-owned shares, the revenue from which would go into the social security fund. The Shanghai Stock Exchange immediately began to slide from its peak at around 2,245 reaching 1,514 by October. The scheme was suspended at that point but when the sell-off resumes, further market slides appear inevitable.

Fund managers are equally concerned by ongoing margin pressure. The CSRC is moving to tighten enforcement, particularly on proprietary trading using clients' money, leading to a decline in profits of securities firms from this revenue source. Changes in rules on investment scope and custodians as well as in civil law will further formalize the fund industry and protect investor interests. Fund promoters will be required to call shareholders' meetings more frequently and over 50% of board members are required to be independent experts with over five years of related experience. Private funds will be legalized and regulated – the number of investors will be between two and 50 and with a minimum investment amount of RMB1 million (a little over $120,000). Trust funds are now expected to revert to trust businesses with a threshold for subscription of RMB10,000. Investors will be able to file lawsuits against fund managers, custodians and related parties for malpractices. These regulations are intended to help monitor fund managers' conduct and reduce malpractice.[3]

On the demand side, the increased presence of institutional investors, as well as high-net-worth individuals with access to international media, will put more pressure on market intermediaries to provide more sophisticated products and services. Domestic issuance will not exceed the capacity of China's retail market to absorb it. By 2005, equities will not exceed 12% of retail assets (as opposed to 17% in Taiwan in 2001). However, both domestic and foreign institutional investors will grow rapidly as insurance companies are allowed to invest in equities, pension reform creates huge pools of retirement funding, open-end mutual funds are introduced, and Qualified Financial Institutional Investors (QFII) are launched. With barriers to equity investment removed, institutional investors could represent up to 30% of the market by 2005.

Competition is also going to heat up. Domestically, the potential entry of commercial banks could add a formidable competitor to the fray. Banks have significant competitive advantages, even against large underwriters, particularly in distribution. China's entry into the World Trade Organization (WTO) will also spur competition. Joint-venture investment banks with foreign ownership limited to 33% are allowed to underwrite domestic shares within three years of WTO accession. Fund management joint ventures with up to 33% foreign participation are also allowed. From December 2004, joint-venture investment banks can conduct domestic share trading while the foreign share in fund management joint ventures can increase to 49%. In 2002, almost every major local securities firm had announced a joint venture with an international major bank or brokerage. HSBC, Fleming, Invesco, Schroders, National Mutual, Credit Suisse, Kleinwort Benson and Merrill Lynch are all already in, or on the point of signing, joint-venture agreements.[4]

Finally, costs will also rise as the cost of top investment bankers goes up and changes in pricing and placement approaches require international-standard investment banking skills. People costs could rise from today's 20% to 30% of revenues to 40%, still some way below the U.S. levels of typically over 50%. In addition, servicing costs will increase, as customers require more in the way of research and customer acquisition. Costs of branch networks will decrease but only very slowly and the IT and systems investments needed to compete are very large.

With all of these pressures, industry margins could drop from 50% in 2001 to 20% in 2005, more in line with the U.S. and Asia. As commissions decline, small players will become uneconomic unless they can justify a price premium through superior products. Proprietary traders who fail to develop true risk-management skills may also find themselves on the wrong side of the market trend. Deregulation of commissions will likely be the first impact on the industry as current commissions are significantly higher than international benchmarks – 40 to 50 basis points versus 10 to 15 in the U.S. With converging prices in the primary and secondary markets for IPOs, a large share of brokerage revenues generated through internal subscription to IPOs will disappear. No change is likely in issuance fees – while China's domestic issuance fees at 150 to 300 basis points are in line with Asian norms, they are substantially below U.S. levels.[5]

But if this outlook is combined with the likelihood of a market drop, things could look even worse. When faced with early withdrawals, firms will have no choice but to unwind the long-term positions they have had to take to sustain high-price stocks, which could occasion a vicious cycle of panic selling, ultimately leading to bankruptcies of highly leveraged firms. Fund managers typically offer a one-size-fits-all product, often guaranteeing returns between 10% to 15%, or a minimum guaranteed rate of return (5 to 10%) plus 20% to 50% profit sharing, and offering little guidance on the nature and type of investment risk they are taking. In a rising market, these guaranteed arrangements look like sure-fire ways to source low-cost capital. But when the market turns, for a firm that has a large number of guaranteed return contracts, even a small drop in performance could mean technical bankruptcy. The failure of GITIC was a salutary indicator that the Chinese government will not stand behind these firms when this happens.

NEW BUSINESS MODELS TO CONSIDER

International experience shows that when investors pile in for a seemingly guaranteed deal, the inevitable outcome is a market collapse when there are no greater fools left. This seems to be exactly what is likely to happen in China. Now as the market moves to a more rational basis, regulators and fund managers need a new business model for the fund management industry.

In principle, the management of risk should be the essence of any financial intermediary. Risk comes in many forms – operating, regulatory, market and environmental are only a few categories. World-class securities and asset-management firms understand and embrace these risks – being able to value, respond to and withstand the shocks of a volatile financial market is the hallmark of an outstanding financial institution. Risk management in its simplest terms means that financial intermediaries understand and are able to withstand market fluctuations they are exposed to – i.e. that they will be able to fulfill their commitments to their clients no matter what the state of the market. Excellent risk management allows the financial firm to profit from market volatility by seeing patterns and building skills to take advantage of these insights.[6]

In the new Chinese capital markets, fund managers will have to make choices about what kind of risks they will be able to manage and, by implication, what customer base and value-added they seek to provide. Fund management is essentially a service business – the winners will be those who provide the best value to increasingly differentiated customer segments. Players have to choose carefully which risks they can afford to take as investors realize that the one-size-fits-all guaranteed product is unlikely to provide security or success in the new market environment.

Building Credibility with Institutional Investors

Serving institutional investors is going to be the natural bent for fund managers and the trading departments of securities firms. Large, relatively sophisticated and active in the market, they would appear to be the best customers. However, serving them will not be easy. Today's salesforce needs to be retrained. New systems should be introduced. And developing the products themselves takes time.

Putting in basic risk-management controls on existing products is a first step. Many companies have only the most rudimentary notions of limits. Regular reports need to be generated and a committee of senior managers appointed to review on a weekly basis the limits in place. Often these reports need to be developed based on new information systems in a multi-year change program.

Another challenge is to develop products that are tailored to investor risk preferences. Some local trusts are already beginning to offer various high-tech, growth and restructuring funds. Potential convertibility of the Renminbi in the next five years could extend these funds overseas, calling for increased investment-management skills. Superior fundamental analysis and portfolio management, particularly in adverse markets, can improve returns. To quote one Chinese fund manager: "Foreign fund management companies can always maintain returns of their portfolios within the expected range under various market situations by being flexible and swiftly adjusting them. But we have no idea how to do this." Risk-management leveraging options or derivatives products can also enable more complex proprietary trading activities with less risk involved than simple position taking. While these products are not yet in the market, their emergence is likely in the next few years.

Finally, restructuring the salesforce is critical. Clients used to guaranteed rates of return will not easily accept new risk-based contracts, even if they contain greater upside. Salesforces will need to have a new level of professionalism as both institutional and high-net-worth individuals will look for specialized knowledge, integrated product offerings and multi-channel access to offset the lack of a "guarantee". Firms must shift customer acquisition away from turnover volume to asset accumulation. Fee income will also be a new focus – China's firms derive less than 10% of their income from fees (exclusive of trading commissions and underwriting fees), as compared to 35% to 45% for U.S. firms. This in turn is likely to require an upgrade to the caliber of people in the salesforce. Today's bankers tend to be well-connected individuals as opposed to experienced client or product specialists. This lack of specialization is reflected in the low personnel costs of Chinese firms. Salaries at Chinese investment banks range from 3% to 10% of those at their U.S. equivalents.

A Choice of Retail Role

Those firms who do not focus on institutional investors face a choice of roles. In retail markets, a split between product development and product distribution is likely. Some players will act as manufacturers of products intended to help investors understand and mitigate risk. Others will be more distributors of products developed by others and differentiate themselves on the quality and breadth of their network.

Regulators are already encouraging open-ended mutual funds to develop safe and effective products for retail investors. Open-end mutual funds started in September 2001 and are expected to remedy the industry's problems of excessive trading volumes, earnings manipulation and trading malpractices. The CSRC selected Hua An and Nan Fang to be the first two open-ended funds. Hua An signed a cooperation with Flemings in late 2000, while Nan Fang formed a cooperation with HSBC, established a quantitative securities analysis system based on EVA and a liquidity control based on ECP.

Things have not gone as smoothly as expected, however. In September 2001, the two open-ended funds were launched with fund sizes of around RMB 5 billion (over $60 million). Bank of Communications and Industrial and Commercial Bank of China were the main distributors of funds. The initial offer was only moderately successful and, in fact, Nanfang was under-subscribed. While retail investors were the main targets, institutional investors emerged as the majority shareholders. An adverse macro-economic environment post-September 11, along with an announcement by the Chinese government of issuance of RMB50 billion in debt, deterred some retail investors. Distribution by Bank of Communications did not adjust city quotas to reflect actual demand. Finally, retail investors have an expected annual return of 30%, much higher than the promised 15% returns of open-ended funds, particularly with perceived high load fees of 150 bps for management (compared to 100 bps in the U.S.), 100 to 200 for purchase, 50 for redemption and 25 for custody.

Distribution reach is also a critical factor in the fund industry. As mutual funds develop, branches will be needed to address the needs of customers who want face-to-face contact. Charles Schwab, for example, boasts 310 branches in the U.S. used primarily for information gathering, account opening, seminars and deposits. New entrants such as commercial banks can leverage their existing branch networks. Large securities firms also have nationwide retail networks that could effectively serve retail investors, who still form the bulk of the market. However, potential fund distributors would be well-advised to seek partnerships with fund manufacturers before investing in new business development. The challenge of retraining existing bank workers is tremendous.

TREADING CAREFULLY AS A FOREIGNER

Foreigners, meanwhile, must tread carefully to establish profitable execution capability. Most are forming joint ventures with domestic fund management firms and seeking to leverage the existing networks of local partners while transferring overseas portfolio investment skills. Picking a local partner, however, should be driven by considerations of which are really ready to change rather than by sheer market size and presence, which may in fact be liabilities in a fast-changing market.

Ultimately, ability to build a talented local skill pool will drive foreign firms' success. Doing so will be a function of the brand and commitment that they display in the China market. Far-sighted players are already trying to develop products to sell directly to high-net-worth Chinese investors with overseas accounts. In doing so they can leverage their existing infrastructure and product knowledge to build the brand and customer base in a low-risk approach.

※　　※　　※

As the market drops and competition intensifies, winning in China's capital market is going to be much more about meeting investor needs and much less about taking big risks. Winners will be those who best understand and execute exactly what their clients want, rather than promising returns that can't be delivered.

6.2 PORTMAN HOLDINGS: BUILDING THE COMMUNITY

An interview with Jack Portman, Vice-Chairman Portman Holdings

The Portman Group is known internationally for its innovative landmark commercial developments. Jack Portman, developer and procurer of business license 003 in Shanghai for Shanghai Center's owner, Seacliff, was one of the earliest investors in China. He and Portman Holdings, a company his father John Portman founded and of which he is still Chairman, have designed and developed some of the most distinctive buildings in China. He shared his experiences and perspectives on the trends and success factors of the real estate business in China.

Q **Let's start by talking about how you got interested in China. How did it happen?**

A Each summer during college, I traveled. In 1969, when I was 20 years old, I traveled for three months through Japan, Taiwan, Hong Kong, Bangkok, Singapore, Bali, Cambodia, India, Cyprus, Egypt, Israel and Greece. That trip exposed me to China, peripherally, for the first time. Initially, it was the existing political process, the separation from the rest of the world, and the ambivalent Russian connection that provoked my fascination with China, a fascination which, even now, is growing.

During that trip, I went on a three-week Sunrise Holding tour in Japan by JTB. I visited the Osaka World's Fair (the predecessor of the World Expo which is going to be held in Shanghai in 2010) and convinced the Fair officials to "loan" me a Russian flag (I was collecting flags). My next stop was Taipei, where I wanted to see first hand what Chiang Kai Shek had done in building Taiwan. On my third night there, I returned to my hotel room and found the police waiting for me. They asked me to give them the Russian flag. Apparently, the maid had gone through my luggage and found it. I told them I was leaving Taiwan the next day so no one would see it. They insisted that I give it to them. So I traded it to them for four Taiwanese flags, one for all of my traveling companions. That was my first-hand experience in learning about the conflict between Russia, Taiwan and China. Next, I went to Hong Kong and, while there, I bought something at the Yue Hwa Department Store, a PRC department store. When I asked them to ship it to me in the U.S., they refused, declaring that they wouldn't ship anything to a "reactionary government" like the United States. I was unaware that the U.S. was a "reactionary government". So again I was exposed, through a direct personal experience, to a very strong attitude which I had heretofore not known existed.

Those two events piqued my curiosity, so when I returned to school at Georgia Tech in the fall, I took a sociology course on the Chinese Cultural Revolution. I passionately absorbed all that I read. When I learned about the concept of sending children, or young adults, from the city to the countryside, and vice versa, so that they would better understand each other, I marveled at the cleverness of such a concept. Now this was during the 1960s, and at that time it seemed to me that this concept was a brilliant way of eliminating the class differences between people. Of course, I wasn't the one who had to endure it, and today this experiment is not considered a success.

Finally, there was Shanghai's aura of mystery, romance and intrigue. With all of these experiences, it created quite an enticing image in my mind of what China might be like, and therefore I was determined to find out more.

After graduation from Harvard Graduate School of Design, I went into our family business and, because of opportunities created by the oil embargo in the early 1970s, soon focused on creating opportunities in the Middle East, going from country to country – Egypt, Israel, Iran, Kuwait, Syria — and doing research on where and how to develop real estate, the process and methods. As I studied (while "holed up" in the old St. George Hotel in Lebanon because of bombings, riots and fires under way in the Beirut streets at that time), it occurred to me that our business, which is to either design buildings or develop them, could be done all over the world.

Around the time Ali Bhutto was in power, I was negotiating a deal in Karachi, working on a hotel casino project. Bhutto was a tolerant Muslim, hence the possibility of a casino. (I should have known better.) From Karachi, I had to make a decision whether to return home through Europe or through Asia. I returned via Hong Kong and Singapore, retracing part of the 1969 trip previously mentioned, and a honeymoon trip in 1973. I was amazed at what I saw compared to what I had seen previously.

In 1977, we had a request from Pontiac Land to compete for an Urban Redevelopment Authority hotel project in Singapore. We won, and this hotel is now the Regent Hotel. The following year, in 1978, I took a research and exploration trip with a colleague, Herb Lembcke, to learn more about the development potential and to meet people in Tokyo, Seoul, Taipei, Hong Kong, Manila, Kuala Lumpur, Bangkok and Singapore. Through various existing contacts which the company had at that time, we met as many new people as we could, people who we felt would have interest in working with us. We were quite fortunate because from that trip, 50% of the subsequent business we have done in those places has been with those people.

We had projects in Hong Kong and Singapore, so we opened an office in Hong Kong and I went there to live in 1979. The Hong Kong office focused on developing business opportunities throughout the ASEAN region and, from Hong Kong, I worked on the Shanghai Center deal in the beginning of '81. Shanghai Center didn't actually begin construction until '84 or '85; then it took another five years to build and finally opened in 1990.

Q **How about the changes between then and today? What's different now?**

A Today there is a great deal of competition; quantity is great; quality is not always so great. Political stability is no longer a concern. Changes do occur. In 1985, we started construction on Shanghai Center. Things looked great at that time. Tenants were very interested. However, in 1989, the Tiananmen Square incident destroyed all enthusiasm. We had just finished a $200 million project and we had no customers. Then, in 1991, Deng Xiaoping took his trip to the South and convinced people that they could do things that they were previously afraid to do. He gave them the freedom to make decisions. Now, everyone wants to do everything. During 1992 and 1993, Shanghai Center had among the highest retail, housing and office rates in the world. We were able to recover what we had lost because of Tiananmen, and because of the slow start. We quickly repaid all of the debt. Now, however, rents are 30% of what they once were. But, they are rising once again.

Consequently, China — Shanghai and Beijing, in particular — are very desirable places to build. Additionally, there is a very strong domestic demand today, and that will quickly dwarf the foreign demand.

Q **And was there enough demand to sustain it all or did you see a shakeout coming?**

A In 1996, I thought there was no way to sustain the market, that the overbuilding situation was going to be so overwhelming that we then began to look for other markets to develop. We picked India over Vietnam, opened an office in Mumbai, and spent seven years there. That experience was a success for our architectural firm since we designed the India School of Business in Hyderabad, and Wellington Mews in Mumbai for the Taj Hotel Group – a truly great organization! But, we were not successful from a development point of view as we were unable to attract any foreign capital to invest alongside of us in India because of legal, political and practical reasons. Maybe some day...

Q **What happened in India, and how do you compare India and China?**

A China is working because *everyone* really wants the system of growth and development to work. You have a political system where decisions can be made quickly and actions taken that are positive. In India, you have what they call a democracy, but it really is a democracy run amuck. With the exception of a few, too many people are trying to suit their own agendas, usually their own personal agendas. No political power is strong enough to enact change when there are so many "vested interests", people who want to keep things the same. They can't make a decision. They are crippled by the political system, and it seems hopeless because the impetus for change does not exist; so India does not get better, and can never compete with China. But in China, everybody wants it to get better. There is so much hope, optimism and enthusiasm here.

Q **The changes in China have been most noticeable in places like Shanghai but do you see it also in the interior?**

A Most of our work is in Beijing and Shanghai so I'm not sure I'm best to answer that question. We have also done architectural projects in Jinan, Hangzhou, Ningbo and a few other cities. The difference between the interior of China and Shanghai, Beijing, and the other coastal areas are that the latter started at a much higher price level – prices are higher, costs are higher. As the domestic economy gets stronger, there are more domestic people with wealth, it will spread out, and these interior cities will grow. In the U.S., even today, the opportunities in Kansas City are fewer than in Washington or Los Angeles. The coastal phenomenon spans from the beginning of time. The middle of the country never gets the same interest – it's less accessible and gets less exposure.

It is more attractive for local people to invest in the interior. Foreigners are mainly interested in big cities because they feel that an exit of their investment will be easier. Real estate is a local business. It's tough for foreigners to be successful on their own. The successful foreigners need to have the right kind of local partners.

Q **What do you look for in a local partner?**

A A local partner needs to have access to land, good working relationships with the municipal authorities, expertise in the development process, or access to capital. Of course, those who have all four of these do not need any assistance from an international developer such as ourselves.

We generally align ourselves with partners who have land and the government relationships. We are responsible for the design, development and management expertise necessary to complete projects, and we of course have access to various capital markets. Most importantly, however, the local partner must have a similar business philosophy and similar development objectives for any partnership to sustain long-term success.

Q **Do you see any changes in government attitude?**

A The government is becoming much more professional, much more sophisticated in its approach to dealing with development. There is an auction system being planned which will make the acquisition of land open and competitive. The difficulty with this is that the large, better capitalized companies such as the Hong Kong companies or international development funds will have a great advantage. The small entrepreneur, from where creativity normally comes, will find fewer and fewer opportunities.

Q **Stepping back, which of your projects do you feel have had the biggest impact?**

A Well, I like all of them. But the Shanghai Portman Centre certainly had tremendous impact because it was the first of its kind in China. The impact was that it made it easy for foreigners to come and work here. An opening market slogan was "Shanghai Centre – Where Anything is Possible" – and it was! It allowed foreigners to bring their money to invest in China. This allowed for development of other industries. Twelve years after opening in 1990, Shanghai Center is still competitive with the newest developments. The just-opened Bund Financial Center, developed by Sinar Mas of Indonesia, has very much helped the Huang Pu/ Bund area. The thing I like about that project is that it injects vitality into what was heretofore a dormant area. Nothing was happening down there, and that project will help start the re-development process. Bund Centre has more area of office space in it than the total area in all of the buildings along the Bund combined. And most of the latter office space is not to international standards.

Q **What do you feel differentiates what you do from other developers?**

A That is a very general question; the answer to which would vary depending on the circumstances. However, we seek the "first strike" advantage.

In addition, I think what contributes to our success is our design-focused development process which is based on a pedestrian, human orientation. Some developers are thinking about square meters, cost per meter and revenue per meter, or the materials on their facade. There is a big difference between "building-to-sell" versus "building-to-hold". We prefer to build-to-hold. We like to develop something that's big enough to sustain itself, where we can create a community within itself, with its own synergy, but also a place which becomes a catalyst for surrounding development. Creating this type of community, creating a "place" rather than a building, is key to our success. Plus, we can do this for less cost.

There is a certain Southeast Asian businessman, very successful in many businesses, who won't go in the Portman Centre because he thinks it is ugly and cheap because the exterior is painted. That's all he sees – because it's a concrete building, it must be cheap. Many Asian developers have a real affinity for marble and granite. It is important to use as good of a quality of materials as possible, but what really matters is what kind of place you have created, the sense of environment, and the atmosphere of the place which the people there enjoy. You can't really get a sense of the atmosphere from driving by a building at 40 miles per hour.

Q **Do you see more opportunities for this kind of development in China? Ten years from now, will there be more communities on this scale?**

A Yes, I think so. Why? The scale of development is increasing as is the number of available users – whether it's companies or individuals. People copy successful concepts, and a lot of these successful concepts have become clichés. We seek to evolve our concepts so that they are fresh.

Q **But will some survive?**

A The better ones will survive because in a way they are not really new – it's the way things have always been. In the old city-states, you had shopping on the ground, some commercial on the first and second floor, and then housing above that. It was the car that started to spread everything out and then created zoning, as we suddenly had the ability to travel distances. Let's live here, let's work there, let's shop somewhere else – it was separated by distance because you had the ability to get from one place to another. But in the process we created sterile, uninteresting environments. Now nobody wants to live there. Today in the U.S., young people don't want to live in the suburbs because they find it boring, even though their parents thought it was heaven. There is no culture or urban life in the suburbs. The urban community puts people face-to-face rather than car-to-car. And since it is more difficult to insult people face-to-face than driving by, it forces people to be more friendly! It isn't the façade of the building which brings people in, but the ground-floor community.

Q **How do you organize in China? How do you connect with the U.S. and your global offices?**

A We have both architecture and development offices in Shanghai. All of our offices are interconnected and interrelated. With email and our FTP site, we can work 24 hours a day. Recently, to complete a design competition, we went back and forth and did in four days what used to take two months.

Q **How about government relations? How do you manage that?**

A It's a lot harder to get access now than in the beginning. Originally when I came to Shanghai, it was simple to set appointments. There were fewer foreigners interested in Shanghai. Today it is the opposite. Shanghai is the magnet of world commerce. The importance of *guanxi* [relationships] cannot be underestimated. A foreigner has a more formal relationship, less off-the-cuff than a local would. In the West, you are evaluated on what you do and how good you do it. In China, there is more and more of this qualitative evaluation, but *guanxi* still plays a role.

Q **Over time, do you see this changing? As people start to have more of a track record, will decisions be more fact-based?**

A Well, we have a solid track record and a lot of people now come and want us to join them. They don't want the money; just the expertise, the name, the brand. They think that makes it easier to sell their projects. But when you have a brand you have to protect it. For that reason, we are selective about the people and the projects on which we work. This business requires a lot of patience, mutual respect and confidence because the gestation period to build the type of projects we build is at least four to five years, and in some cases as much as 10 years.

Q **Last question. What do you know now that you wished you had known when you started?**

A I wish I had built upon our momentum which we had established during the 90s rather than diverting our focus to other areas of the world.

6.3 TRANSFORMING THE MEDIA

China's media industry is a paradox – it is the largest market in Asia yet the poorest performing. Years of state subsidies and control have left it peculiarly underdeveloped, with a dearth of high quality content and a plethora of local channels. But change is knocking at the door as consumers, fresh technology and domestic and international competition are all pushing the industry into a competitive market environment. Winners in this new market will be those with distinctive content able to find and target a programming segment. Content will be king in China and media players need to start now to capture their audience.

MEDIA TRADITIONALLY A PROTECTED SECTOR

China's multimedia industry has historically been one of its most protected. The state has funded it directly in line with political priorities. Cable subscription fees are set at artificially low levels – basic subscription fees run to around RMB 8 (less than $1) to RMB 15 (less than $2) per month. Thus China has a well-developed cable television (cable TV) network, which now reaches over 90 million households to achieve a penetration of well over 30%. Satellite TV reaches an additional 230 million households, achieving in total a 95% penetration rate and making China's total television household market the largest (almost 60%) of the Asian total.

Not surprisingly, then, China's media companies lack any experience of developing and marketing programs under competitive conditions. Chinese cable TV systems are typically owned by local or provincial entities. These systems are in turn closely related to affiliated program consolidators, thus creating a tidy local monopoly on distribution. Local government control of media has also meant that few companies have developed economies of scale. Most of China's 2,000-plus producers are small scale and unable to effectively launch new products. Only one media player, Central China Television (CCTV), has national reach. As a result, China's various media entities have little commercial incentive or ability.

This lack of incentive is particularly evident in content – few local media companies have developed a reputation for quality content. Even when pushed by the government to fill local content quotas, media companies have often resorted to importing cheap product rather than invest. In part, this is due to the culture of piracy that permeates the industry. Today licensed goods amount to less than one-eighth of the total CDs sold in China and less than one-tenth of the videos. In 1998, MPAA ranked China as the fifth-biggest piracy market, with annual losses due to piracy running to $120 million.

Instead, media companies today act more as conduits for both government propaganda and for government investment, which is in turn biased to hardware and infrastructure assets. China was one of the world's largest spenders on communications and media infrastructure in 2000 and 2001. Investment funds are used to expand physical networks both through own-build and acquisition. Media companies have also been among the most aggressive state enterprises in developing real estate around their core media holdings.

As a result, total sales of entertainment multimedia are under $2 billion and less than 0.1% of GDP, compared to 0.4% or even greater in the U.S., Japan and Korea. Even these low levels of multimedia revenues, though, have been enough to create attractive conditions for the local broadcasting monopolies. Total multimedia-industry profits amounted to $500 million in 2000, and the largest media groups took the greater share, which was promptly remitted to their governmental masters.

BUT NOW THE MARKET WANTS MORE

Now, however, the cosy conduit monopoly is being challenged. Consumers are demanding more from the industry. With the growth of cable, and the entrance of DSL and satellite, competition for the audience will increase. Expanding distribution capacity and new media allow for increased channel selection and imply fragmenting audiences. Even within the traditional media sector competition is increasing, as with the support of government larger players are buying up smaller ones.

Overall spending on entertainment in China is increasing rapidly and is expected to continue to do so in line with trends in other developing countries such as Taiwan (Exhibit 6.3). Steady growth in GDP and disposable incomes, increased spending on leisure activities by individual households, and increasing participation of global and local investors in the media have driven growth in total entertainment spending (including eating out) from $4 billion in 1990 to $64 billion in 2000. These factors will continue to drive demand growth in double digits. If growth continues at 10% per annum, China's entertainment market could top $100 billion in 2005.

This growth implies an enormous potential profit pool for multimedia. China's backbone national fiber-optic network is growing rapidly and the number of cable TV subscribers will grow from 100 million to 150 million over the next few years. The State Administration of Radio, Film and Television (SARFT) projects that total media revenues, including advertising, will grow to over $28 billion in 2005. While the 40% annual growth rate of the past decade in TV advertising may not be sustainable, rising incomes, growth in regional/local networks and continued increases in rate cards should all contribute to a rising level of advertising spending, probably around the 15% rate to about $5 billion. Television advertising today amounts to less than 10% of the Asian total and, at $2.7 billion, is only $1 billion ahead of that in Hong Kong and Taiwan.

In addition, pay-TV and broadband subscription revenues are expected to be a major incremental source of media revenues, rising to $15 billion by

Exhibit 6.3   Growing wealth should lead to increased spending on entertainment

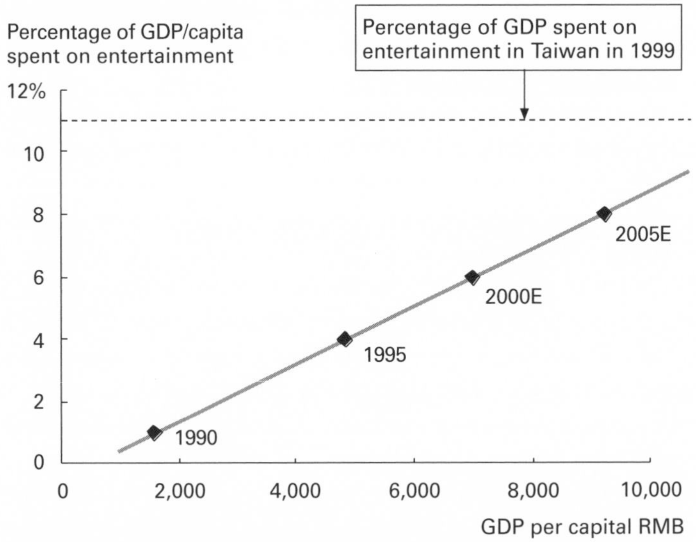

Note: Assumes 8% growth on the EIU forecast Yr2004 GDP figure from Yr2004 to Yr2005

Source: China Statistics, EIU, National Income in Taiwan (DGBAS)

2010 according to Goldman Sachs.[7] Satellite Direct-to-Home broadcasting, meanwhile, could reach 40 million, primarily in rural areas.[8] Direct-to-Home satellite could account for another $2.5 billion in revenues. Terminal devices are another major opportunity as set-top boxes and cable modems become standard issue items for consumers, accounting for around $3 billion in revenues. Finally, basic cable subscription will be about $3 billion.

The growing pie, however, is also attracting competitors. Internationally, new channels and technology create new entrants. BSkyB's rapid expansion, building on its position as the U.K.'s first pay-TV provider, is a case in point. In China, most telecom companies are actively investing in distribution access. China Telecom is actively rolling out a Digital Subscriber Line (DSL) service. CNC Broadband is laying fiber to the curb and China Mobile Broadband is supplying Internet services over local cable TV networks and has formed cooperative joint ventures with network operators such as Big Sky Network Canada. These telecom companies are also already seeking to acquire sources of bandwidth-intensive content to fill their pipes – some have even begun to move into content production and packaging. China Mobile and China Unicom have developed mobile portals to control the mobile customer interface.

Traditional hardware players are also seeking to develop into media players through their control of the set-top box and other access devices. In Shanghai, Shanghai Audio Video owns the Shenhua football team and its Broadband division is exploring educational and health-related content-development opportunities. AOL and Legend Computer have formed a joint venture to develop their own content-based channels.

In parallel, the government has begun to invite foreign investment from major global media groups who had already begun to position themselves to enter the market in the early 2000s.[9] Guangdong was chosen in late 2001 as the pilot for reform when Phoenix TV and AOL Time Warner (AOLTW) received permission to operate cable networks in return for expanded access for CCTV's cable programming in the U.S. In publishing, foreign book publishers are gradually being allowed in. Competition in distribution may even be allowed as the *People's Daily* has launched a competitive venture to Xinhua in partnership with a Hong Kong firm.

Finally, competition among media groups themselves is increasing at the local level. With government support, larger companies are acquiring smaller ones to form powerful regional media groups. By late 2001, four had been formed in Shanghai, Shandong, Hunan and Beijing, each with assets of over RMB3 billion. Their assets spanned radio, TV, film and, in some cases, print, Internet, advertising and cable. For example, the Hunan Media Group includes businesses related to advertising, program production and

Alternative Media Opportunities

Book and magazine publishing is a relatively underserved market with many unaddressed niche markets. Providing differentiated content to individual customer segments could be a terrific opportunity to revolutionize publishing, particularly with the removal of restrictions on foreign investment in distribution. Book, magazine and newspaper publishing combined amounted to $4 billion to $5 billion in spending in 2001. There is a total of 600 publishing houses, most subscale and specialized, and almost all state-owned. While China publishes almost seven books per person, mostly educational in nature, margins are still high in the largely educational market.

Newspaper publishing seems more challenging – only four out of 100 people receive a daily newspaper. Newspapers operate as quasi-government agencies and have their daily page count approved by local government authorities. The newspaper market is, however, geographically fragmented, with no national newspaper chains and with 2000 local newspaper agencies, often leading to significant local competition. Thus, advertising revenues are small and profits are low.

In the online space, no portals currently break even and consumers generally pay only for access, not for content. Online media was a relatively small market in 2000 with $1.5 billion in revenue. The largest segment is Internet access, wherein many small players compete. It is a highly regulated market where establishing local relationships, investing to build scale and a customer-oriented operation are keys to success. The total profit pool is over $100 million, most of which comes from Internet access. However, as technology and infrastructure develop, the total online market could reach $11 billion, driven by Internet access. Those able to find the killer application could still be fortunate.

Outdoor advertising, while growing fast at over 15% per annum, is highly fragmented – 80% of outdoor media carriers are owned by small advertising agencies, competition between agencies is fierce and there is almost no regulatory restriction on foreign investment. Several foreign players are already seeking to capture advantaged positions through early acquisition of the best sites. Successful players compete largely on talent and large agencies able to attract the best talent were able to capture most of the industry's total profit pool of about $200 million in 2000.

Finally, there are also opportunities in the less glamorous parts of the value chain. Commercial pre-media is growing fast. With about $1 billion in sales in 2000, this is an emerging segment with no established market leaders and is benefiting from the fast growth of industries such as financial services, real estate, retail and airlines. The private sector's role in private direct delivery of magazines and the like is expected to increase to 30% by 2005 in what is a small, local but very high-growth business.

distribution as well as cable network construction and operations. Group subsidiaries were listed on the Shenzhen Stock Exchange as early as 1999 and $54 million was raised. This and subsequent offerings have been used to fund the acquisition of various CATV networks within Hunan, boosting its subscriber base to 2.5 million. Future plans include developing international marketing capabilities while continuing to acquire over 40 county networks and upgrading current networks.[10]

CONTENT WILL BE KING

Globally, in competitive media environments only one strategy – of leveraging distinctive content across markets and formats – has proved successful. AOLTW, Disney and BSkyB all win by leveraging their scarce content assets across a wide range of distribution assets to create uniquely valuable offerings. For example, AOLTW's cartoon development feeds the Cartoon Network. The Cartoon Network is in turn distributed through Time Warner Cable, AOL and AOL Anywhere (wireless). This allows cross-subsidization to support growth business, content synergies across platforms, significant cross-promotional opportunities, and negotiation of better deals for subsidiaries by the conglomerate.

The alternative, of playing as only a conduit, is both unattractive and unsustainable even in China. Without quality content, no channel can maintain its distinctiveness. Today, Chinese channels are already starting to compete for advertisers' dollars based on the popularity of their content and in so doing opening up their prime viewing slots to content from third parties.

Multiplexes are a good example of why content matters even in China. The demand for quality movie houses in China can almost be taken for granted. China's movie theater industry is woefully inadequate – literally thousands of new cinemas remain to be built. Yet in the 1990s, box office revenue declined by 17% per annum to only RMB 800 million ($96.6 million) in 1999. China has a much lower number of cinema visits per capita than other countries at comparable levels of economic development.

This stagnation was directly caused by government constraints. Historically, government policies allowed the import of only 10 foreign films a year. These films made up over 80% of the box office in China, a poor reflection on the quality of local content. Furthermore, film distribution rights were granted exclusively to one player, China Film and its regional subsidiaries. This monopolistic structure made it difficult for cinemas to source and offer a wide selection of high-quality movies. Limitations on high-quality content in turn made investment in new cinemas and cinema upgrades unattractive.

Now with WTO entry, the ceiling on foreign content is being gradually lifted. As important, domestic distribution is being liberalized and domestic co-productions are being encouraged. With the content barrier lifted, multiplex projects are springing up in every major city. In the few cities where they already exist, box office revenues are rising dramatically, indicating that at least some people would prefer to see the movie with friends rather than watch the DVD at home. Making money on the investment, however, depends very much on the ability to access content.

In China, few players so far appear to be taking the content-driven approach seriously. Traditional state-enterprise program-makers lack a market orientation as they implicitly assume that their wages will be paid regardless of whether their product finds a market or not. The large state media groups in many cases have difficulties in ensuring their content is what the market wants – they act far more as loose confederations of independent assets than as integrated media companies. Multinationals for their part appear to believe that geographic monopolies on content distribution make developing content itself less of a priority – quite different from how they operate in their home markets.

This is a mistake. Current conditions appear to make a content-based approach not only possible but, in fact, essential to gain a return on distribution and infrastructure assets. An improved intellectual property environment in China supports higher valuation of content. Audiences are increasingly discriminating in their preferences. For example, channels such as Hunan Satellite are gaining in share across China based on distinctive content. Hunan Satellite TV has achieved a share of 14% in Beijing and 4% in Shanghai based on distinctive drama and entertainment content. There will also be a massive demand for content to fill up the infrastructure investments already made. With this new distribution capacity already in the ground (or air), broadcasters will have incentives to seek fresh content and earn a return on their capital. Otherwise, infrastructure assets could quickly become commodities, with marginal cost driving pricing. In hardware, the same dynamics that have driven aggressive price-cutting in TVs could apply to the new generation of access devices.

THE WINNERS ARE NOT YET DECIDED

Since developing distinctive content can be a multi-decade challenge, it would be shortsighted not to start the effort now. Developing content requires a deep understanding of a target audience's needs combined with a solid artistic and commercial talent base. Domestic content also needs to be able to meet the requirements of interactive TV and broadband. The proliferation of access devices will increase the complexity of content production and distribution. Traditional media groups, multinationals and entrepreneurs all need to decide where and how they will build their position.

Reforming Traditional Media Groups

Traditional Chinese media groups which today own their own film and production studios, as well as cultural troupes and venues, need to start by creating real organizational accountability for content and market development. Similar to the BBC's transformation in the 1990s, these groups must define internal markets for production and programs, while at the same time building recognizable brands around their program and channel assets. In a market-based internal bidding process, program-developers should start to take a more entrepreneurial approach to defining their distribution strategy. Channels, meanwhile, should no longer blindly take whatever is made for them. Rather, programs should have to compete to take their place in the lineup. Likewise, program resource providers must compete for the program-makers' budgets.

Local media groups also have the option of acquiring content. Internationally, content developers are usually skilled dealmakers. Thematic channels like Discovery have built a strong brand through a web of alliances and acquisitions, leveraging in-depth knowledge of the needs of a specific segment. Over the space of seven years, the Discovery Channel acquired three other major channels and two retail chains, while expanding globally and launching two new channels of its own, as well as developing alliances to provide its content over broadband media and develop a branded travel package. Chinese media companies also need to become better at acquiring unique content. While M&A is still in its early stages – some transactions have been done in cable TV and outdoor advertising – now is the time to identify and negotiate with up-and-coming talent.

Localizing the Foreigners

For foreign players, while the notion of success through content is familiar, the issue is how to get it done in China. Lessons from other industries show that localization is essential to success – for example, Motorola's handset leadership is intimately linked to its local R&D position. Localization, however, requires a deep understanding and commitment to the local market. Unless the global media companies are truly committed to putting leadership and resources on the ground in China, they too will miss the chance to compete.

To paraphrase Tip O'Neill, the late Speaker of the U.S. House of Representatives, all content is local. Top-rated television programs in China and globally are local – starting with news, entertainment and sports. Simply transferring in global content won't work. Initial efforts by Star TV simply repackaged mainstream U.S. content and beamed it in English over a wide footprint. Not surprisingly, this had limited impact in China. More effectively, Phoenix, a Chinese-language satellite broadcaster, has had terrific success, achieving between 4% and 12% audience shares in Beijing, Shanghai and Guangzhou.[11]

Focusing the Entrepreneurs

Finally, entrepreneurial content players need to invest with a specific audience in mind. This may be more difficult than it seems, as there is a dearth of market research data and processes in China. Systematic understanding of the market and its needs hardly exists. And viewer preferences vary dramatically across the country and across socioeconomic segments. In Shanghai, 16–24-year-old males overwhelmingly watch sports while women in the same age bracket are hooked on MTV and international news. As a result, much of the local content produced today fails to strike a chord in audiences.

Entrepreneurs also have to find distribution and exhibition outlets, as well as build merchandising capability. The value of content is maximized through its coordinated release through film, TV, the Internet and, particularly, via merchandising. In developed markets merchandising can account for over 50% of the revenues of a theatrical release.[12] However, in China, traditional content licensing deals offer only marginal returns. Local content players need to develop the same quality control and marketing skills that global players use to protect and promote their characters. In the absence of these, having a cash-generating part of the business is essential if only to survive the long wait between releases. This could be anything from outdoor advertising to magazine sales.

Phoenix Rising

Phoenix Chinese Channel, a joint venture between the News Corp-controlled Star TV and PRC parties, has been the most popular foreign channel in China. Phoenix is broadcast as a free-to-air (unencrypted) channel and can be picked up by anyone with a C-band satellite dish. Foreign satellite distributors and cable channels in Guangdong province also carry Phoenix, where more than 16 million Phoenix viewer households are located. Phoenix has been distributed in Guangdong since 1997 with the express approval of the local cable authority and the tacit consent of national authorities. Nationwide an estimated 700 of China's estimated 3,000 cable-TV operators carry Phoenix to the viewer. Cable operators have had to weigh the benefit of carrying a popular channel such as Phoenix against the risk of regulatory sanction. That so many have chosen to carry it implied at least implicit endorsement by the authorities of Phoenix's signals. Advertisers certainly approve – Phoenix has an advertising base of $80 million annually, 80% of which originates from China. In late 2001, Phoenix's Guangdong downlinks were finally made official, in return for helping to promote CCTV 4 in the U.S. and Europe where Phoenix has its own presence.

⁂ ⁂ ⁂

While incumbent media groups start with an advantage of the existing subscriber base, their hold on the Chinese market is by no means assured. The successful media player of China's future will need both compelling content and a solid grasp of the realities of dealing in a semi-regulated sector. Whether this new player will be foreign or domestic is something the Chinese consumer is unlikely to care much about so long as the quality of what he or she gets improves dramatically.

REFERENCES

1. Chile and Singapore are the models for this move. However, internationally, there are no examples of large economies like China achieving a smooth transition from closed to open financial markets. Rather, Japan shows what happens when banks prove unable to manage their Non-Performing Loans (NPLs) and remain technically insolvent. While social issues remain largely stable, there is generally no growth. Korea and Mexico show that the transition can go faster, but with significant turbulence as the stock market bubble bursts, exchange rates fall and social unrest ensues. In either case, the implication would be a substantial fall in investor confidence and turmoil in the markets.

2. The local branch of the security company acts as much as a gossip mill as a place to take orders. Most individual retail traders are often unemployed and spend over six hours per day on the premises of the securities company. In fact, the average holding period for stocks in China is only 2.2 months compared to 10 in the U.S.

3. As early as November 14, 1997, the State Council announced the Provisional Rules for the Administration of Securities Investment Funds to regulate the mutual fund industry. Promoters were to have had three years' experience in securities investment and have been continuously profitable, with a minimum paid-up capital of RMB 300 million (over $36 million). Typical backers included securities companies, trusts and fund managers. A maximum investment of 80% was allowed in equities and at least 20% in government and corporate bonds and deposits. Reforms accelerated with the bankruptcy of the Guangdong International Trust and Investment Corporation (GITIC) in the late 1990s. In May 1999, the China Securities Regulatory Commission announced plans to close the existing investment trust funds with assets of RMB 9 billion (over $1 billion) and restructure them into new funds.

4. Prior to WTO entry, China International Capital Corporation (CICC) was the only joint-venture investment bank granted domestic and overseas listing licenses thanks to its strong government backing. Foreign investment banks were not allowed to underwrite domestic listings, with the exception of the Bank of China International (BOCI), the Hong Kong-based investment-banking arm of the Bank of China. However, prior to WTO entry, some banks had already begun to offer advisory/counseling services for Chinese players and most of the global leaders had representative offices. By 2001, 22 firms had acquired B-share brokerage licenses and Goldman Sachs and Morgan Stanley had become lead underwriters for China's major mid-1990s international IPOs (for example, China Mobile, Unicom, PetroChina).

5. Overseas fees are a bit higher, reflecting the complexity and that the lead underwriters of overseas IPOs are typically foreign investment banks.

6. See *Facing up to the Risks* by Dominic Casserley.

7. Goldman Sachs Equity Research, 8/31/2000.

8. Credit Suisse First Boston, China's Broadcasting Sector.

9. News Corp, in particular, has been a leader in developing the Chinese market. It established a partnership with CCTV to broadcast CCTV-9 on its networks in Australia and the U.S. in exchange for access to Guangdong Cable. It also invested $60 million in CNC, one of three fixed-line operators in China, and holds 38% of Phoenix TV, a Chinese-language TV station. A News Corp subsidiary providing access technologies for pay-TV set up in Beijing and signed an agreement to provide interactive RV services for CCTV's sports channel. It also signed a deal with a subsidiary of the regulator SARFT to provide front-end systems, access technologies, EPG and STB operating systems to the national cable network in exchange for profit-sharing. Finally, it teamed up with Legend, China's leading PC maker, to provide software solutions in STBs manufactured by Legend. This web of alliances bespeaks an aggressive commitment to the market and a strong belief in its growth potential.

10. Credit Suisse First Boston, China's Broadcasting Sector.

11. Credit Suisse First Boston.

12. At Disney, intellectual property is owned by the corporation, not by business units, and there is a commitment to exploit key properties across all platforms. There is active coordination and sequencing of product release across platforms and the CEO and Vice President of Synergy ensure maximum capture of linkages.

7
Success Factors in Investment

The opportunities may seem boundless but capturing them has never been easy. China has successfully attracted over $40 billion in Foreign Direct Investment (FDI) in each of the past 20 years, and in 2002, China was the world's largest destination for FDI surpassing the United States. China's accession to the WTO now means a proliferation of new investment opportunities for foreign multinational companies (MNCs) across different industries. However, a "winner-take-all" structure characterizes most Chinese industries and participating in and winning the investing game here requires both a competitive strategy and on-the-ground capability to execute it. The next three to five years may represent the most attractive window of opportunity for MNCs to win in China. If they do not, it will not be long before they see Chinese competitors emerge globally.

Investors also have to think more comprehensively about how they compete in the market. Alliances have been the dominant form of FDI in China since the initiation of the "Opening to the Outside World" policy in 1978. Twenty years later, however, maturing local companies, more accessible markets and progress towards a more stable regulatory environment had negated much of the initial rationale for alliances. At the same time, fundamental imbalances in partner contributions have grown over time, rendering existing alliances unstable. In China, most joint ventures are between potential competitors, 50:50 deals are in the substantial minority, and both Chinese and multinational companies face cash constraints in the enormous Chinese market. No surprise then that many of the joint ventures signed in the early 1980s are now being restructured. In this context, executives should take a hard look at their current and prospective China alliances, to assess their rationale and restructuring potential.

7.1 INVESTING IN POST-WTO CHINA

China was a favored destination for corporate investment in the 1990s. And its ongoing funding needs could ensure that opportunities will persist. But how well investment will fare is often difficult to assess. The well-publicized failures of the past have given investors some cause for concern. Still, those willing to make the first move, frame innovative strategies, and align corporate commitment and investment in building a local organization are well placed to succeed in this challenging market.

CHINA AS THE WORLD'S INVESTMENT CHOICE

Since the early 1990s China has attracted substantial FDI. With an estimated FDI of $40 billion in 2001, China is the second-largest host country for FDI, accounting for about 10% of total global FDI and 40% of total FDI to developing economies. Between 1995 and 2001, an accumulated FDI of over $400 billion flowed into many sectors in China. Foreign-funded enterprises in fact now represent 16% of the total economy, 48% of exports and are growing at over 20% per annum. Telecom, automotive, energy and electronics are among the largest sectors for FDI in China. Among the investors are Motorola, BP, Samsung, Volkswagen, Nokia and GE, each of whom has invested over $1 billion to date.

For foreign companies the initial lure was market access. The size of the domestic market and its promising growth potential attracted the electronics companies relatively early on. Chinese mobile subscribers have been growing at 30% per annum, as have handset sales. Today, China is almost as large a market for Nokia as the U.S., and Motorola derives 20% of its global revenues from China. Likewise, pharmaceuticals and consumer-goods companies were among the first into the country.

Early investors also saw China's potential as a low-cost manufacturing base. Most of the $40 billion per annum of FDI coming to China now goes into manufacturing and industry and is repeat investment from businesses already present. These must have had good experiences to be reinvesting. It may be too much to claim that China will become the sole manufacturing center for the world. But it is clearly becoming an essential component of a global manufacturing network. In the high-tech industry, more than 70% of components such as motherboards, keyboards and mice are now made in China. Given its cost advantage, Taiwanese companies in particular and, to a lesser extent, Japanese companies have begun to move operations to the mainland.[1] The wave of announcements from Sony, Mitsubishi, NEC and

Fujitsu in 2002 is only the visible crest of the wave. Today, China makes 24% of the world's washing machines, 30% of its air conditioners and 16% of its refrigerators. China's exports are rising and are expected to continue to grow. In particular, higher value-added industries such as machinery and electronics, chemicals and precision instruments are expected to grow at 15% rates.

One consequence of China's attractiveness as a market and a manufacturing base is the hollowing out of Taiwan's high-tech manufacturing sector. Today, most leading Taiwanese manufacturers (for example, Delta, Quanta, Honhai, Wistron) produce around 90% of goods in China, over 70% of which in turn is dedicated to export. And these investment decisions are taken by chief executives who are inherently highly conservative towards China and who seem to be willing to gamble on its stability. Even Taiwan's semiconductor producers are now moving to China. Around one million Taiwanese (mainly males of working age), nearly 5% of the population, are believed to be working in China today and more university graduates from

Exhibit 7.1 Investments are making China a major manufacturing base for the world

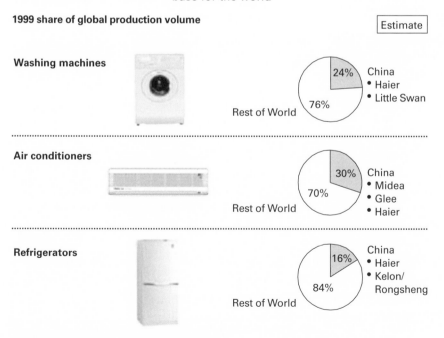

Source: Alliance magazine; literature search

Taiwan now want to live in Shanghai than in Taipei. The belated response from the Taiwanese government is a weak attempt to restrict highly talented Taiwanese individuals from working in China.

More recently, global companies such as Microsoft and Siemens have recognized the value of China's intangible assets such as R&D resources and have built global R&D centers here.[2] Unlike in Latin America and much of Eastern Europe, investors are not just building factories but also research centers. Motorola for one not only manufactures phones in China, but also designs them. Ericsson has invested over $200 million in R&D and human resources in China and has a total R&D headcount of over 400. It built its first software R&D center in Shanghai and a 3G experimental network in Beijing. Microsoft has an annual budget of $80 million for its research institute for language and for research in 3G basic technology.

Finally, companies have begun to discern China's advantages as a global service center. Multinationals such as HSBC and GE Capital are starting to build global service centers here to serve customers worldwide more efficiently. HSBC's 250-employee service center in Guangdong serves Hong Kong and the U.K. with data-processing services. Microsoft has invested $10 million to set up a Greater China Tech Support Center in Shanghai and has since invested an additional $50 million to cover global customers.

With all this investment, someone must be making money. In fact, the overall performance of foreign companies in China has improved dramatically. According to the U.S. Department of Commerce, profits of China-affiliates of U.S. companies grew from $0.1 billion in 1990 to $1.5 billion in 2000. Foreign investors in China have been able to achieve similar pre-tax profit margins as local competitors, and capture a substantial share of industry profits. In 2000, the average pre-tax profit margin for all Foreign Invested Enterprises (FIEs) was 5.6%, compared to 5.1% for domestic companies. In total, FIEs captured about 30% of the profits of industrial enterprises in China. In sectors where they have made particularly large investments, foreign players are able to capture a disproportionate share of the profit pool. In electronics and telecom equipment, FIEs account for over 65% of the estimated industry pre-tax profit pool. In passenger cars, they have captured almost 95%.

All FIEs are not success stories, of course. Whirlpool entered China in 1994 only to withdraw three years later with a loss of over $100 million (it has since re-entered). Peugeot entered China in 1985 but backed out of its joint venture in 1997 with a loss of $100 million. Carlsberg set up its second factory in Shanghai in 1998. In 2000, suffering a loss of $10 million, it sold it to local competitor Qingdao Beer.

What lies behind these failures? Two main causes: poor strategic assessments and weak execution. A host of factors can doom a strategy to failure: ignorance of regional differences leading to overestimated markets; lack of understanding of consumer dynamics resulting in unsuccessful products; underestimation of the impact of an unfavorable industry structure; lack of preparation for government intervention; poor assessment of complex distribution; or just poor timing. Poor execution is at least as notable a reason for failure. Investors simply fail to apply the same rigor and discipline to implementing their strategy in China as they would elsewhere in the world.

PURSUE FIRST-MOVER ADVANTAGE

Acting quickly to gain and maintain first-mover advantage is one big requirement that China winners have got right. Those first in have had the opportunity to build a sustainable leadership position against both local and multinational entrants. Coke got in first in the premier coastal provinces and cities and now holds sway there. Pepsi, a second-comer to the market, has had to settle for leadership in second-tier markets like Chengdu, Kunming and Fuzhou. The timing for early moves differs by sector. In consumer goods, initial entries were made in the mid-1980s and led to many early successes. The story is different for capital-intensive industries like energy and chemicals. Interest and effort in these sectors have come much more recently, and in many the role of first-mover remains to be taken.

To understand the Chinese market and find out where first-mover advantage may lie, companies should start by assessing its multiple segments. To illustrate, investors who believe the market starts and ends with Guangzhou, Beijing and Shanghai will be missing the major opportunity. In fact, Tier 3 cities and rural areas are likely to be the fastest growing segment of the market over the next five years. In home appliances, these two segments are likely to account for more than 55% of the market. Players need to aggressively expand in these areas while keeping a strong presence in Tier 1 and 2 cities.

Another important task is assessing with which product and brand to enter. Many players assume that their global product will be appropriate for China and that global brands can sell themselves. In fact, current demand is largely for mid- to low-end products. In most segments, the high-end amounts to no more than 15% to 20% of total demand. And while consumers are becoming more brand conscious, companies still need to invest aggressively in building their brands in China. Total advertising spending has risen from less than RMB20 billion ($2.4 billion) in 1995 to over RMB70 billion ($8.5 billion) in 2000. This level of spending is needed to introduce the brand to a market that is already becoming saturated with information.

In some industries, aggressive local competition may rule out a first-mover position. Many Chinese industries already suffer from overcapacity, resulting in price and profit falls. In air conditioners, overcapacity is 121% of demand, in microwaves it is 45% of demand, in refrigerators 39%, in washing machines 30% and in color TVs 150%! TV prices have fallen by 19% annually from 1997 to 2001, refrigerator prices by 6% and washing machine prices by 7%. Today, a 21-inch color TV retails for US$115, an Ericsson mobile phone for $70 and a large Samsung refrigerator for $85.

Such fierce price competition has brought about consolidation and the emergence of strong domestic players. In air conditioners, the number of players has dropped from 415 in 1996 to 94 in 2000; in refrigerators, the players have declined from 187 to 40. Likewise, in color TVs, the share of the top six players increased from 35% in 1994 to 80% in 2000, led by Changhong, TCL, Konka, Hisense and Skyworth. In PCs, Legend has led the consolidation and now boasts a 30% market share (foreign competitors IBM and Dell have only 4% to 5% apiece). In washing machines, Haier, Little Swan and Rongshida split 60% of the pie, while in air conditioners Midea, Gree and Haier again dominate. Multinationals resolving to compete in these industries cannot assume they will be first movers. Rather, they must learn how to play the game in China.[3]

Even where a foreign player has achieved a first-mover position, it may come to naught since occasionally the government will intervene to support domestic producers. In mobile phones, the government has supplied RMB 4 billion (around $483 million) in R&D funding to domestic companies and allocated a quota for purchases to 10 selected domestic companies. MNCs, meanwhile, face regulatory constraints such as limits on the import of finished products, no new approvals of foreign mobile-handset manufacturers including joint ventures, a requirement to authenticate seals on each handset and enforcement of an export and domestic content ratio.

FRAME INNOVATIVE STRATEGIES

To mitigate these risks and to sustain advantages that a first-mover position has endowed, foreign investors must develop an innovative strategy, sometimes at odds with global precedent. Successful multinationals often start by defining a strong home base. In China, territories are set mainly by word of mouth (for consumer companies) or by local sourcing preferences (industrial companies). Product logistics in turn often drive territory design. Waterway access is usually the best alternative. Road transport has historically been good for up to 200 to 400 kilometers – although this may expand with new infrastructure investments. Thus, currently territories are generally the home province plus easy-to-reach parts of nearby provinces. Building a strong home base can facilitate a national rollout. P&G began by building a strong position in Guangdong province. It then made two key acquisitions in Chengdu and Beijing. The competitive edge it gained in its home market could then be leveraged in its national rollout, that is, cash, people, experience and an established pull-and-push system.

Beyond geographic focus, winners also figure out where the chokepoints in the industry lie. In a market with as many inefficiencies as China has, big strategic moves can pay off. Partnering with the end-customer is still possible in some industries where the government has not yet withdrawn. Some examples illustrate how: In the early 1990s Baker Hughes established a joint venture with China National Petroleum Corporation to supply oilfield equipment, securing a dominant share of the market early on. CP Pokphand of Thailand has led vertical integration along the value chain of poultry feed, processing and even chicken retailing.

Even where structural advantage is not directly achievable, tailoring global products to local requirements is usually a good move. In consumer goods, Coke has introduced tailored China products. In technology, the first handset Motorola designed outside of the U.S. was in China.

The Motorola Story[4]

Motorola, the number-one investor in China's telecom industry, is one of the success stories of foreign investment in China. Motorola set up a representative office in Beijing in 1987 focused on industrial electronics. In 1990, it established its first manufacturing facility in Tianjin and set up Motorola University. By the mid-1990s, Motorola had established 18 R&D centers and moved its North Asia headquarters from Hong Kong to Beijing. This commitment helped it to become the only foreign company with a license to manufacture CDMA handsets, in the late 1990s. Today, Motorola has a multi-billion-dollar business in China, including mobile handsets, network equipment, pagers, two-way radios, semiconductors, auto electronics and accessories. It has also invested over $3 billion to date in eight joint ventures and 26 subsidiaries, and employs over 5,000 people in China. Finally, Motorola has consistently aspired to lead the market wherever it participates. In mobile handsets it has kept pace with the market's blistering 40% annual growth and now shares the lead with Nokia; each company has more than 30% market share.

Four key factors are behind Motorola's success. First, its product strategy is highly localized. Motorola provides a broad range of products but with an increasing focus on low-end products, the key to demand in China. It has invested heavily in local R&D, both to increase localization of content and to speed rollout of new products. It has wide distribution coverage even in Tier 3 cities, closely tracks channel orders to manage production schedules, and is best-in-class in channel support. Finally, Motorola has made and kept a commitment to training and continuous localization of the management team: 75% of its team is now local due at least in part to the company's investment in training.[5]

The success of Motorola's A6288 mobile shows the importance of developing a product tailored to the Chinese market and of getting advertising and distribution right. According to Charles Weng, the Director of Motorola's Beijing Design Center, "This is the first ever Motorola handset wholly developed outside the U.S. The Accompli A6288 is the result of a 14-month development effort by 148 engineers." Key features include GPRS, Chinese and European handwriting recognition, Java (J2ME)/WAP Support, and PDA functions. With 18 R&D centers in China and a headcount of over 800, Motorola has one of the largest commitments of any multinational in China to Chinese R&D. It also maintains the highest advertising spending among competitors and captures the highest brand awareness.[6] Its market share across regions and Tier 1, 2, and 3 cities is also relatively consistent due to its wide distribution coverage.

Shadow management is another particularly important part of strategy in a market as fragmented and logistically challenging as China's. Procter & Gamble exerts direct control over its third-party distributors to ensure that its products make it to market in a cost-effective fashion. Distributors typically handle mainly physical tasks – invoicing and marketing are the responsibility of a manager assigned to work closely with each distributor. And while credit collection remains the distributor's responsibility, a proprietary salesforce in each distributor reports to the manager, not to the distributor, to ensure full-time dedication. This arrangement obviously benefits those consumer companies able to offer a broad product portfolio.

On the other hand, direct-to-retailer approaches are also becoming more important. Modern formats are growing rapidly and now account for over 35% of sales. The number of new hypermarkets to be opened by the players currently in the market alone is expected to triple to over 160 by 2005. China is rapidly improving its infrastructure – the total length of the road system, for example, increased by 12% annually over the 1990s. This has led to dramatic reductions in logistics costs. In one consumer-goods industry, logistics costs per kilometer-ton dropped by over 30% in the late 1990s. This means the traditional first, and second-tier distributor structure is under threat. Companies need to take on more of the challenge of going directly to the retailer, with the attendant implications for logistics and marketing support.

Finally, M&A is an option that is only just emerging in the Chinese market. In 2001, China attracted $45 billion in FDI, of which only 5% to 6% was from foreign M&A, a modest figure compared to the estimated 80% of total transnational investment made through acquisitions worldwide. Historically, joint ventures were the only vehicle available for foreign investment in China – in any case, there were few attractive assets for sale. Regulations are now being finalized to allow foreign companies to acquire state and private enterprises. Observers expect this to kick off a boom in Chinese M&A. "The birth of the regulations will be conducive to attracting more foreign investment in the years to come," says Professor Lu Jinyong of the University of International Business and Economics. "Also, in the coming five years mergers and acquisitions between foreign companies and domestic companies, and between different domestic companies will also increase as a result of the regulations." Emerson Electric's acquisition of Huawei's power-supply business is a case in point. The minority stakes that Anheuser-Busch has taken in Qingdao Beer and that Interbrew has taken in Zhujiang Beer point another way to a creeping acquisition path.

PLAY TO WIN, NOT PLAY TO PLAY

Winning in China also requires a corporate commitment to "play to win", not "play to play". MNCs fall into three stages of business-building: experimenter, strategic investor and dominant local player. In the first, the level of corporate commitment to China can be low to moderate. The primary objective is to establish a presence, become familiar with the market and operations and assess the risks and rewards of taking the next step. That next step – to become a strategic investor – requires a much greater level of corporate commitment. In one survey of leading MNCs, the strategic investors planned an investment of $200 million on average over the next five years as compared to $25 million for the experimenters. These investments are typically needed to build a broader presence through sales or facilities, seize a first-mover advantage and develop local management capability. Only a few companies in our experience have stepped up beyond the strategic investor role to make China a central corporate priority and in so doing secure a dominant market share, shaping industry structure and conduct to achieve sustained superior returns.[7]

To illustrate the transition from experimenter to investor, one office-equipment manufacturer invested a total of US$15 million in the 1980s to understand the market. It viewed the investment as a small price to pay for a ticket to entry and set a breakeven target of five years. The company invested in a single venture manufacturing two core products with a marketing focus on industrial cities and a heavy reliance on the local partner, especially for sales and distribution. Its own executives were largely fly-in-fly-out. After a decade of this, the manufacturer decided the time was right to bring the China operations to a world-class level, in part spurred by the threat of competitor entry. It launched three additional ventures with at least 10 core products, bought out distributors, and launched its own regional salesforce. Annual investment jumped to $50 million and a major buildup was made of both local and expatriate personnel.[8]

Investors also increasingly realize that as they increase the magnitude of their investments in China they need to take care of execution themselves; relying on the partner is not a recipe for success. The percentage of foreign investment in the form of a Wholly Foreign Owned Enterprise (WFOE) (as opposed to a joint venture) has risen from less than 30% in 1992 to 47% in 2000. Likewise, companies that originally entered through a joint venture have progressively restructured their participation to either take control or exit. China Schindler, for example, moved from a 25% stake in 1980 to 65% in 1995 and then to 100% in 2001.

Leading this kind of ramp-up in investment often requires creating and empowering a China center (as opposed to leading China out of corporate headquarters). In the initial experimentation phase, it is important that the business units define their own strategic aspirations. But in the business-building phase, a strong center is often needed to coordinate and support business units in setting up ventures. Over time, business units may then integrate China into their global operations.

Responsibilities of the China team can include coordinating local relationship management (speaking with one voice); providing shared services; supporting business development by centralizing scarce legal, valuation and negotiation skills and leading cross-business initiatives; and coordinating investments to capture synergies and build consensus with headquarters. In some cases, a team approach is employed where the China country executive coordinates with local business unit heads. This typically happens in companies where global lines of business are strong. Focused leadership by the China CEO may also be possible where the business is quite regional in nature (for instance, retailing) or where very senior local leadership is required to manage the size of the business.

Closely aligned with the need for a strong local coordination group is the requirement for a structured relationship-management program. Multinationals should take care not to let global business units confuse government decision-makers. Rather, the best practice is to map PRC governmental positions and their corporate equivalents to ensure a close fit in terms of both seniority and availability. For example, the chairman of a typical multinational would be able to meet directly with State Council members on an annual basis, whereas the CEO could be expected to be in China between two to four times a year and meet with ministers and provincial governors. The China chief representative, on the other hand, would typically be on the ground full time and be able to meet with directors of government bureaus and senior state-enterprise leaders regularly.

INVEST IN PEOPLE

This may be true of all countries but is more so in China: investing in people is key to success. The top operating challenge for most foreign companies in China is human resources. The cost of skilled human resources is increasing at 30% per annum, as is the turnover rate. Among the three types of workforces foreign companies need, skilled talent is the hardest to find. The pool of potential workers is vast since workers released by the restructuring of SOEs are adding to the national pool of economic migrants. There is also a relatively large and fast-growing pool of college graduates to serve as management trainees.[9] Middle/top managers who have post-graduate experience, however, are scarce.

Successful companies do invest in building local human resources, both

Growing China Pioneers

In the mid-1990s, McKinsey set out to understand what differentiated successful from unsuccessful multinationals in their development and use of expatriates in China. To that end, we conducted an extensive confidential survey of the senior managers of primarily large Western companies with sizable China operations (that is, earning average revenues of $85 million). We found wide differences in performance, both self-reported and actual, which allowed us to group companies into successful and unsuccessful segments. Interestingly, almost two-thirds reported profitability, which in itself was a criterion, but not the only one, for success.

Four key lessons emerged from the successful companies: select true pioneers; proactively manage the HR pipeline; give personal attention to development; and offer the next challenge to retain employees. Senior managers at successful companies fit a well-defined personality type. Generally optimistic, driven and adaptable, they are pioneer-type personalities and invariably appear more successful than others. Most successful companies hire general managers with international experience, not Asia specialists. Many are volunteers – 52% as opposed to 28% for unsuccessful corporations – and are typically employed for a longer period (three-plus years) as opposed to an average two years in unsuccessful companies. Successful corporations also reported that they paid their managers more than unsuccessful companies. Average compensation was around $350,000, including housing and other bonuses, for a net $50,000 increase in compensation for moving to China.

Successful companies also anticipate and prepare better. While two to six expatriates appears to be a minimum complement for any size of operations, there is a clear relationship between size and expatriate requirements as the number of employees grows. Employees per expatriate initially tend to be relatively low, at around 10 to 20, but by the time total employment reaches 1,000, the ratio appears relatively stable at between 80 and 120. Even at these levels of demand, successful companies do a better job of managing handovers, involving managers in the actual negotiations and feasibility studies of their prospective companies, and handling mobility issues. Once these managers are assigned roles, personal attention from senior management is the most effective tool for developing China expatriates. CEOs visit China almost 40% more often a year at successful than unsuccessful companies. Successful companies also delegate operating decisions to China. For example, 78% of the 10 most successful companies reported freedom to select their own machinery, compared to just 36% of unsuccessful companies.

Finally, successful companies recognize that their senior managers in China are among the most at risk in their corporation. China pioneers are happy (away from home) and 46% are likely to leave within two years rather than return to headquarters. They fear a loss of independence and are skeptical about their future career on return (while most feel that coming to China has increased their external market value). Consequently, successful companies are modifying their rewards systems and increasingly offering a greater range of global entrepreneurial roles in order to ensure retention of these critical global resources.

expatriate and PRC nationals, and do not rely on their local partners to do it for them.[10] One consumer-goods company set ambitious goals to achieve $1 billion in sales over a five-year period, building from a $70 million current business. When it did its calculations, however, it realized this meant increasing the China workforce from 200 to 2,000. Recruiting and developing this level of resources leaves no choice but a focused investment of expatriate resources. In this same company, 90% of top management is expatriate, as is 40% of marketing, 25% of finance and 5% of sales. These resources are certainly expensive, even when recruited locally, and so rigorous performance management is essential to get value for money. On the other hand, relying on local partners to do the work results in a vicious cycle of poor skills, weak organization, poor recruiting and business performance, and a reluctance to invest more to solve the problem.

※　　※　　※

Winning in China is no pipedream, even if many companies have tried and failed. Clearly, there can be no guaranteed recipe for success. But companies that are willing to move first, frame innovative strategies, aim high – that is, play to win — and invest in people have won most of the battle.

7.2 RESTRUCTURING ALLIANCES

Alliances have been the dominant form of FDI in China since the initiation of the Opening to the Outside World policy in 1978. Twenty years later, however, maturing local companies, more accessible markets and progress towards a more stable regulatory environment have removed much of the initial rationale for alliances. Indeed, over 50% of new FDI in Shanghai is now in wholly-owned and contractual joint ventures.

At the same time, fundamental imbalances in partner contributions have grown over time, rendering existing alliances unstable. Globally, complementary skills, 50:50 contributions and the ability to evolve beyond original expectations mark successful alliances. In China, most joint ventures are between potential competitors, 50:50 deals are in the substantial minority, and both Chinese and multinational companies face cash constraints in the enormous Chinese market. No surprise then that many of the joint ventures signed in the early 1980s are now being restructured.

In view of these risks in alliances, executives should take a hard look at their current and prospective China alliances, to assess their rationale and restructuring potential. Paying attention to the details could prevent pain later. Even successful ventures can go wrong as markets, partners and competitors all evolve.

Why Breakups Happen

Alliances are coming apart for three reasons:

Divorce due to incompatibility. Globally, incompatible objectives among competitors who are in an alliance appear to be one of the most common reasons for split-ups. In one deal between a global leader and the leading Chinese company in its industry, the global company sought and obtained both a 55% stake and contractual control of marketing rights. However, startup losses and differences in management strategy created tension among the partners. The Chinese company lost patience, figured it could run the business better, and is now seeking return of marketing rights and government approval for a split.

Divorce due to inequity. Lack of balanced contributions also dooms some alliances from the start. In one of the largest and earliest direct investments in China, the multinational company contributed equipment but took only a 25% stake, and left many of the day-to-day decisions to its partners. These decisions were often not well thought through. Eventually, as a result of a badly mistaken pricing outlook and significant cost overruns, cash pressures mounted on all the partners. The multinational viewed the returns as insufficient compensation for the risks of its position and succeeded in obtaining a Chinese buyout after six years.

Divorce due to inaction. Even if they succeed initially, some alliances never truly grow up — usually because one party has entered into it only as a tool to gain market access and sees limited growth potential. To illustrate, in one China deal the multinational partner achieved a minority stake in an early-mover venture which allowed for profitable sales of imported components. However, over time, market growth was slow and pressure from the local partner grew for greater investment. Unwilling to make the additional commitment, the multinational proactively withdrew from the deal, leaving the local group to seek other partners.

DIFFERENTIATE BETWEEN PARTNERS AND FRIENDS

One of the most common pitfalls is to mistake friendships for partnerships. In China, companies typically have relations with both government authorities and enterprises (Exhibit 7.2). The former are there to provide access, resolve regulatory disputes and occasionally intervene to expedite project execution. The latter are the companies one has to work with day to day, who should provide personnel, contacts and cash to the venture. Expecting an approval authority to do the venture's marketing, or an enterprise to secure government licenses, is usually a mistake.

Companies must take care to truly understand the need for and interests of both government friends and day-to-day partners. With government entities, the first question is why they are really needed. Only in sectors where government intervenes directly is there likely to be much mileage in getting a government entity directly involved in the business. Functional bureaux like the Ministry of Foreign Trade and Economic Cooperation (MOFTEC) will generally not make policy exceptions for individual companies. Even where government is directly involved, it is important to understand the direction of reform. Many industries nominally controlled by central planning entities have been corporatized in the last few years – steel, oil and gas, and

Exhibit 7.2 Understand differences in partner type

Type of partner	Example	Nature of value-added	
		Access to opportunities/entry	Project execution/operations
• "Mother-in-law" (government decision authority)	• State Planning Commission • Provincial governments • National ministries	• Approve project • Allocate funds • Allow markets to be opened • Assist with foreign-exchange issues • Grant fiscal concessions	• Expedite project execution
• "Day-to-day partner"	• State-owned enterprises (local operating companies of national corporations) • Private and collective enterprises	• Provide market access	• Provide operating personnel • Provide marketing/distribution/transportation capability • Provide physical infrastructure (land, plant) • Provide supplies and locally controlled resources

automotive, to name a few. In these sectors, the government is unlikely to be aggressive in promoting a foreign agenda. Finally in those sectors where government still can be directly leveraged (for example, healthcare), the challenge is to understand exactly what it will take to make a competitive offer and what the government is prepared to give in return. Volkswagen's offer to localize production of the Santana in the 1980s in exchange for guaranteed marketing and support in component localization was one such offer.

With day-to-day partners, there is no substitute for research to understand not only technical capabilities (which is usually done) but also business aspirations, partnership track record, and organizational depth (which typically is not done). Three examples show why. A CEO struck a deal during a one-time trip, trusting a friend's introduction. The partner turned out to be a major supplier and distributor, but soon also became a major competitor. The head of a global business unit negotiated a joint venture with the local leader to get market share quickly. But conflicts with the partner on product-line priorities and salesforce control soon emerged. A business development manager chose the "best" partner (provided it was located in Shanghai), resulting in an expensive base of operations. In all cases, it was marry in haste, repent at leisure. Best practice due diligence typically includes conducting site visits to check physical location; interviewing key partner executives to assess their management philosophy, business aspiration and execution skills; collecting, interpreting and synthesizing the Chinese partner's financial and accounting information to codify its operational and financial strength; and visiting retailers and distributors to assess and evaluate the Chinese partner's true marketing skill.

PLAN FOR SHIFTS IN THE POWER BALANCE OVER TIME

An alliance between partners whose skills are truly complementary can last a long time. However, shifts in power can occur over time and destabilize and end the partnership. Global players tend to have more power when global brands, world-class technology, global scale, or financial depth are key industry success factors. Local players will be favored when relationships with local suppliers, customers or regulators are essential, and when global competition is relatively weak versus local producers. In an emerging economy, these factors can change rapidly as markets evolve and skills are transferred.

In China, these power shifts have been particularly dramatic. Many alliances in the country were predicated on a technology-for-market swap.

Local companies would bring marketing skills and foreigners would contribute world-class equipment and cash. Unfortunately, some foreign companies have found that their Chinese partners lack any real marketing capability, often because the state distributors they used to sell to have gone under. As a result, of 14 leading multinationals we interviewed, 50% said they had recently increased or were about to increase their equity share in their joint ventures. In the words of one: "If your ultimate goal is 100%, the closer you start, the less pain you have to go through later." Likewise local companies have sometimes found their foreign partners unwilling or unable to continuously inject cash and technology. To quote the chairman of a leading local group: "Their initial technology was not suited to the Chinese market and they have proved unwilling to reinvest to rebuild share."

For companies considering new ventures, the implications of power shifts should be considered in the negotiation. Likely buyers should choose smaller companies as partners and avoid setting acquisition prices as bargaining power will increase over time. For example, one venture succeeded in reducing the initial buyout price by 20% by timing the offer to coincide with increases in the partner's cash needs in other businesses. Likely buyers should hold both management and financial control, which in best-practice experience requires over 67% of the equity. Buyers should also consider keeping key value drivers out of the alliance while ensuring the key elements of the alliance's business system itself can be absorbed at a later date. For example, one logistics firm separates its customer-relationship staff from the day-to-day transportation-service joint venture to preserve its marketing capability outside the venture, but ensures common electronic data interchange systems and standards.

Potential sellers, on the other hand, should seek to strike pre-sale agreements to earn acquisition premiums. Many Chinese firms are now routinely seeking such agreements by tying buyout price to market multiples. Sellers should also seek to obtain skills that can be transferred outside the venture but keep the business itself separate from the parent to allow a clean sale. Chinese firms often achieve this by actively rotating managers from the partner for two- to three-year periods. These managers then go back to the parent company to start up new businesses, often competing with the venture.

FIT THE ORGANIZATION TO THE BALANCE

Equity arrangements alone cannot ensure an alliance goes the way you want it to. Equally important are fitting the softer organizational elements of structure, skill transfer and human resources to the alliance's evolution.

Stable and unstable joint-venture organizations differ radically. Stable alliances are characterized by independent organizations, with their own board and direct control over their own business activities. Often they develop their own unique business identity, complete with separate names, logos, uniforms and personnel systems. Unstable ones typically feature direct intervention by partners into day-to-day business activities, and a rudderless board. The multinational that seeks to tell its joint venture's salesforce what to do is a good example of instability.

Setting up a supposedly stable – that is, independent – organization when it is clear the joint venture is unstable due to radically imbalanced partner contributions creates lots of problems. To illustrate, strong joint-venture boards can effectively block multinationals seeking to coordinate multiple joint ventures to improve the effectiveness of multiple salesforces (one consumer-electronics company, for example, has 15 joint-venture salesforces for the same customer base) and reduce the overheads associated with having literally dozens of joint-venture general managers. After exhausting negotiations with each venture partner and its board, some multinationals have achieved centralized sales and marketing cost centers, with joint ventures still acting as profit centers. However, only those who started with the endgame in mind have achieved centralized sales profit centers that allow them to treat production joint ventures as contract manufacturing cost centers.

Good planning in skill transfer and human-resource management is also key to alliance success. The simple rule of thumb is, import, don't export, skills. Other rules to keep in mind are: Set clear and measurable objectives for learning and skill-building up front. Define boundaries in advance for transfer of skills, technology and other "soft assets" to protect strategic interests. Develop methods to reward staff from the parents whose primary role is not with the alliance but who are critical for transferring skills to the joint venture (for example, technology managers). Designate "gateway keepers" who ensure that alliance boundaries are respected (for instance, that sensitive technology is not transferred unintentionally) and track what information is shared and received. Put enough people into the alliance to ensure learning and systematically transfer them to leverage specific knowledge and skills.

In China, the last point is particularly relevant. Many companies have learned the hard way that under-investing in expatriates and relying on the local partner is counterproductive. In the short term, skills do not improve, leading to a weak China organization and poor performance. This in turn makes it difficult to hire top-notch talent, perpetuating the skills gap. The parent becomes reluctant to throw good money after bad, making it ever more difficult to summon up the courage to send out yet another expensive expatriate. In our experience, this situation more than any other drives multinationals to leave China.

NEGOTIATE FROM THE TOP

Even with foresight and good planning there may be no alternative to a tough restructuring negotiation. In these situations, consider direct action from the top.

The best restructuring negotiation is prepared well in advance – in fact, even in the initial deal structuring. Negotiations in China are protracted events, often lasting several years, that both set the guidelines for cooperation and let the parties get to know one another. Given this opportunity, far-sighted MNCs clearly signal their intentions and prepare for likely restructuring by including equity put-and-call options in the joint-venture contract, ensuring management control, and carefully defining the joint venture's scope. To illustrate, provisions can also be inserted into contracts that put pressure on a partner to agree to restructuring – for example, identifying early on events that require a unanimous resolution approving joint-venture termination, if they occur. (It must be noted, though, that the binding nature of these clauses is yet to be tested.) Experienced negotiators say: "Timeliness of negotiations is not critical; avoiding major concessions is key."

Planning ahead is particularly important in China as joint-venture restructuring or divestment is legally valid only with the consent of both partners and the original approval authority. The 1996 Foreign Invested Enterprise Liquidation Measures promulgated by MOFTEC and other relevant regulations appear to indicate five circumstances where early joint-venture termination is possible: failure to subscribe capital, divestment by one party, bankruptcy, termination for cause (that is, *force majeure* or breach of contract of a magnitude to prevent continuation of the business) and liquidation by unanimous board consent. In all cases, a unanimous board resolution is required.

If your partner is not in agreement with your restructuring proposal, reopening negotiations usually is best done at the partner-to-partner level. The same issues of partner selection and long-term strategy tackled in the initial negotiation need to be addressed. Venture managers may have an understanding of the issues, but typically lack both internal and external credibility to make the tough decisions. Where the joint venture is clearly being looted by one partner, the other partner should not try to fight from inside but appeal directly to the top. A final cautionary tale: One multinational relied on government goodwill and installed the former general manager of its Chinese partner as the joint-venture CEO. As it happened, the GM embezzled and transferred funds to the Chinese partner. After two years of fruitless discussions by local expatriate managers, the MNC CEO appealed directly to the city government, who ousted the GM within a month and agreed to the joint venture's restructuring.

✳   ✳   ✳

Restructuring alliances in China is likely to be a significant trend. With adequate preparation, restructuring can be an effective tool for developing a sound business platform. Without it, the process is likely to be a challenging and expensive test.

An Alliance Self-Assessment

To assist you in identifying the implications for your enterprise, we suggest a few questions for self-assessment:

1. Have you considered the impact of alternative industry scenarios on the power and attractiveness of your prospective government friendships?

2. Have you conducted site visits to your prospective day-to-day partner, interviewed their executives and analyzed their businesses to assess partnership skills?

3. In planning your business development strategy, have you assessed whether you and your partner are now living up to each other's expectations, and whether and how this might change?

4. Have you considered changes in equity structures over time and negotiating conditions at the likely restructuring point?

5. In structuring your venture organization, have you matched organizational independence, board composition, and joint-venture scope to foreseen venture stability?

6. Do you design skill-transfer mechanisms to avoid excessive leakage while meeting joint-venture business needs?

7. Have you invested sufficiently in people to run the business on its own if you plan to absorb it in the future?

8. In preparing for restructuring for negotiations, have you designed your contract to identify early termination and divestment points and conditions?

9. Have you secured the consent of your partner to the possibility of restructuring in the future?

10. Have you involved your CEO or at least made him aware of his important role in restructuring negotiations?

REFERENCES

1. A worker's annual salary on the mainland can be one-tenth that of his Taiwanese counterpart. Even Western players such as Whirlpool and HP use China as an export base; over 30% of their production is dedicated to exports.
2. This complements moves by Chinese companies to build their own research capabilities. Companies like Huawei, ZTE and Datang all have thousands of researchers on the payroll.
3. In refrigerators, multinationals' share has grown from 3% in 1997 to over 20% in 2000, reflecting a new commitment by the leading Korean and European players.
4. Large companies are not the only winners in China. EFF, a German mid-sized company (total revenue in 2000: US$45 million), is another winning example. EFF has a product focus on high-end electro-mechanic security locks. It set up a representative office in Beijing in 1995 and started with 10–15 product types; sales were $0.4 million in 2000 through its one representative office and four staff. EFF has experienced profitable growth since entering China with EBIT of over 10% and sales growing at 77% annually since 1998. It now sells over 30 product types, and by focusing on the high end is able to capture a disproportionate share of the profit pool. EFF has 50% of the high-end market but 5% of the total. Consequently, its profits are almost 20% of the industry's total profit pool.
5. Motorola University contains four programs: Asian Impact for Motorola (AIM) – a regional solution to develop senior managers from Asia; China Accelerated Management Program (CAMP) for promising local PRC managers; Motorola Management Foundation Program (MMFP) – to train new managers and develop their skills in management, problem solving, communication and leadership; and Motorola High Tech MBA (TMBA) – enables high-performing staff in Motorola China to earn an MBA degree with an emphasis on high technology at Arizona State University.
6. In 2000 Motorola spent almost $30 million on advertising for mobile phones and captured 88% brand awareness, compared to Nokia's 81% and Ericsson's 72%.
7. Volkswagen could be termed one of the few genuine stage-three multinationals in China, with over a 40% share of the passenger car market through its joint ventures in Shanghai and Changchun. An aggressive localization program, achieving 100% in Shanghai, and being the largest foreign employer in the auto industry, with over 5000 employees in Shanghai alone, has made Volkswagen profitable since year one. Profits, however, have all been reinvested in the venture.
8. As counterpoint, multinationals who make the initial manufacturing investment but then limit sales and marketing expenses to assure profitability and rely on local partners and distributors, often find they lose consumer and channel support, do not build strong organizations and consequently perform poorly.

9. China graduates over 50,000 computer science students each year (compared to 25,000 in the U.S. and 30,000 in India). At least 7,000 Chinese students studying overseas return to China each year, a figure rising to 20% since 1990. Unofficial estimates believe there are more than 300,000 Chinese students studying abroad at any given time.

10. Many foreign enterprises see no choice but to develop senior managers internally. Motorola has a "Technology MBA" with Arizona State University and Qinghua University in Beijing. Ericsson's China Academy offers a 14-month part-time MBA in association with the Australian National University. Nokia supports an MBA program between Beijing University and Kellogg School, while Nortel offers a mini-MBA through INSEAD.

8

A Closing Word

C hina's economy is undoubtedly in the throes of a painful transition. Dramatic changes are happening across the board. Old industrial companies will go under. Entire swathes of the service sector need to be reinvented. And the social costs and pressures caused by the dislocation of hundreds of millions of people are immense. All this at the same time as an entire generation has had its expectations raised by two decades of almost uninterrupted growth. Political scientists say that revolutions usually happen when things are getting better, not when they are at their worst. However, there is no going back now. China's leaders are on a bicycle that goes in only one direction. Only by continuing to improve capital and labor productivity can the Chinese government generate the revenues it needs to provide social benefits. And only by continuing to open up the funding and distributive functions of the economy to market forces can it increase productivity. These pressures reinforce each other and leave Chinese leaders no fundamental choice other than continued reform.

No economic system is immune from challenges and China has its share: growing income inequities; possible social dislocation, given large-scale lay-offs due to reform-induced restructuring; and the lack of an adequate pension system for an ageing population. First, there is the potential for mass lay-offs as domestic industries restructure in the move to the market economy. This includes a potential loss of livelihood for those dependent on agriculture due to a flood of cheap imports if current protections are removed with WTO accession. China already faces social stresses from millions of rural people without jobs. Currently, rural workers relocate to manufacturing centers for three to five years, accumulate some capital through saving and then return to the countryside, perhaps to run a small business of their own. This cycling of low-skill, but highly committed, labor is the basis for many of the manufacturing clusters in Guangdong province. Manufacturing needs to keep growing to ensure China's large rural workforce can be accommodated.

Second, China's public pension scheme will need to support a rapidly ageing population but the current public pension scheme may have insufficient funds and the traditional family mechanism is unlikely to be effective because of the one-child policy.[1] Those over 65 years of age will amount to 16% of the population by 2030, compared to 7% in 1998. Current public pensions cover less than 30% of the total working population. Few private companies have participated outside of foreign-invested enterprises. Employees of privatized state enterprises have lost their previous pension coverage and those in rural areas often never had it. Assuming total retirees grow at the historical rate of 3.85% to 2010, coverage of public pensions remains at 82% and average benefit payments remain at 75% of the average working salary of the urban working population, pension payouts will amount to $79 billion by 2010. Contributions will lag behind at $52 billion given salary trends, workforce participation, and if contribution trends stay constant. The size of the public pension fund gap will amount to over $100 billion by 2010, requiring either a cut in benefits or that the government make up the shortfall.[2]

The third potential shock lies in the countryside. Reform has inevitably led to a growth in income inequality, particularly between urban and rural sectors. After initial rapid growth, rural incomes have stagnated since the mid-1980s. Government investment in the countryside has also been limited, focusing instead on developing the coastal regions. These have received by far the bulk of foreign and domestic investment, benefiting as they do from an educated populace, capable politicians and special government policies. The lack of rural investment is compounded by a policy of avoiding massive urbanization – China today has a disproportionately low urbanization rate compared to its emerging-market peers. Given the high reliance on local governments to provide basic social services, this stagnation has in turn a direct impact on the well-being of China's rural populace, which still makes up over 60% of the population. Spending on education, healthcare and public works in poor areas is constrained by the lack of funding, leading in some cases to the reappearance of poverty levels not seen since pre-Revolution days. The worst of these sufferings appear in the far interior of the country where poverty is often compounded by official malfeasance and corruption, as highlighted in the floods of the summer of 2001. Zhu Rongji was embarrassed to find that the dam that he had visited a few weeks earlier had given way – state-specified steel had been substituted with low-quality materials.

The risk to the system comes in the potential for an underclass of rural migrants to appear. The Chinese government's lack of investment in the countryside has in fact created a rural migrant workforce numbering in the hundreds of millions. China's *hukou* (residence card) system restricts its people from living and working in cities not of their origin. Talent is thus prevented from moving to places where it can best be utilized. Employers seeking talent must buy residency for qualified individuals, imposing an unnecessary cost on businesses. Historically, Chinese empires have always fallen when an agricultural disaster has prompted peasants to move in great numbers on the cities. Such an event could conceivably lead to a similar scenario in today's China.[3]

Finally, there are political risks. Today, successful entrepreneurs are recognized as the leaders of the economy and lauded in the press as China's heroes. Jiang Zemin himself has announced that entrepreneurs can be Party members and that stock markets are a socialist institution. Jiang's Three Representations – modern technology, the people, and advanced culture – that define his vision of what the Party should stand for imply a squarely technocratic vision of China where business stands shoulder to shoulder with a modern Party in raising China's standard of living. On the flip side, with the passage of the Bankruptcy Law in the late 1990s, banks for the first time had the legal right to seize the collateral of a defaulter. Those dissatisfied with their personal fortunes will constitute an increasingly disaffected portion of society.

Another issue of concern is the lack of alternative power structures or control mechanisms other than the Party, given the lack of civil institutions. There are no unions and no way for workers to mobilize on a mass basis. The military now has limited political influence and has been successfully pushed back from its emerging role as a business conglomerate over the last five years. Student bodies that 15 years ago might have become an alternative center have become completely apolitical and business-focused to the extent that they had to be prompted by the government to demonstrate after the Belgrade bombing. This could be a problem for China since civil institutions provide a cushion against social convulsions that could follow if the Party's authority is weakened.

Endemic corruption in China could also unhinge progress if left unchecked. Corruption, exemplified by the high-profile cases in Guangdong and Fujian, results from a lack of transparency and insufficient checks and balances. Observers note that corruption poses the greatest threat to the Party's leading role in Chinese society. The Party handles thousands of cases each year but with barely any impact. Even in the early years of reform, there were many major scandals ranging from car smuggling in Hainan to the fixing of futures contracts in Shanghai. Jiang Zemin has put the fight against corruption at the top of his agenda. But the current efforts may be too little, too late, in the face of a morass of official embezzlement and fraud.

To manage all of these risks, what government must now do is continue to force the pace. Continued economic growth and rising productivity can provide the funds needed to manage these risks. But the tendency to slip backwards and avoid hard decisions will mount as new elites emerge. The real threat may not be from the well-known industrial cliques but, rather, from surprising new sources. For example, unlike 20 years ago, China now has many rich people. These people for now are still subservient to the government. But it will be only a matter of time before at least some start to try to play a more active role to defend their own vested interests. The corruption scandals in Xiamen and elsewhere will then only be the tip of the iceberg.

Imagine an economic journal reviewing China's position in the year 2022. One could hear two very different stories. In the optimistic version, China of 2022 will be one of the world's largest economies, second only to the United States as an economic powerhouse. Its GDP per capita now firmly in the middle tier of developing economies, the transition to a service economy will be well under way. Urbanization will have made steady progress with over 50% of the population. Labor productivity has been rising, though still significantly below international norms in the service sector. The key engine of growth will be a dynamic private sector, with less than 10% of the economy in state control. China could boast the world's second-largest stock market. China's coastal regions are still likely to be leading development but China will be globally integrated, with exports amounting to over 10% of world trade and its imports of raw materials creating the largest market for many commodities. Still one of the largest recipients of FDI, China will also have substantial holdings of international capital. Economic wealth will lead to dominance in the Asia region. Domestically, China's politics will have taken a back seat to the need for a transparent, accountable rule of law.

The pessimistic version has China as still an important country but nowhere near being a global economic power. Development still places it firmly in the ranks of the emerging market economies and productivity increases have been lagging since the early part of the century. Initial moves to corporatize and list state enterprises were thwarted by the lack of liquidity in the domestic stock market coupled with the continuing failure of bank reform and pressure on the government to provide social payouts to the growing pool of pensioners. Rural-urban inequities have led to wide disparities in incomes, a huge floating population and high social costs incurred in the enforcement of migration policy. China's role in world trade has stagnated as, while its imports of raw materials grow, trade sanctions and the failure of its companies to develop new technologies have led to a tough competition with India and other low-cost labor-based exporters. Domestically, foreign investment has dropped dramatically as the government has refused to allow foreign companies to take over "strategic" sectors, even after WTO entry. And corruption has become a huge and endemic problem in not only business but society as a whole.

The decisions being made today will determine which of these pictures will emerge as the true one in 2022. Responsibility for ensuring that the success scenario is enacted lies squarely with both government and corporate leaders.

REFERENCES

1. Severe embezzlement of individual accounts led to an accumulated shortfall of over $12 billion by 1999 and the lack of a unified provincial pension fund has resulted in multiple accounts for individuals. Balance of pension funds has remained stable at around $9 billion from 1997 to 1999. Government contributed $1.2 billion in 1999 to maintain this.

2. To reform, China's government has studied many models with alternative mixes of private and public contribution and fund-management approaches. The Singapore CPF model appears to be the most attractive to Chinese regulators. This would allow workers to set up individual accounts. The money from these accounts would be invested by a single financial institution, probably government controlled. Confirmed elements in 2001 included mandatory contributions, where employees contribute 8% of salaries to individually funded accounts, and social fund includes up to 20% of salaries contributed by employers. The government itself will manage investments of the individual funded accounts.

3. The government has finally realized this risk and with the launch of the "Go West" campaign in 2000 has made development of the interior a priority.

Index